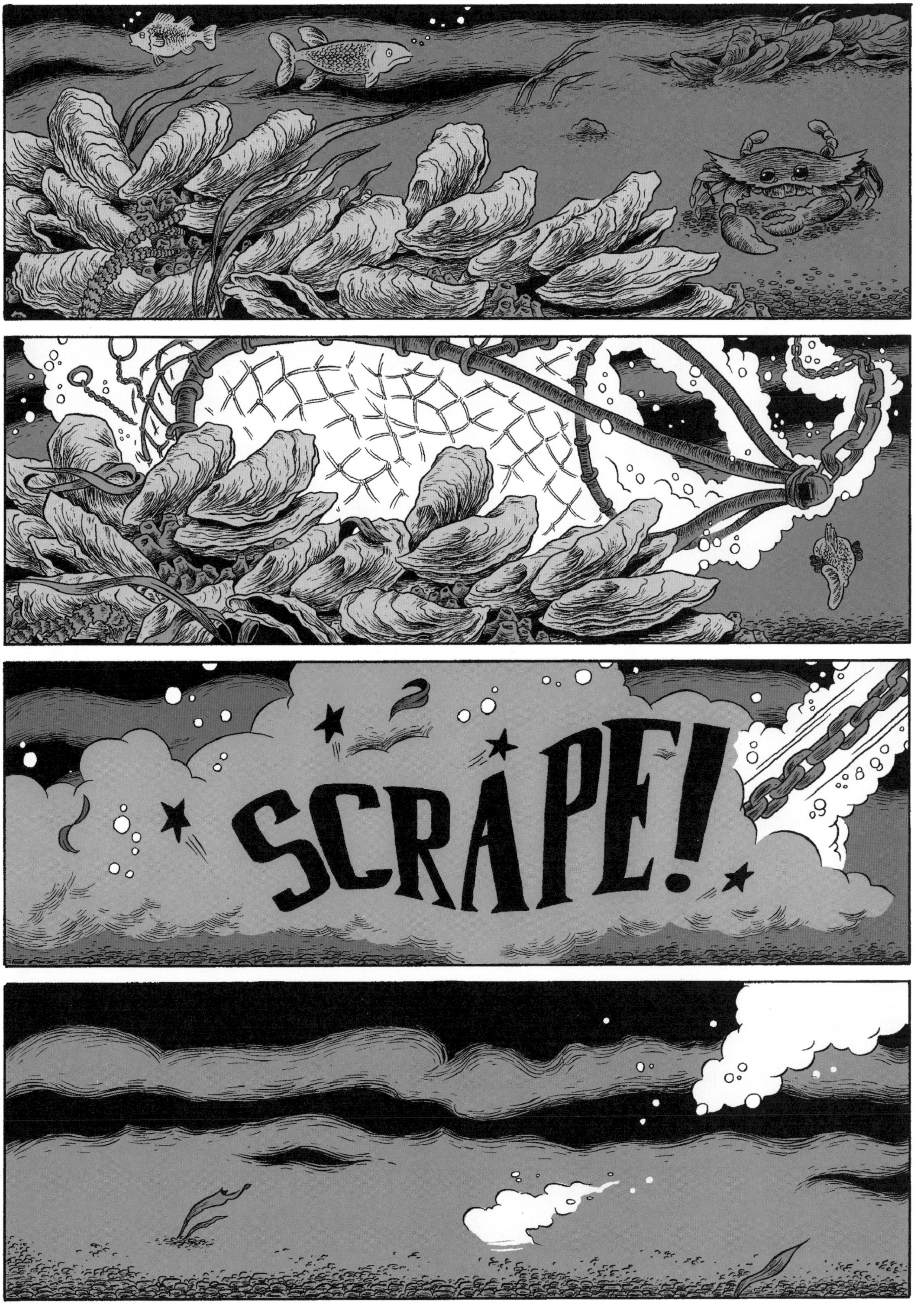
SCRAPE!

OYSTER WAR

WRITTEN AND ILLUSTRATED BY
Ben Towle

DESIGNED BY
Elaine Lin

EDITED BY
Robin Herrera with Ari Yarwood

PUBLISHED BY ONI PRESS INC

Joe Nozemack, publisher
James Lucas Jones, editor in chief
Cheyenne Allott, director of sales
Fred Reckling, director of publicity
Troy Look, production manager
Hilary Thompson, graphic designer
Jared Jones, production assistant
Charlie Chu, senior editor
Robin Herrera, editor
Ari Yarwood, associate editor
Brad Rooks, inventory coordinator
Jung Lee, office assistant

onipress.com
facebook.com/onipress
twitter.com/onipress
onipress.tumblr.com
benzilla.com | @ben_towle

First Edition: September 2015

ISBN 978-1-62010-262-6
eISBN 978-1-62010-263-3

Oyster War, September 2015. Published by Oni Press, Inc.
1305 SE Martin Luther King Jr. Blvd., Suite A, Portland, OR 97214.

Printed in China

Library of Congress Control Number: 2015932778

1 2 3 4 5 6 7 8 9 10

CHAPTER ONE

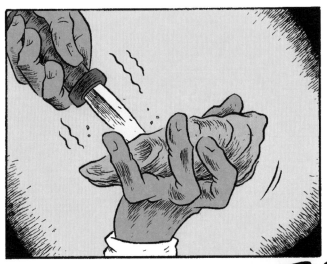

POP!

SLORP

TOSS

Delicious.

Now we can give you an *official* welcome...

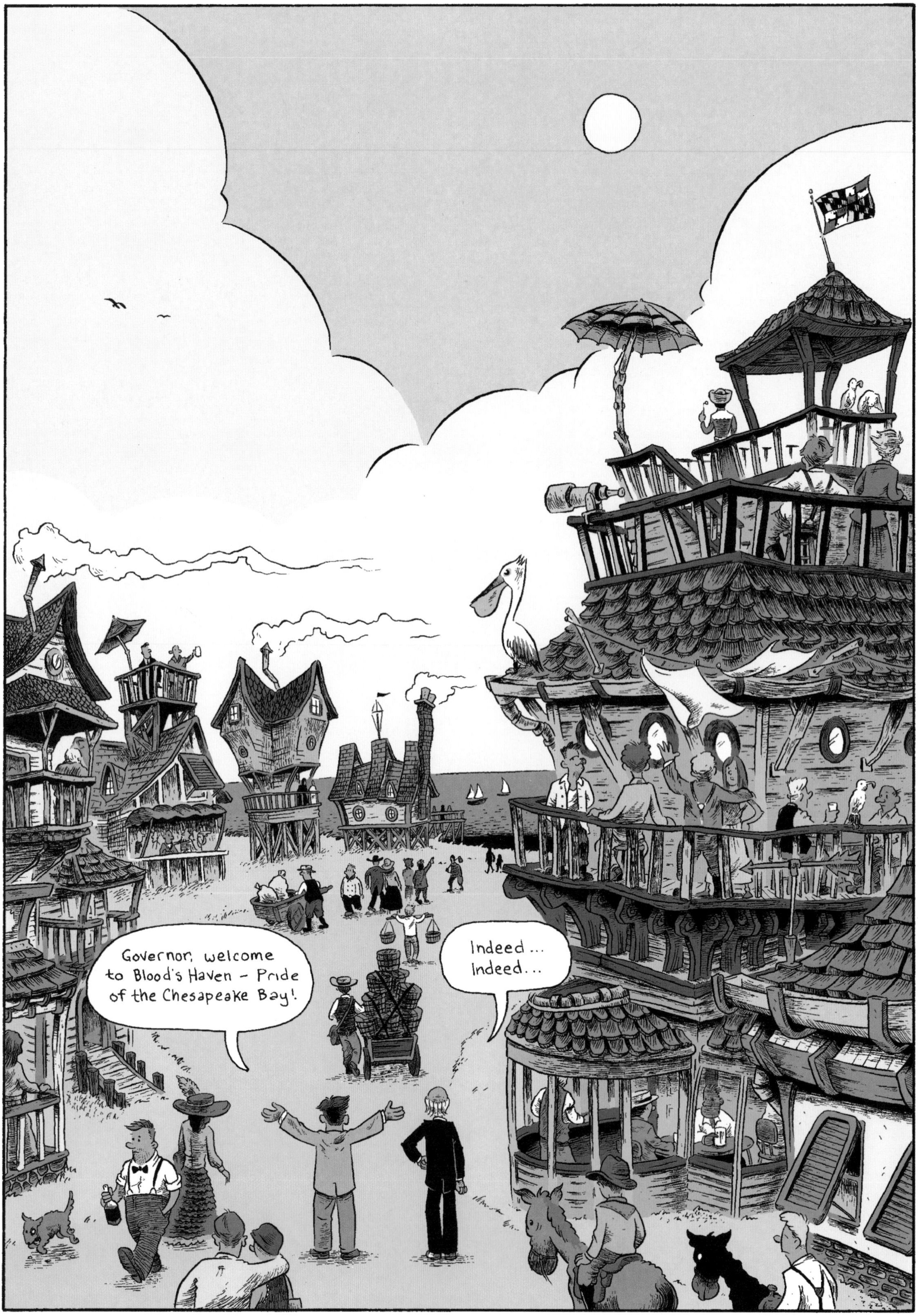
Governor, welcome to Blood's Haven - Pride of the Chesapeake Bay!
Indeed... Indeed...

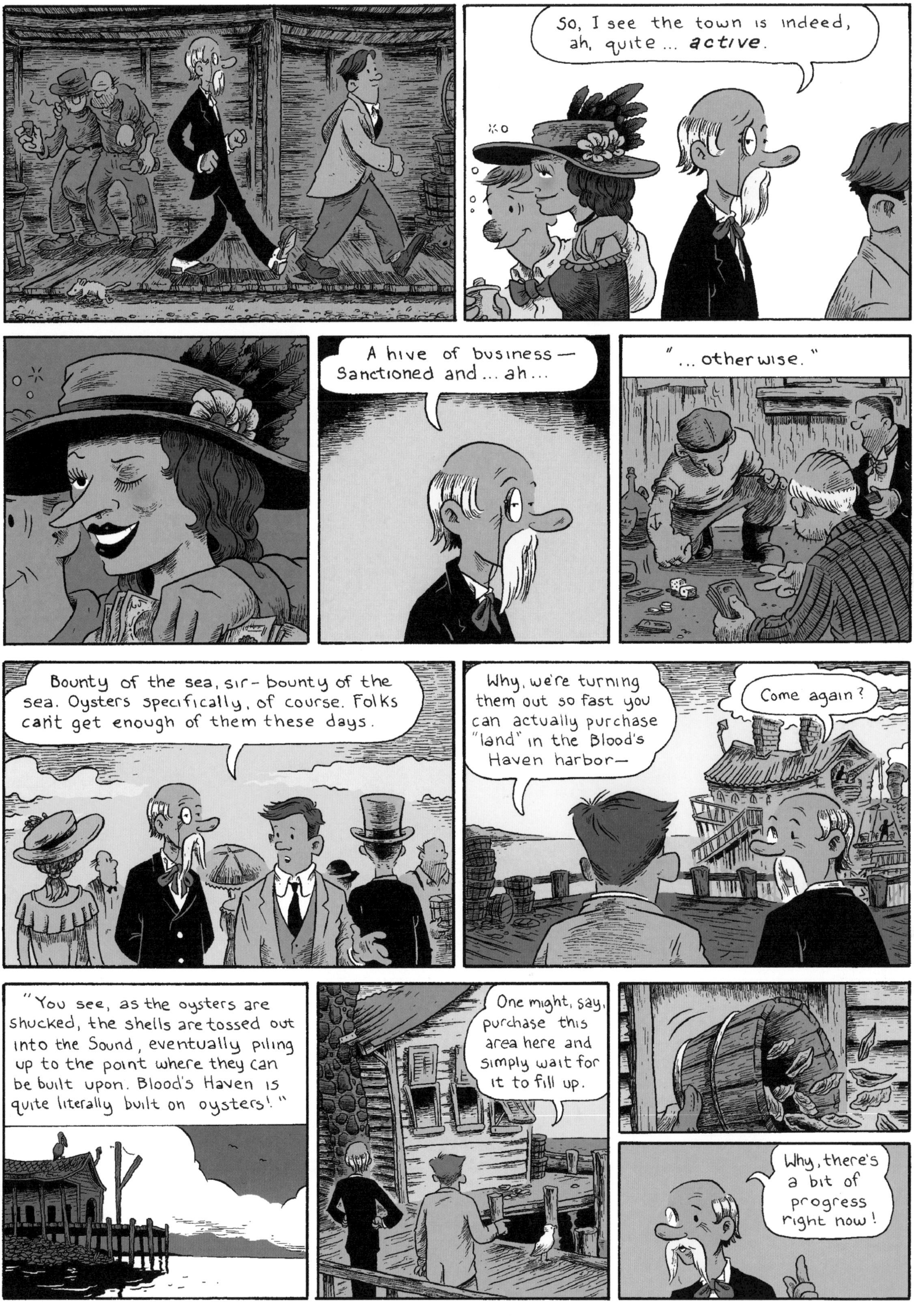

So, I see the town is indeed, ah, quite ... active.
A hive of business — Sanctioned and ... ah ...
"... otherwise."
Bounty of the sea, sir - bounty of the sea. Oysters specifically, of course. Folks can't get enough of them these days.
Why, we're turning them out so fast you can actually purchase "land" in the Blood's Haven harbor—
Come again?
"You see, as the oysters are shucked, the shells are tossed out into the Sound, eventually piling up to the point where they can be built upon. Blood's Haven is quite literally built on oysters!"
One might, say, purchase this area here and simply wait for it to fill up.
Why, there's a bit of progress right now!

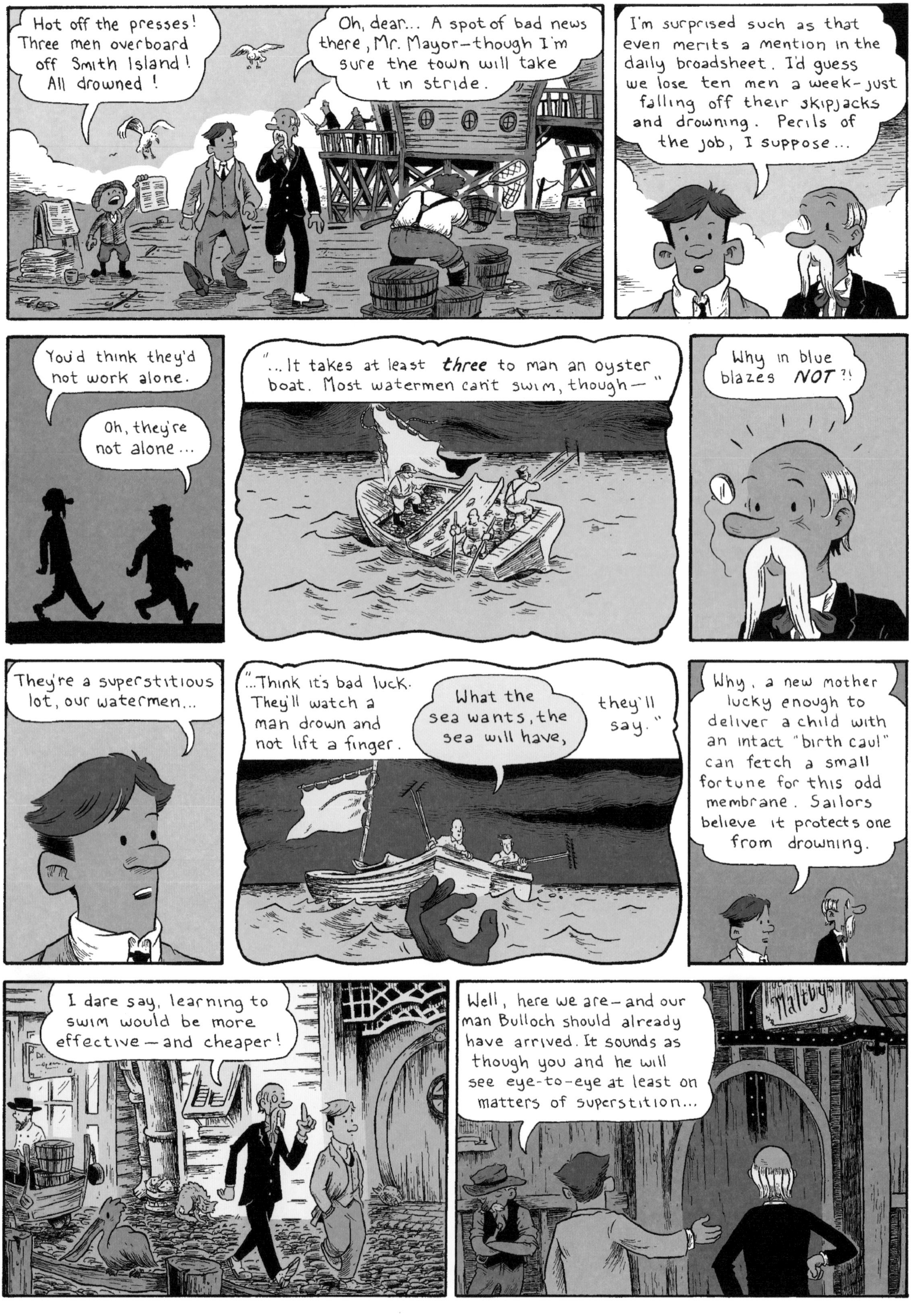
Hot off the presses! Three men overboard off Smith Island! All drowned!
Oh, dear... A spot of bad news there, Mr. Mayor—though I'm sure the town will take it in stride.
I'm surprised such as that even merits a mention in the daily broadsheet. I'd guess we lose ten men a week—just falling off their skipjacks and drowning. Perils of the job, I suppose...
You'd think they'd not work alone.
Oh, they're not alone...
"...It takes at least *three* to man an oyster boat. Most watermen can't swim, though—"
Why in blue blazes *NOT*?!
They're a superstitious lot, our watermen...
"...Think it's bad luck. They'll watch a man drown and not lift a finger.
What the sea wants, the sea will have,
they'll say."
Why, a new mother lucky enough to deliver a child with an intact "birth caul" can fetch a small fortune for this odd membrane. Sailors believe it protects one from drowning.
I dare say, learning to swim would be more effective—and cheaper!
Well, here we are—and our man Bulloch should already have arrived. It sounds as though you and he will see eye-to-eye at least on matters of superstition...

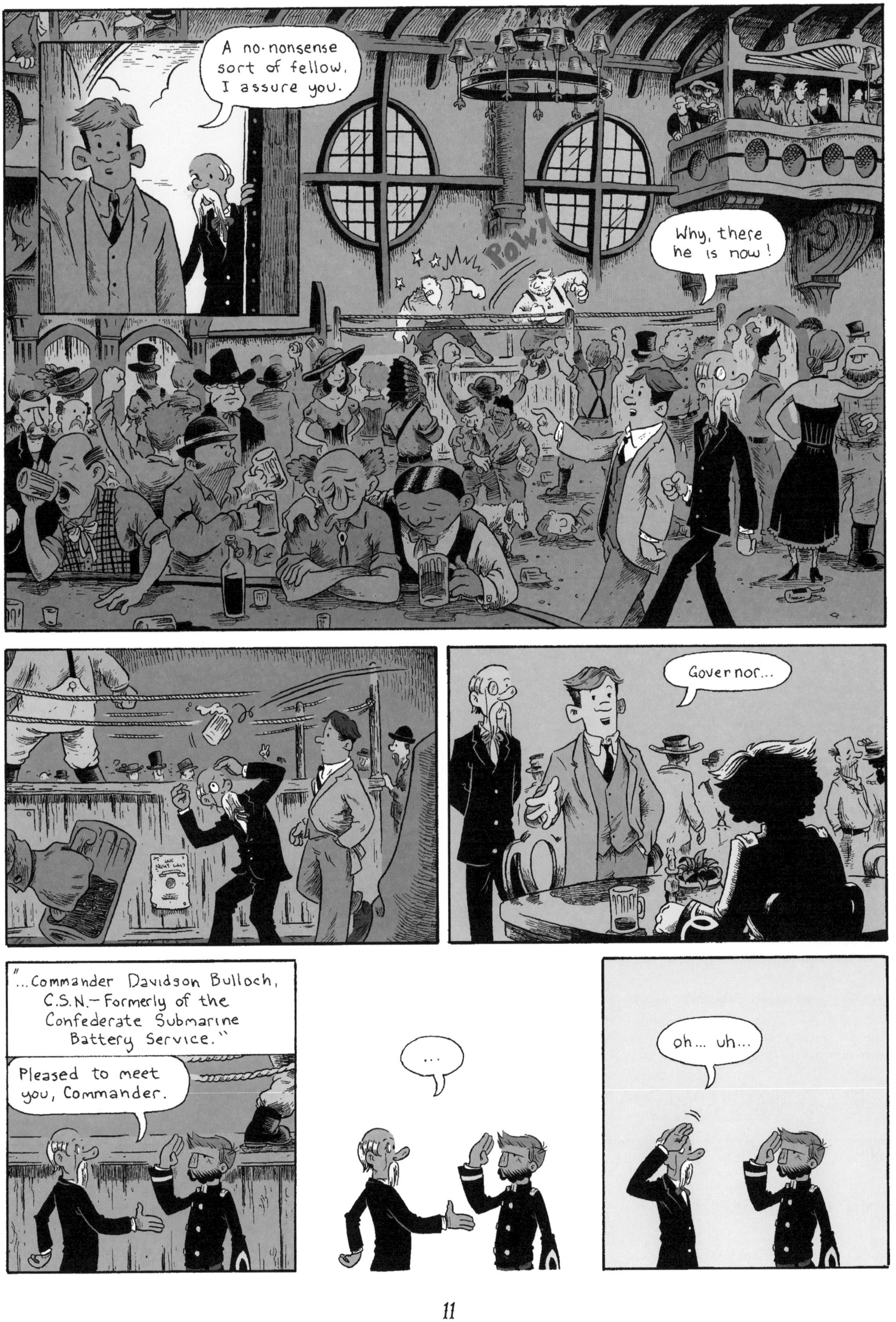
A no-nonsense sort of fellow, I assure you.
POW!
Why, there he is now!
Governor...
"...Commander Davidson Bulloch, C.S.N.—Formerly of the Confederate Submarine Battery Service."
Pleased to meet you, Commander.
...
oh... uh...

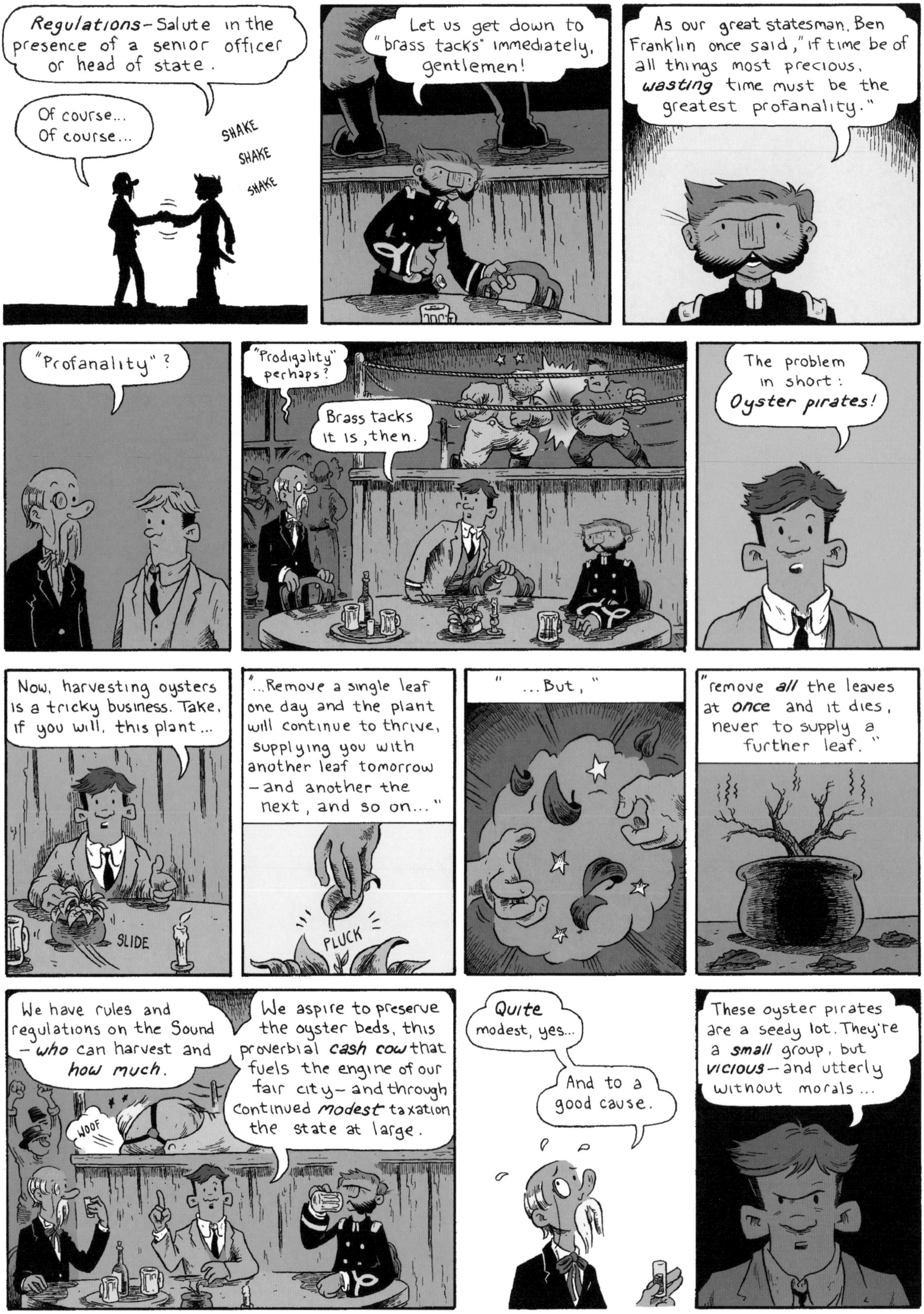
Regulations- Salute in the presence of a senior officer or head of state.
Of course... Of course...
SHAKE
SHAKE
SHAKE
Let us get down to "brass tacks" immediately, gentlemen!
As our great statesman, Ben Franklin once said, "if time be of all things most precious, wasting time must be the greatest profanality."
"Profanality"?
"Prodigality" perhaps?
Brass tacks it is, then.
The problem in short: Oyster pirates!
Now, harvesting oysters is a tricky business. Take, if you will, this plant...
SLIDE
"...Remove a single leaf one day and the plant will continue to thrive, supplying you with another leaf tomorrow -and another the next, and so on..."
PLUCK
" ...But, "
"remove all the leaves at once and it dies, never to supply a further leaf."
We have rules and regulations on the Sound -who can harvest and how much.
We aspire to preserve the oyster beds, this proverbial cash cow that fuels the engine of our fair city- and through continued modest taxation the state at large.
WOOF
Quite modest, yes...
And to a good cause.
These oyster pirates are a seedy lot. They're a small group, but vicious- and utterly without morals...

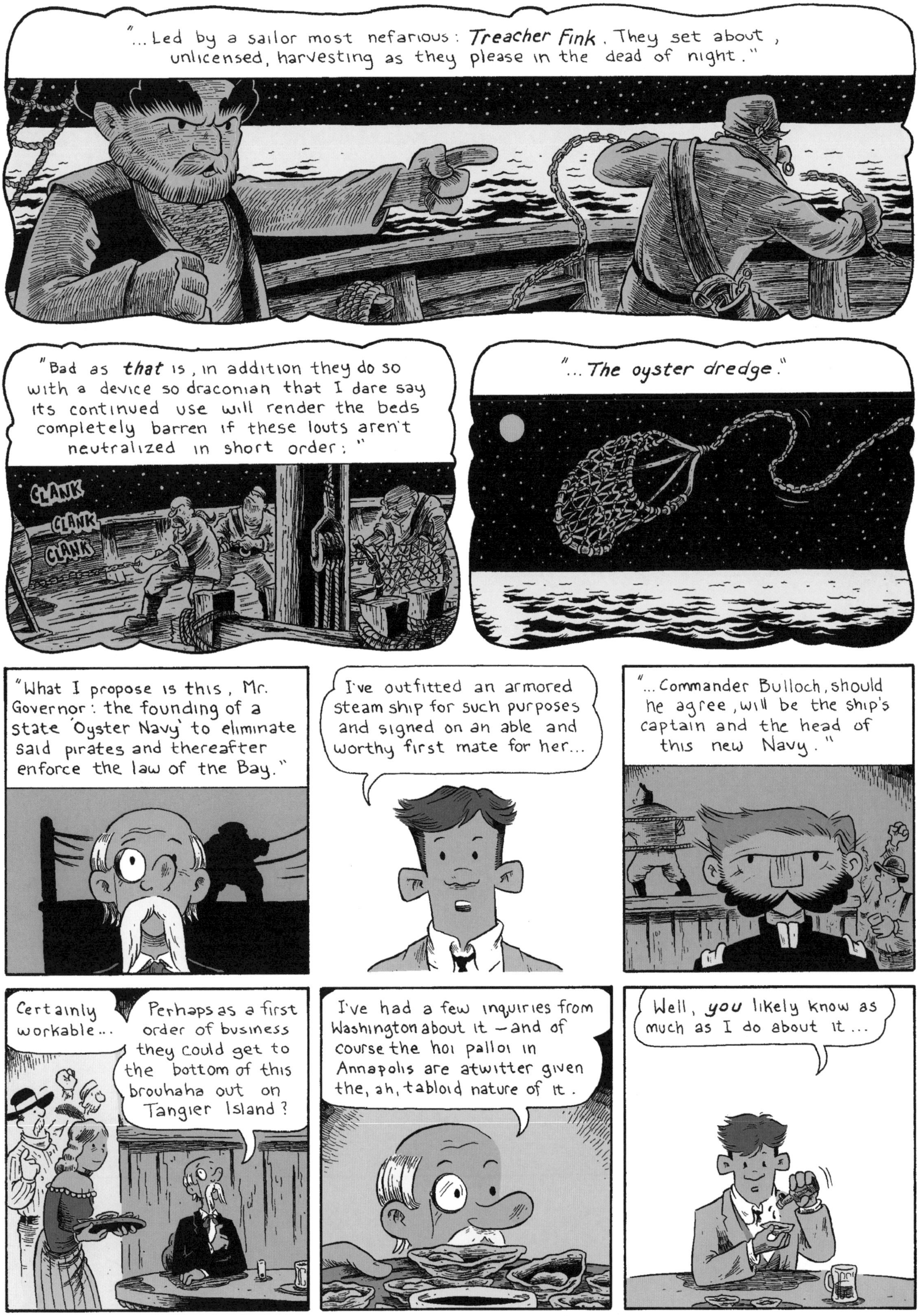
"...Led by a sailor most nefarious: Treacher Fink. They set about, unlicensed, harvesting as they please in the dead of night."
"Bad as that is, in addition they do so with a device so draconian that I dare say its continued use will render the beds completely barren if these louts aren't neutralized in short order:"
CLANK
CLANK
CLANK
"...The oyster dredge."
"What I propose is this, Mr. Governor: the founding of a state 'Oyster Navy' to eliminate said pirates and thereafter enforce the law of the Bay."
I've outfitted an armored steam ship for such purposes and signed on an able and worthy first mate for her...
"...Commander Bulloch, should he agree, will be the ship's captain and the head of this new Navy."
Certainly workable...
Perhaps as a first order of business they could get to the bottom of this brouhaha out on Tangier Island?
I've had a few inquiries from Washington about it — and of course the hoi polloi in Annapolis are atwitter given the, ah, tabloid nature of it.
Well, you likely know as much as I do about it...

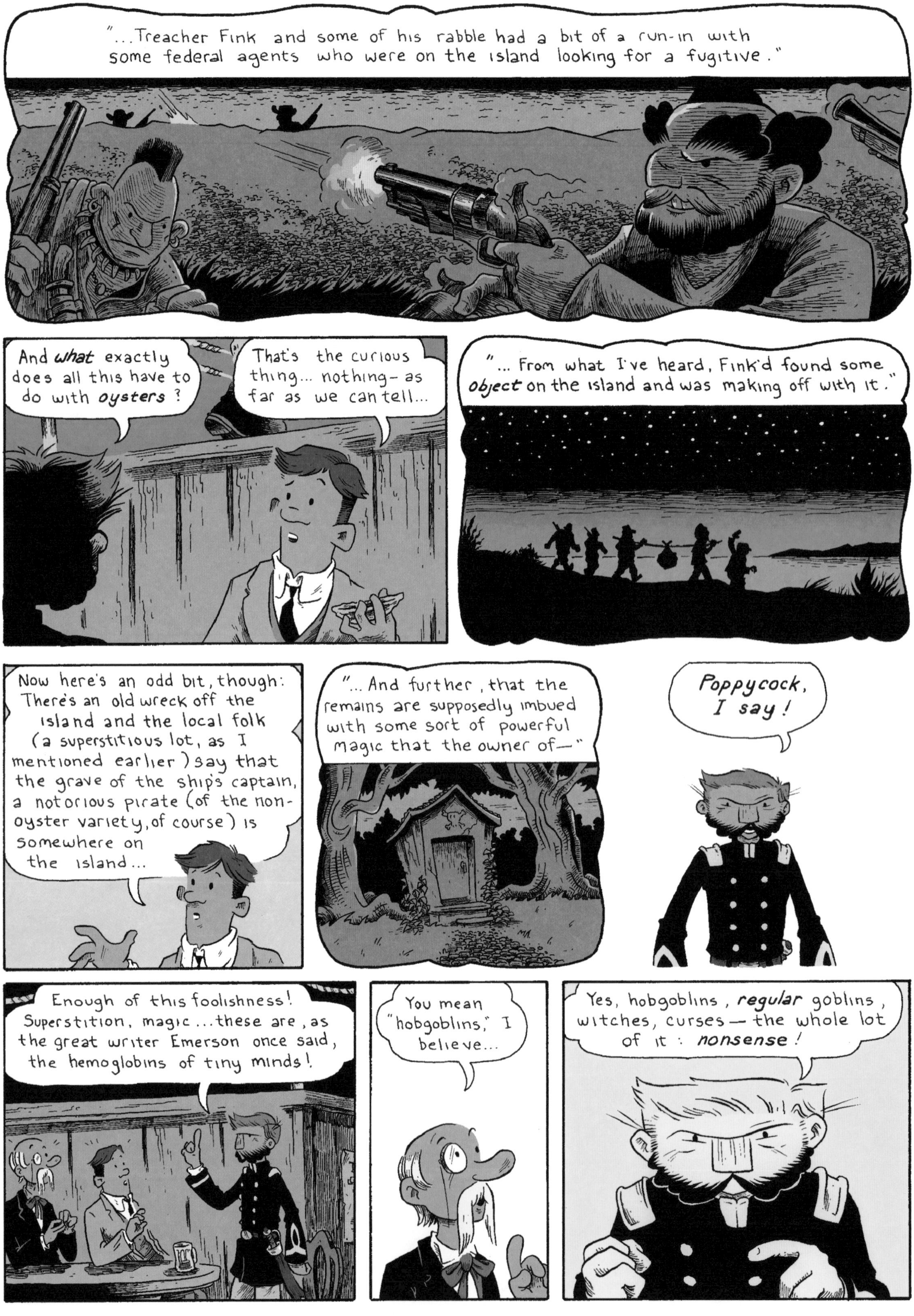
"...Treacher Fink and some of his rabble had a bit of a run-in with some federal agents who were on the island looking for a fugitive."
And *what* exactly does all this have to do with *oysters*?
That's the curious thing... nothing– as far as we can tell...
"... From what I've heard, Fink'd found some *object* on the island and was making off with it."
Now here's an odd bit, though: There's an old wreck off the island and the local folk (a superstitious lot, as I mentioned earlier) say that the grave of the ship's captain, a notorious pirate (of the non-oyster variety, of course) is somewhere on the island...
"... And further, that the remains are supposedly imbued with some sort of powerful magic that the owner of—"
Poppycock, I say!
Enough of this foolishness! Superstition, magic... these are, as the great writer Emerson once said, the hemoglobins of tiny minds!
You mean "hobgoblins," I believe...
Yes, hobgoblins, *regular* goblins, witches, curses — the whole lot of it: *nonsense*!

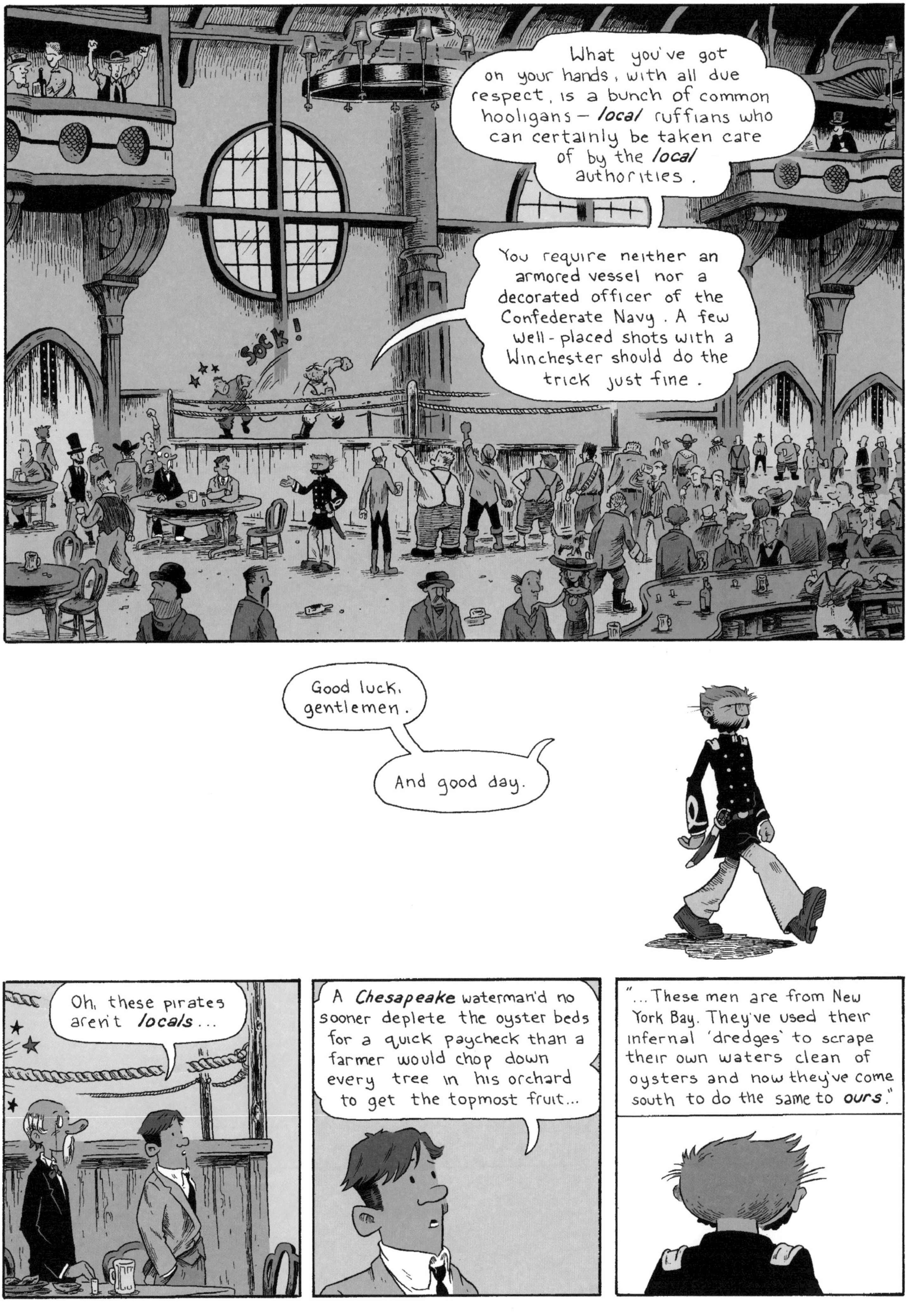
What you've got on your hands, with all due respect, is a bunch of common hooligans — *local* ruffians who can certainly be taken care of by the *local* authorities.
You require neither an armored vessel nor a decorated officer of the Confederate Navy. A few well-placed shots with a Winchester should do the trick just fine.
SOCK!
Good luck, gentlemen.
And good day.
Oh, these pirates aren't *locals*...
A *Chesapeake* waterman'd no sooner deplete the oyster beds for a quick paycheck than a farmer would chop down every tree in his orchard to get the topmost fruit...
"...These men are from New York Bay. They've used their infernal 'dredges' to scrape their own waters clean of oysters and now they've come south to do the same to *ours*."

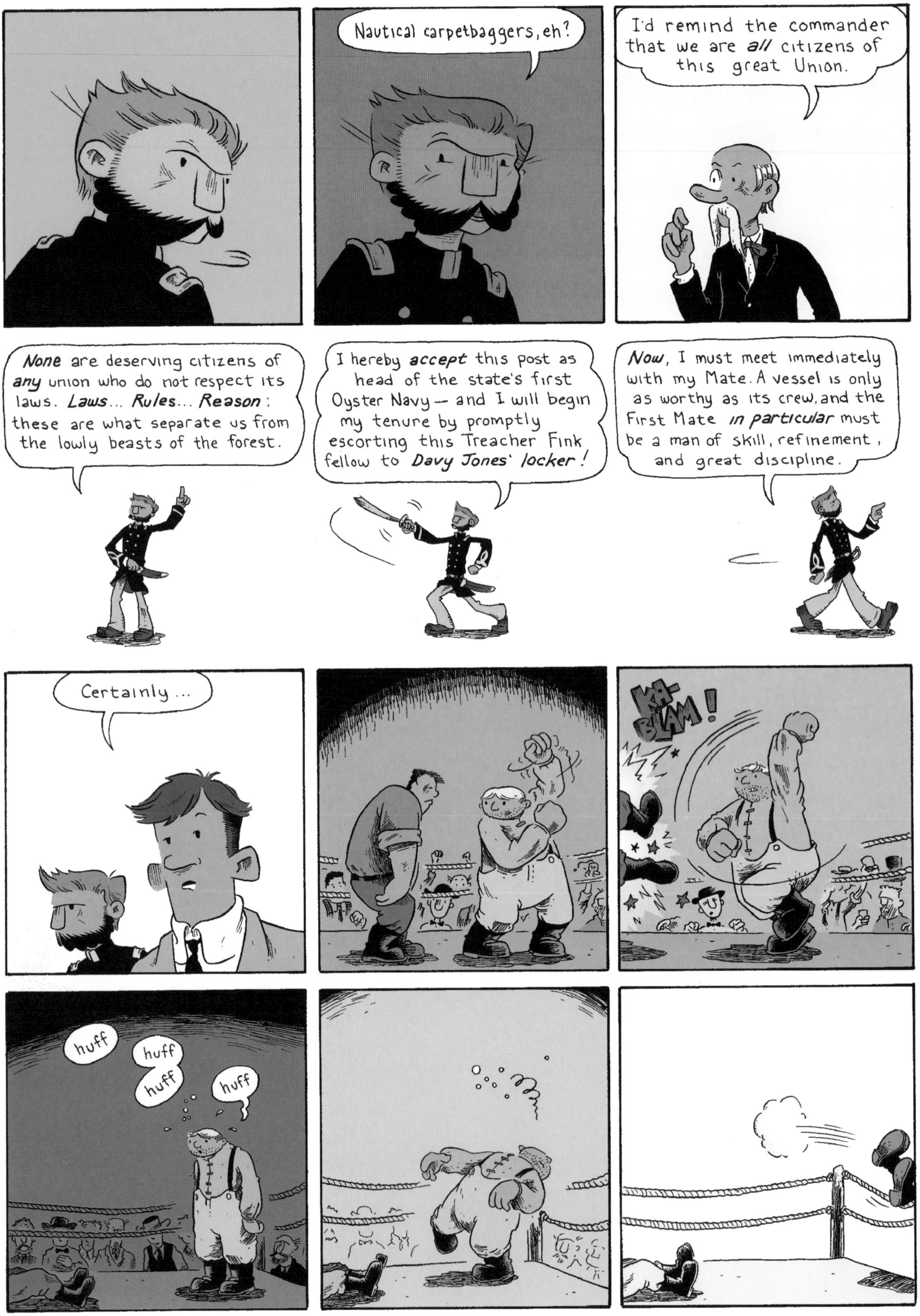
Nautical carpetbaggers, eh?
I'd remind the commander that we are *all* citizens of this great Union.
None are deserving citizens of *any* union who do not respect its laws. *Laws*... *Rules*... *Reason*: these are what separate us from the lowly beasts of the forest.
I hereby *accept* this post as head of the state's first Oyster Navy — and I will begin my tenure by promptly escorting this Treacher Fink fellow to *Davy Jones' locker*!
Now, I must meet immediately with my Mate. A vessel is only as worthy as its crew, and the First Mate *in particular* must be a man of skill, refinement, and great discipline.
Certainly...
KA-BLAM!
huff
huff
huff
huff

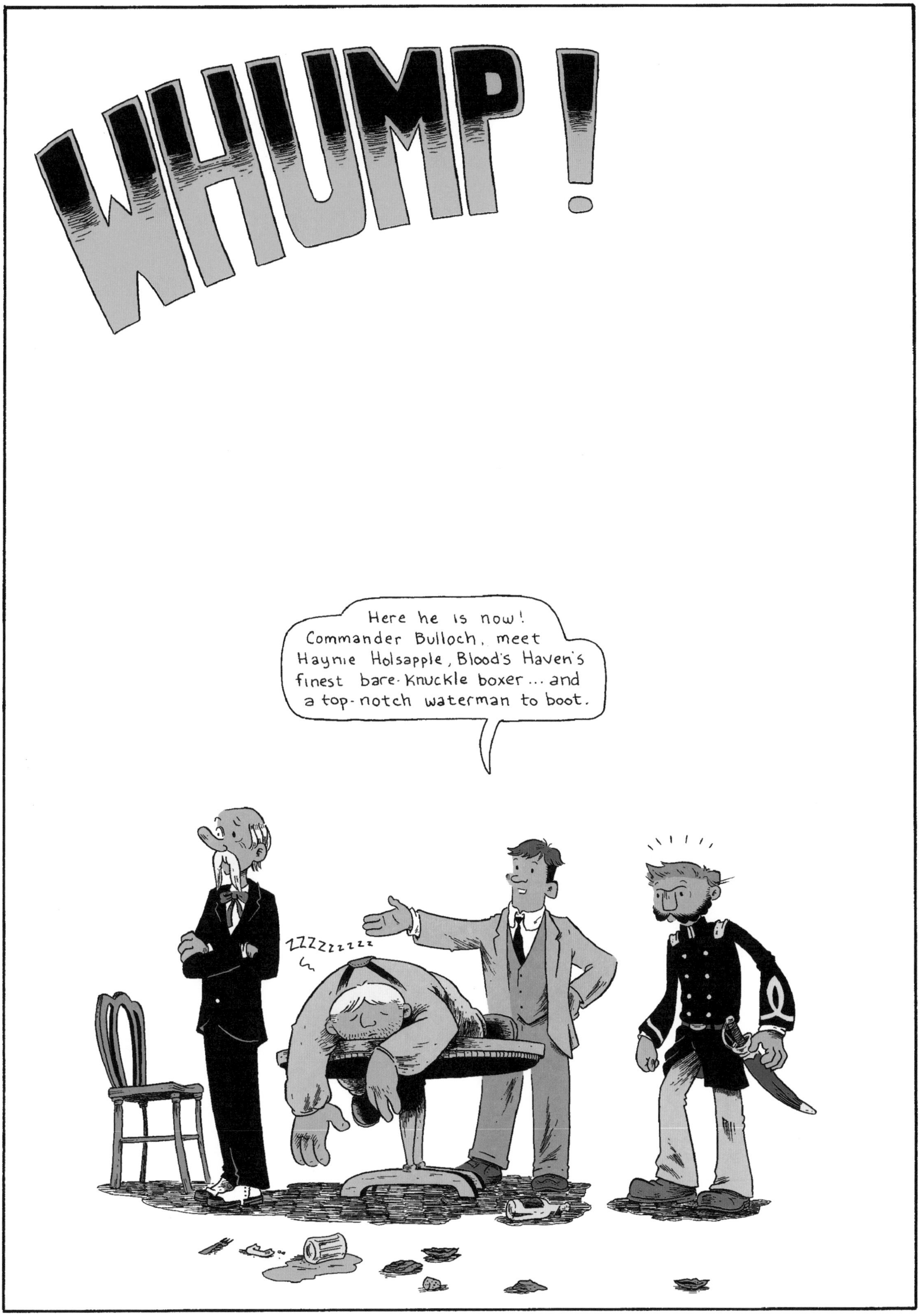
WHUMP!
Here he is now! Commander Bulloch, meet Haynie Holsapple, Blood's Haven's finest bare-knuckle boxer... and a top-notch waterman to boot.
ZZZzzzzz

CHAPTER TWO

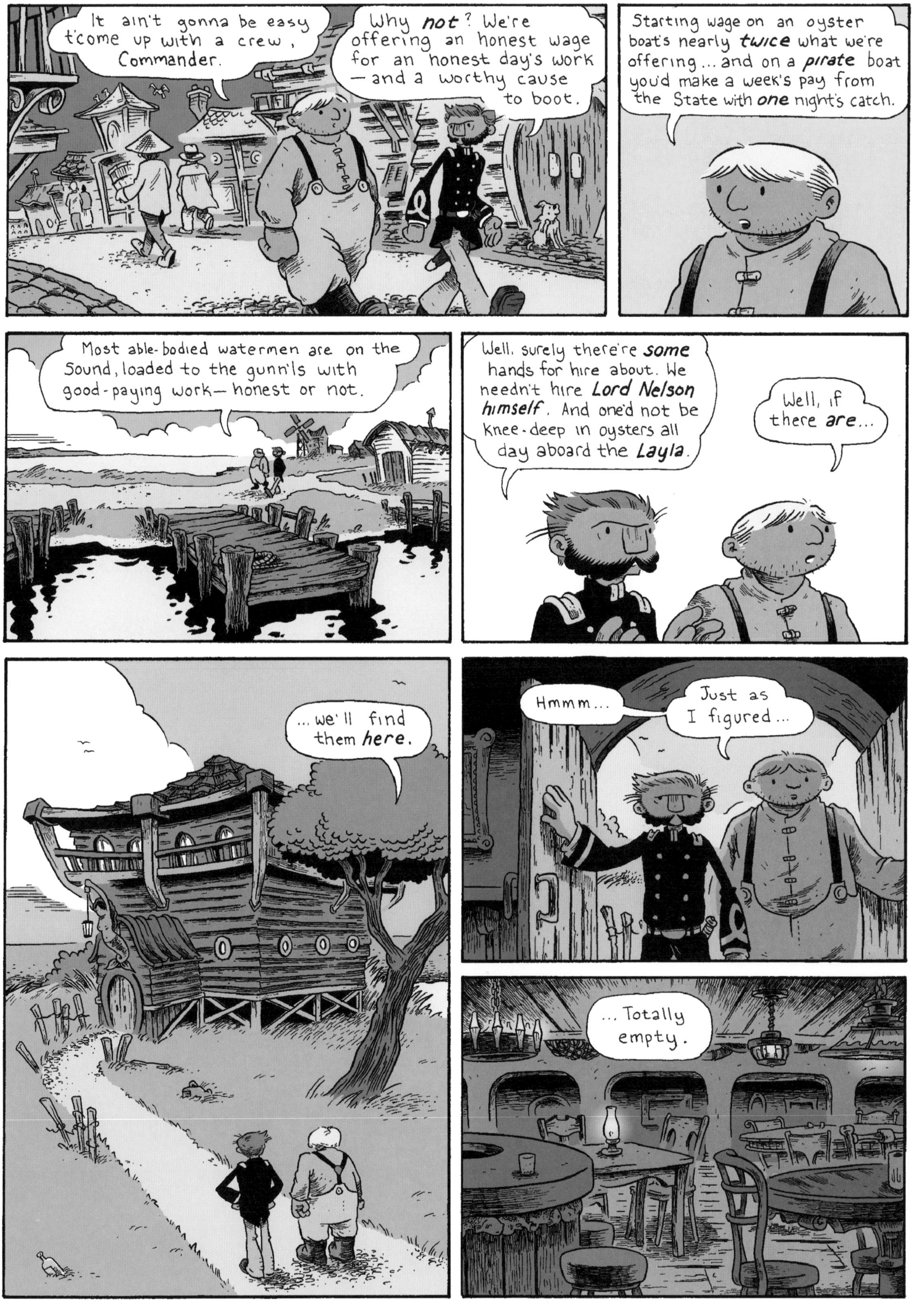
It ain't gonna be easy t'come up with a crew, Commander.
Why *not*? We're offering an honest wage for an honest day's work — and a worthy cause to boot.
Starting wage on an oyster boat's nearly *twice* what we're offering... and on a *pirate* boat you'd make a week's pay from the State with *one* night's catch.
Most able-bodied watermen are on the Sound, loaded to the gunn'ls with good-paying work— honest or not.
Well, surely there're *some* hands for hire about. We needn't hire *Lord Nelson himself*. And one'd not be knee-deep in oysters all day aboard the *Layla*.
Well, if there *are*...
...we'll find them *here*.
Hmmm...
Just as I figured...
...Totally empty.

Well, not **totally** empty.

Tick...

"Tick"?

"That's Philip Tickbourne. The place **might as well** be empty."

He'd be manning a dredge for the blackest pirate in the Sound right now if he weren't knee-deep in **whisky**.

A bit of "Dutch courage" isn't unheard of now and again among men of the sea, I suppose...

I'm **off** the sauce, you galoot, and sober as the day I was **born**.

And I know this Sound like the back of my hand.

YOINK!

SNIF
SNIF

Hell's bells. It's coffee.

Beggars cannot, as they say, be choosers.

Be at the docks tomorrow morning— 6 am sharp. Name of the boat's the *Layla*.

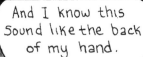
One down... at least **five** to go.

If it's like you say—any port in a storm— I **might** be able to fill out the roster. But these folks'd be a bit... "off the beaten path."

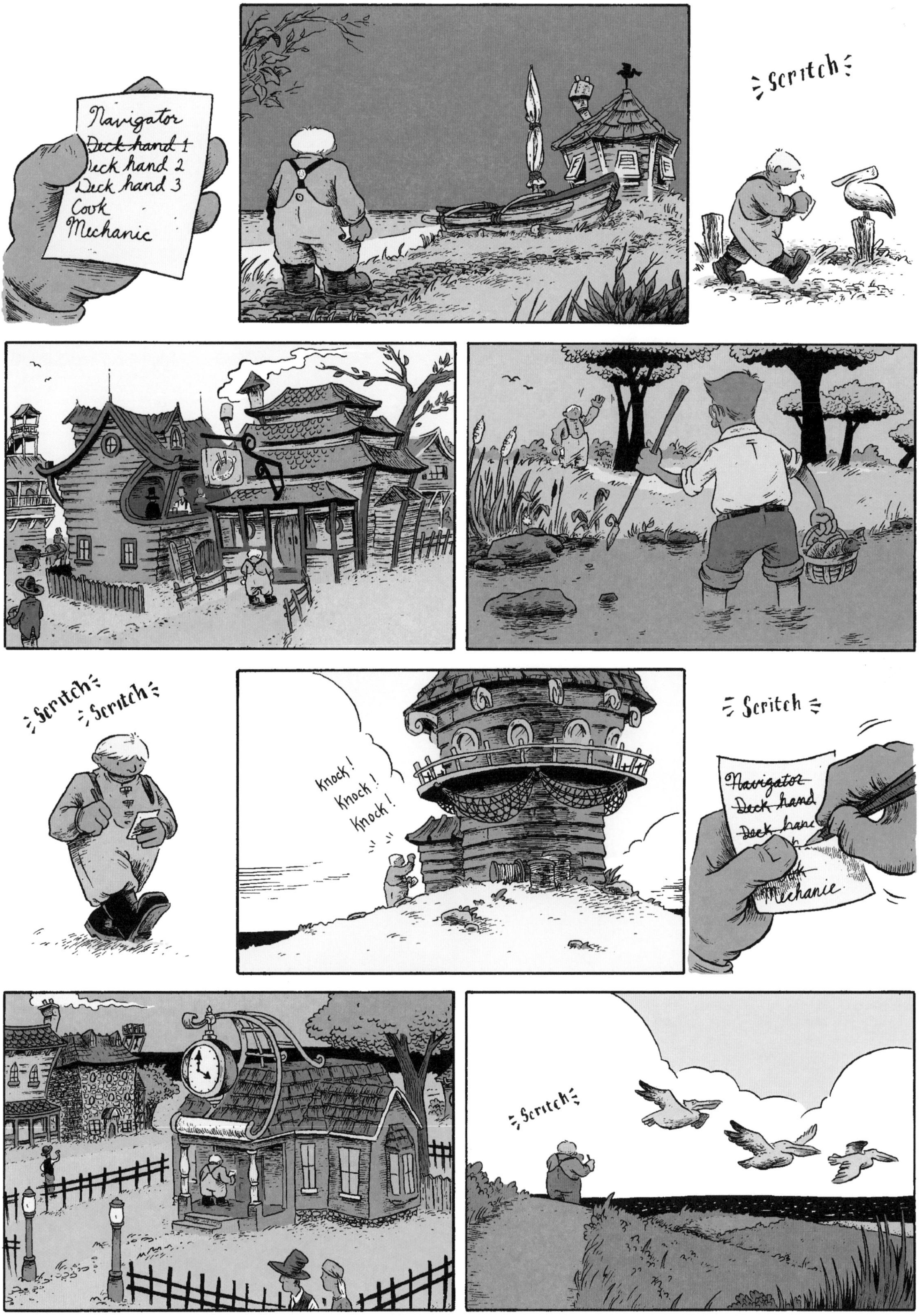
Navigator
Deck hand 1
Deck hand 2
Deck hand 3
Cook
Mechanic
Scritch
Scritch
Scritch
Knock!
Knock!
Knock!
Scritch
Navigator
Deck hand
Mechanic
Scritch

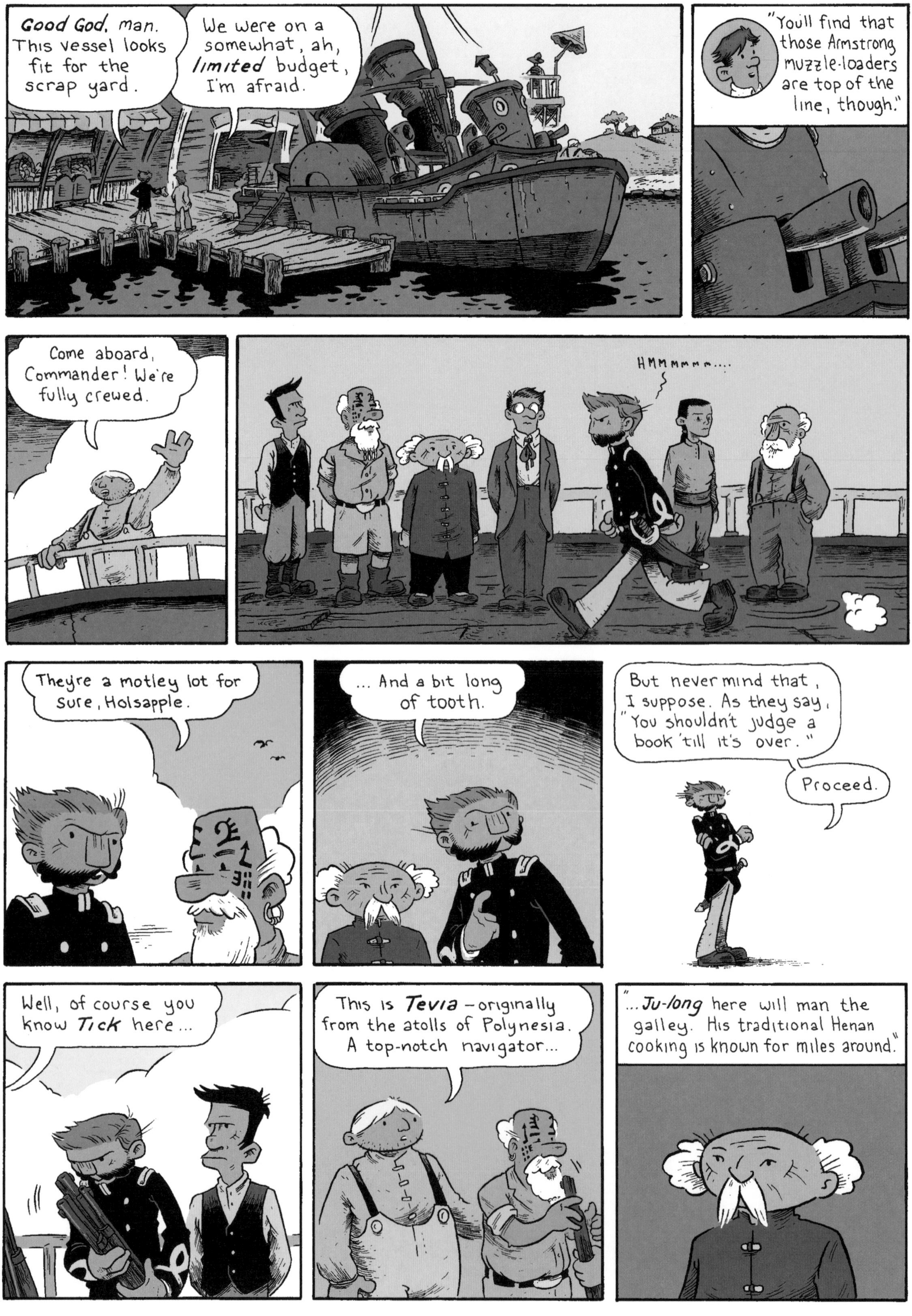

Good God, man. This vessel looks fit for the scrap yard.
We were on a somewhat, ah, limited budget, I'm afraid.
"You'll find that those Armstrong muzzle-loaders are top of the line, though."
Come aboard, Commander! We're fully crewed.
HMMmmmm....
They're a motley lot for sure, Holsapple.
... And a bit long of tooth.
But never mind that, I suppose. As they say, "You shouldn't judge a book 'till it's over."
Proceed.
Well, of course you know Tick here...
This is Tevia – originally from the atolls of Polynesia. A top-notch navigator...
"...Ju-long here will man the galley. His traditional Henan cooking is known for miles around."

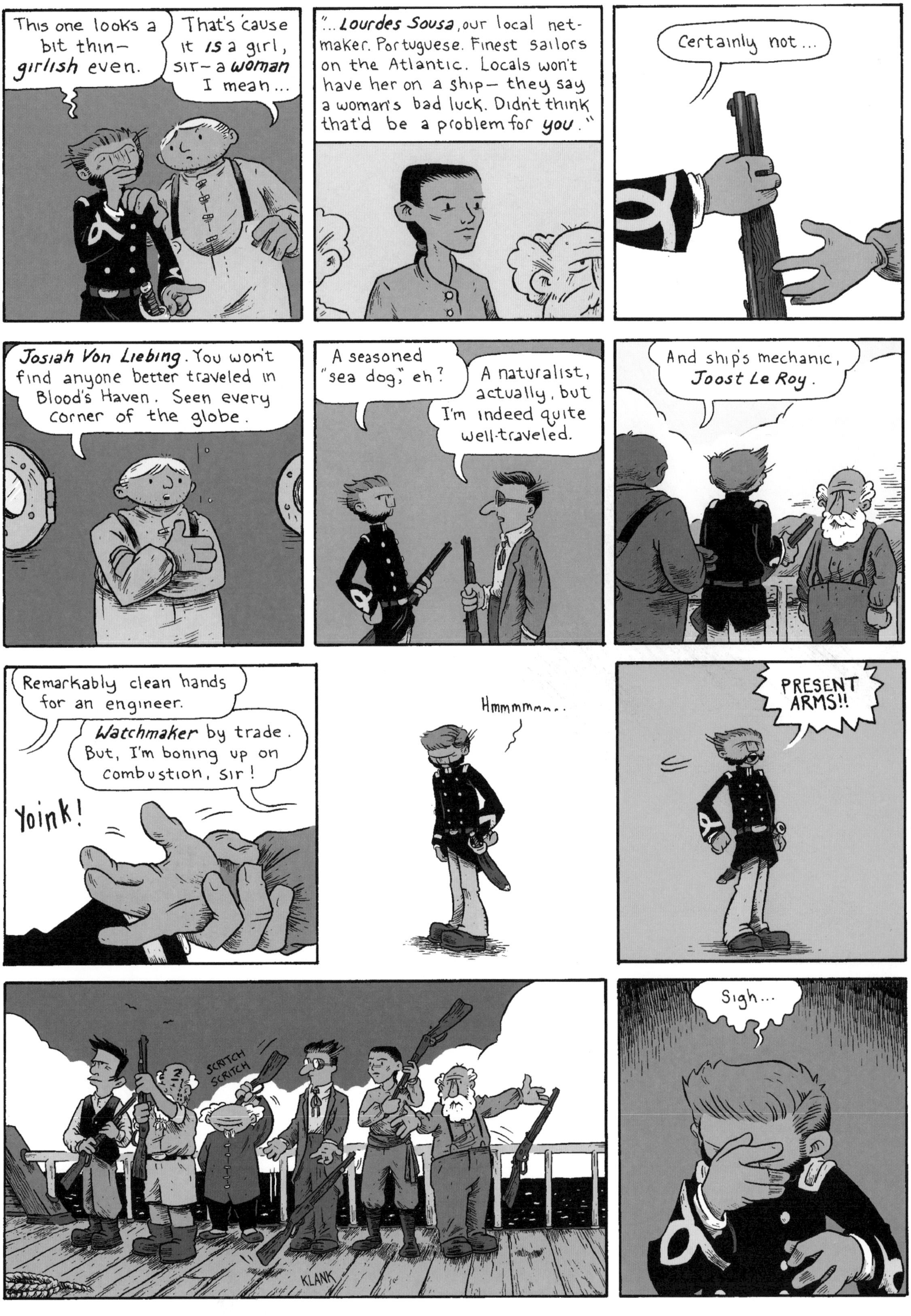

This one looks a bit thin— girlish even.
That's 'cause it IS a girl, sir— a woman I mean...
"...Lourdes Sousa, our local net-maker. Portuguese. Finest sailors on the Atlantic. Locals won't have her on a ship— they say a woman's bad luck. Didn't think that'd be a problem for you."
Certainly not...
Josiah Von Liebing. You won't find anyone better traveled in Blood's Haven. Seen every corner of the globe.
A seasoned "sea dog," eh?
A naturalist, actually, but I'm indeed quite well-traveled.
And ship's mechanic, Joost Le Roy.
Remarkably clean hands for an engineer.
Watchmaker by trade. But, I'm boning up on combustion, sir!
Yoink!
Hmmmmm...
PRESENT ARMS!!
SCRITCH SCRITCH
KLANK
Sigh...

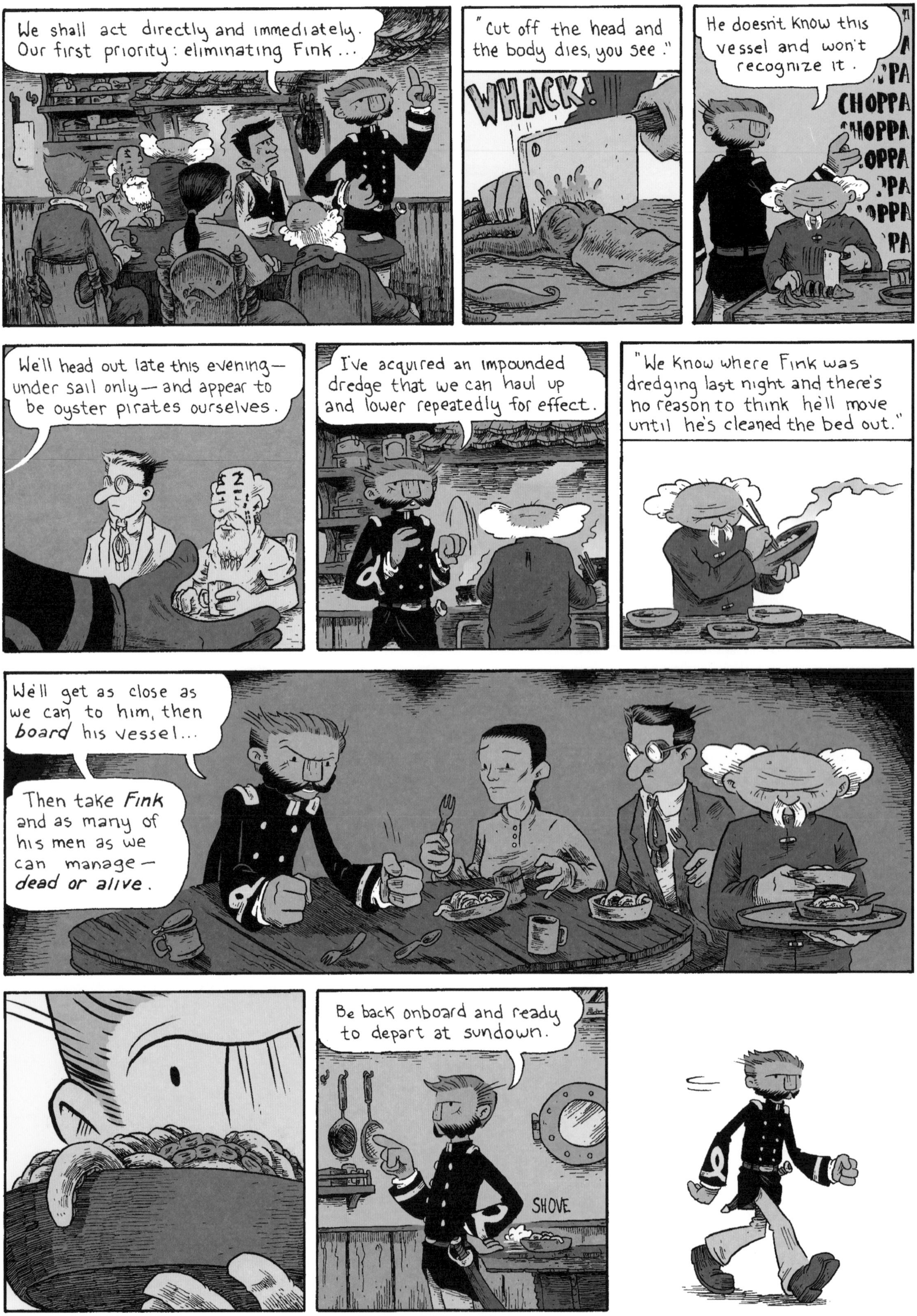
We shall act directly and immediately. Our first priority: eliminating Fink...
"Cut off the head and the body dies, you see."
WHACK!
He doesn't know this vessel and won't recognize it.
CHOPPA
CHOPPA
We'll head out late this evening— under sail only— and appear to be oyster pirates ourselves.
I've acquired an impounded dredge that we can haul up and lower repeatedly for effect.
"We know where Fink was dredging last night and there's no reason to think he'll move until he's cleaned the bed out."
We'll get as close as we can to him, then *board* his vessel...
Then take *Fink* and as many of his men as we can manage— *dead or alive*.
Be back onboard and ready to depart at sundown.
SHOVE

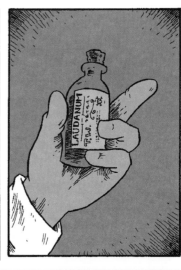

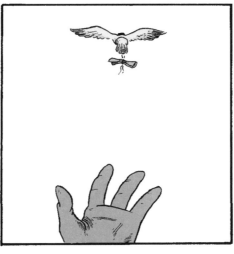

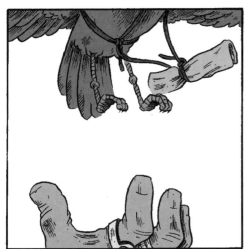
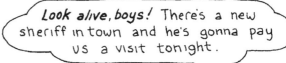

Hmmmmm...

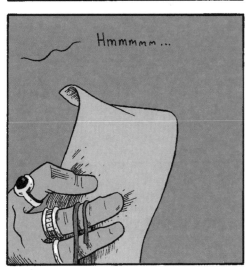

Look alive, boys! There's a new sheriff in town and he's gonna pay us a visit tonight.

CHAPTER THREE

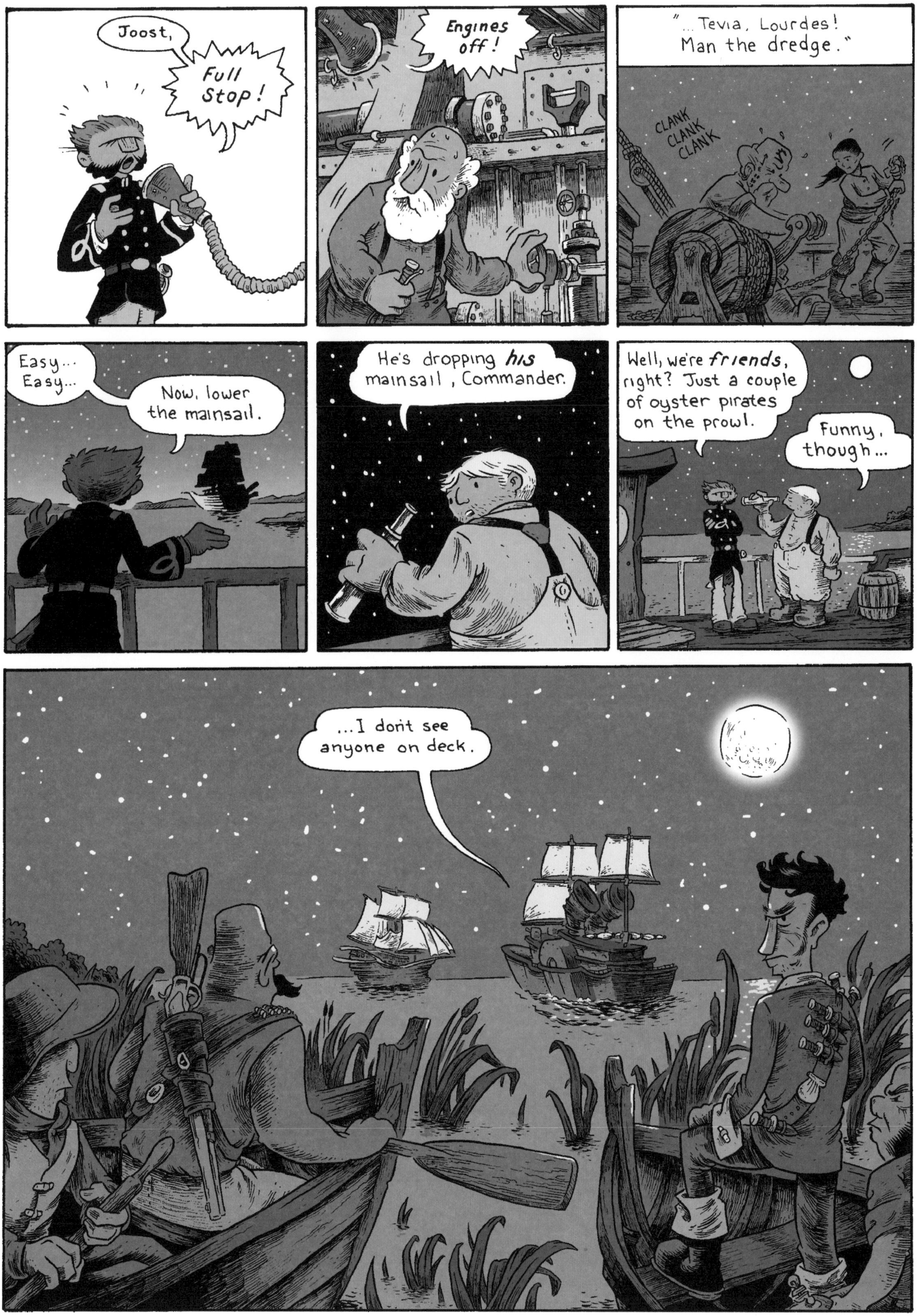
Joost,
Full Stop!
Engines off!
"...Tevia, Lourdes! Man the dredge."
CLANK CLANK CLANK
Easy... Easy...
Now, lower the mainsail.
He's dropping his mainsail, Commander.
Well, we're friends, right? Just a couple of oyster pirates on the prowl.
Funny, though...
...I don't see anyone on deck.

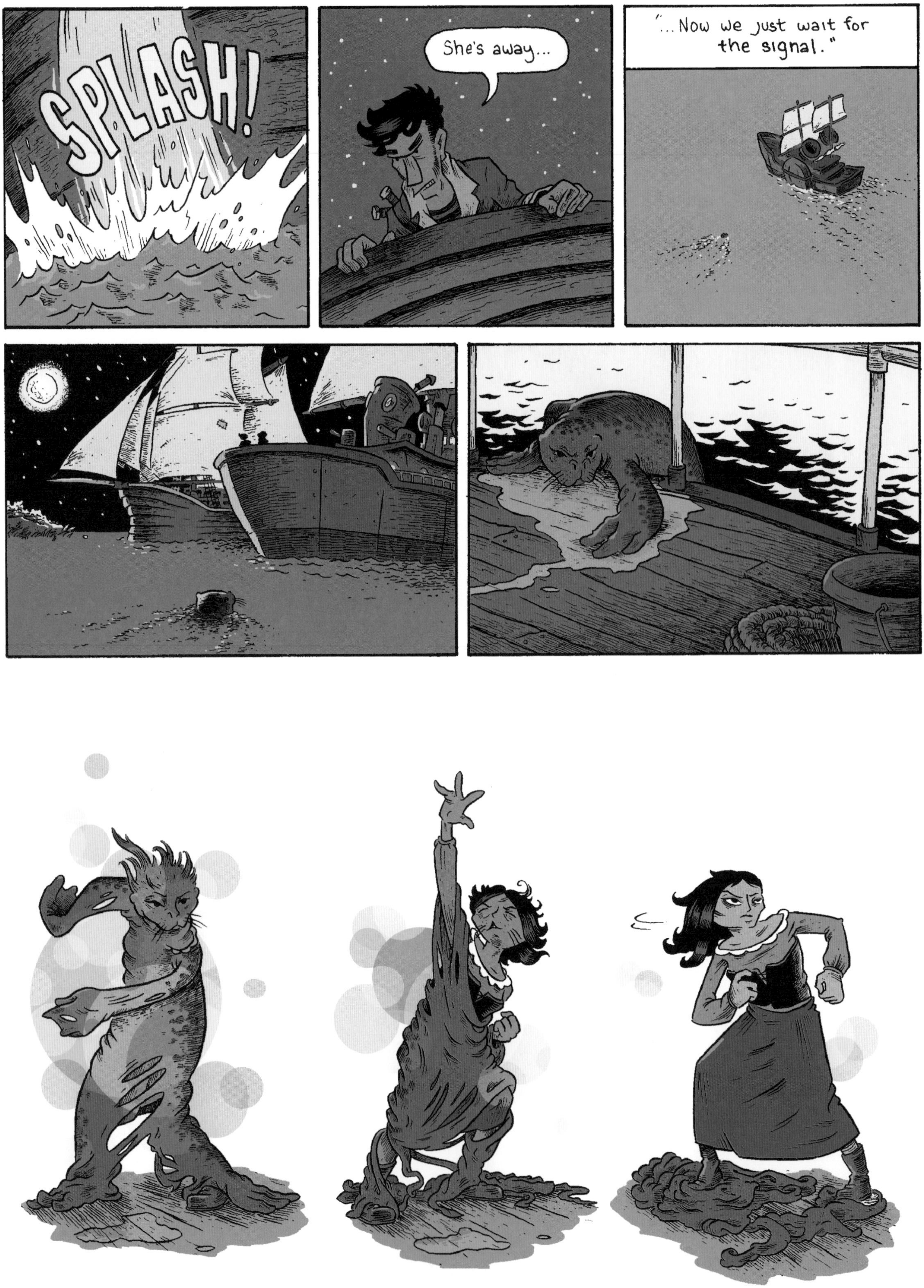
SPLASH!
She's away...
"...Now we just wait for the signal."

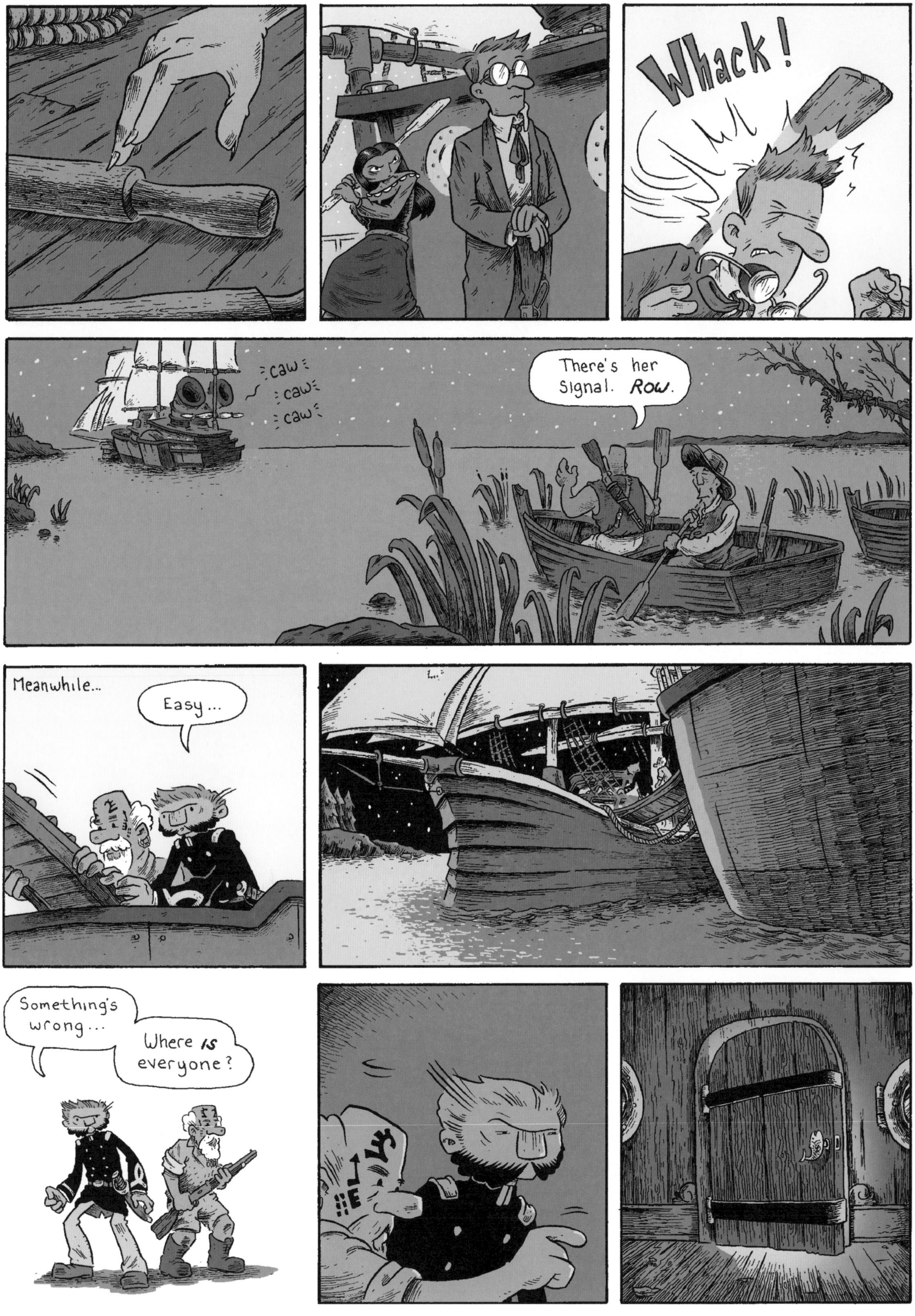
Whack!
caw
caw
caw
There's her signal. ROW.
Meanwhile...
Easy...
Something's wrong...
Where IS everyone?

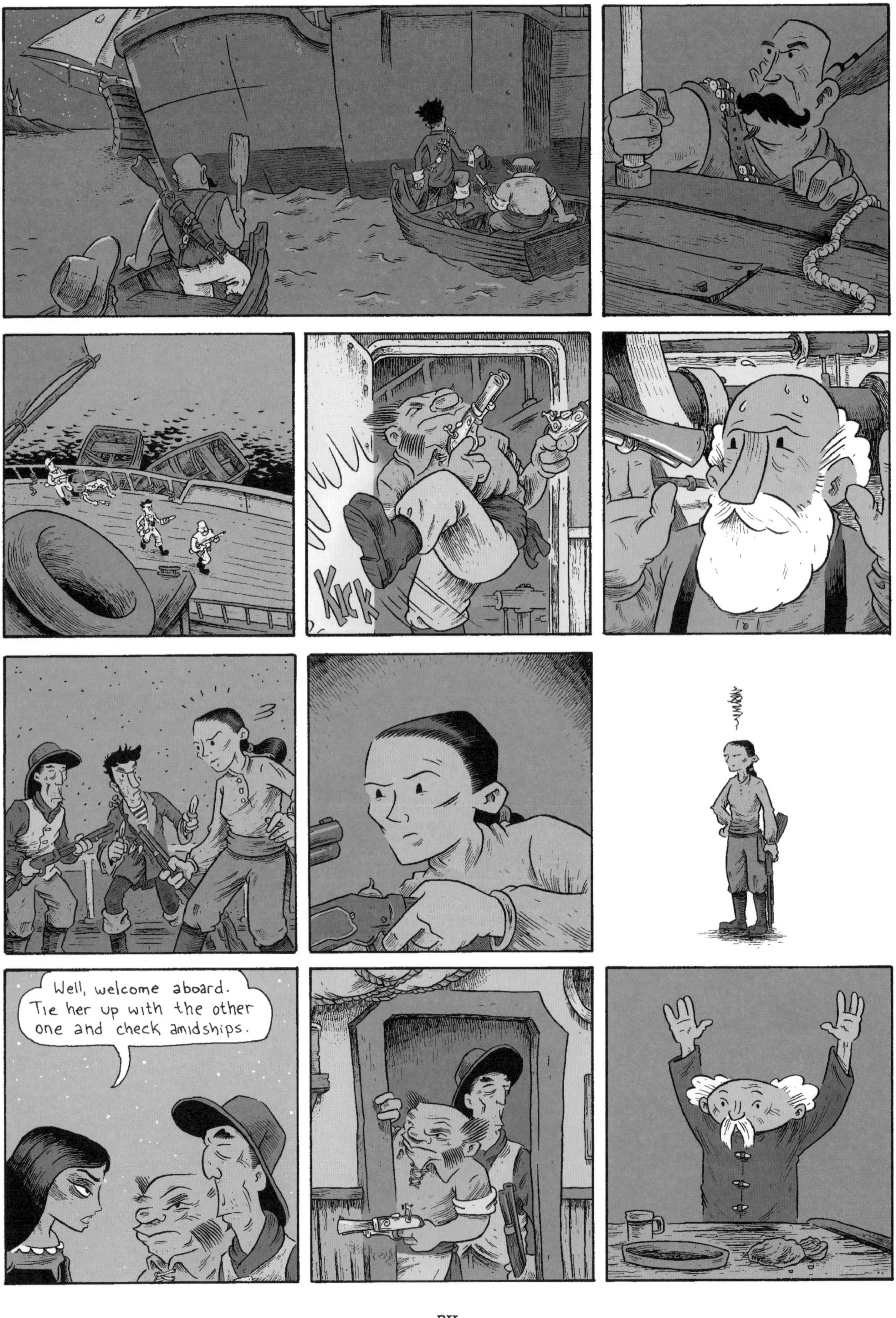
KICK
Well, welcome aboard. Tie her up with the other one and check amidships.

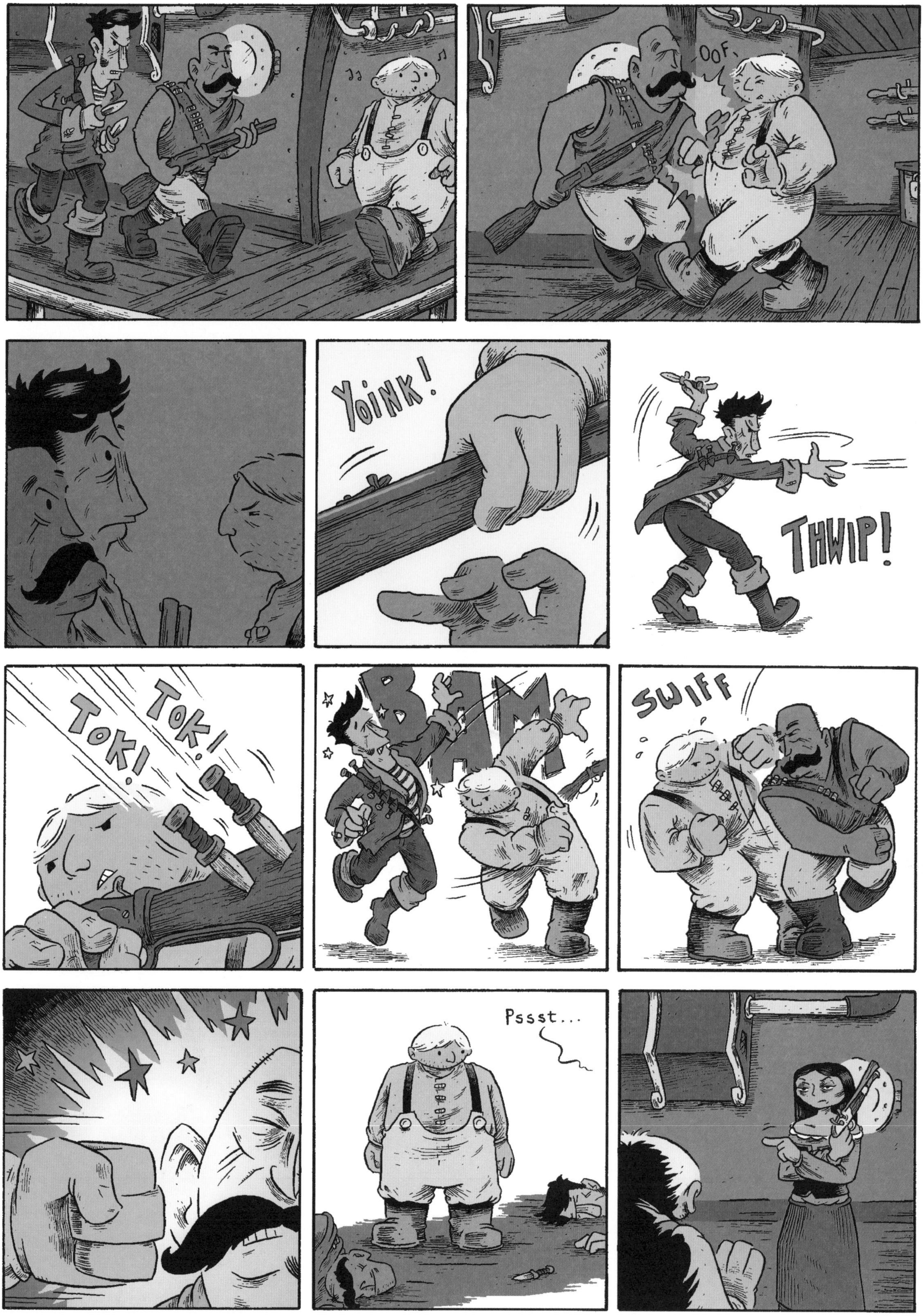
OOF
YOINK!
THWIP!
TOK!
TOK!
BAM
SWIFF
Pssst...

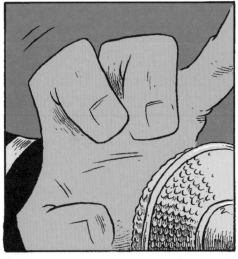

SNAP!

CLICK

BING!

THWIP!

POW!

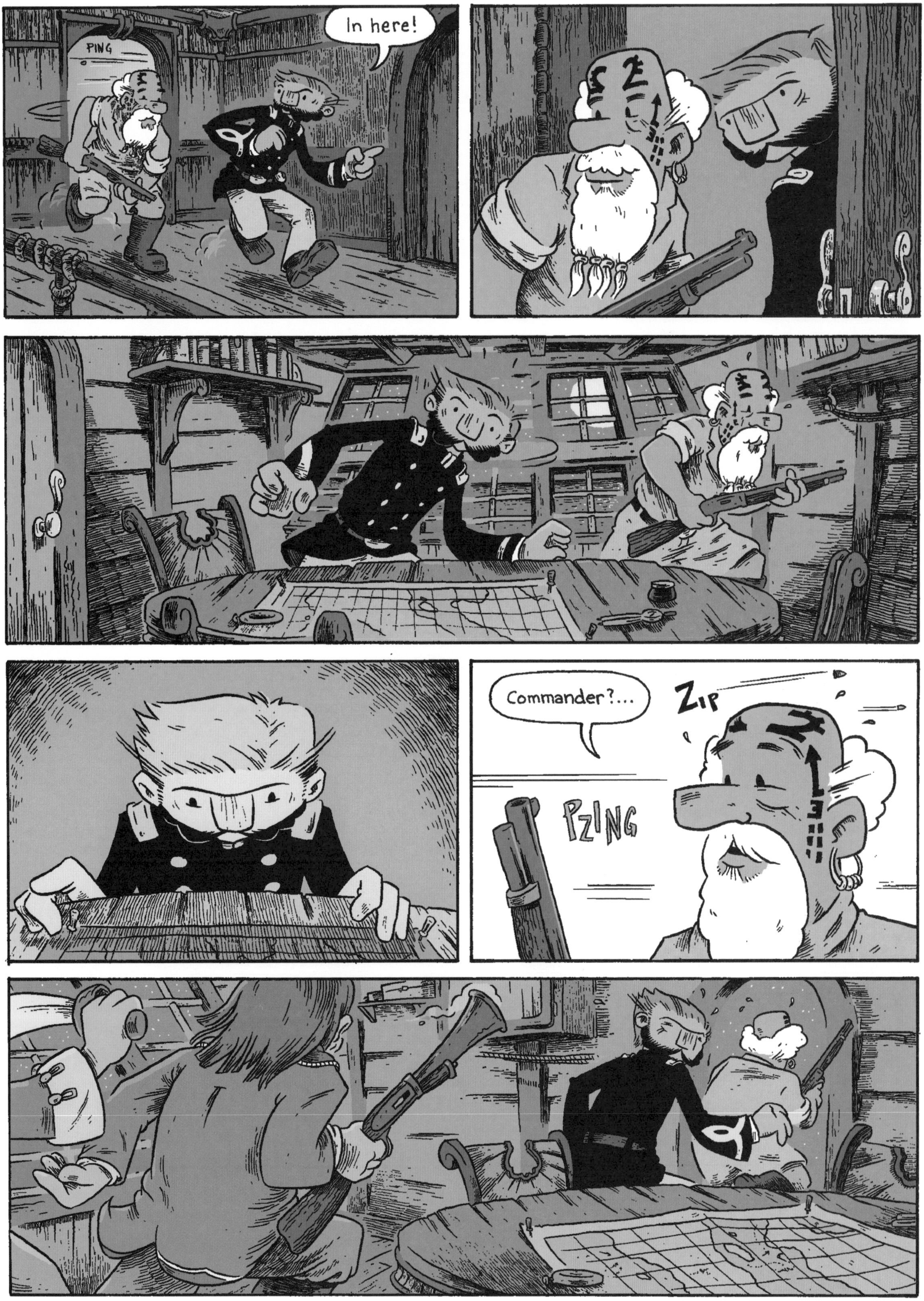
PING
In here!
Commander?...
ZIP
PZING

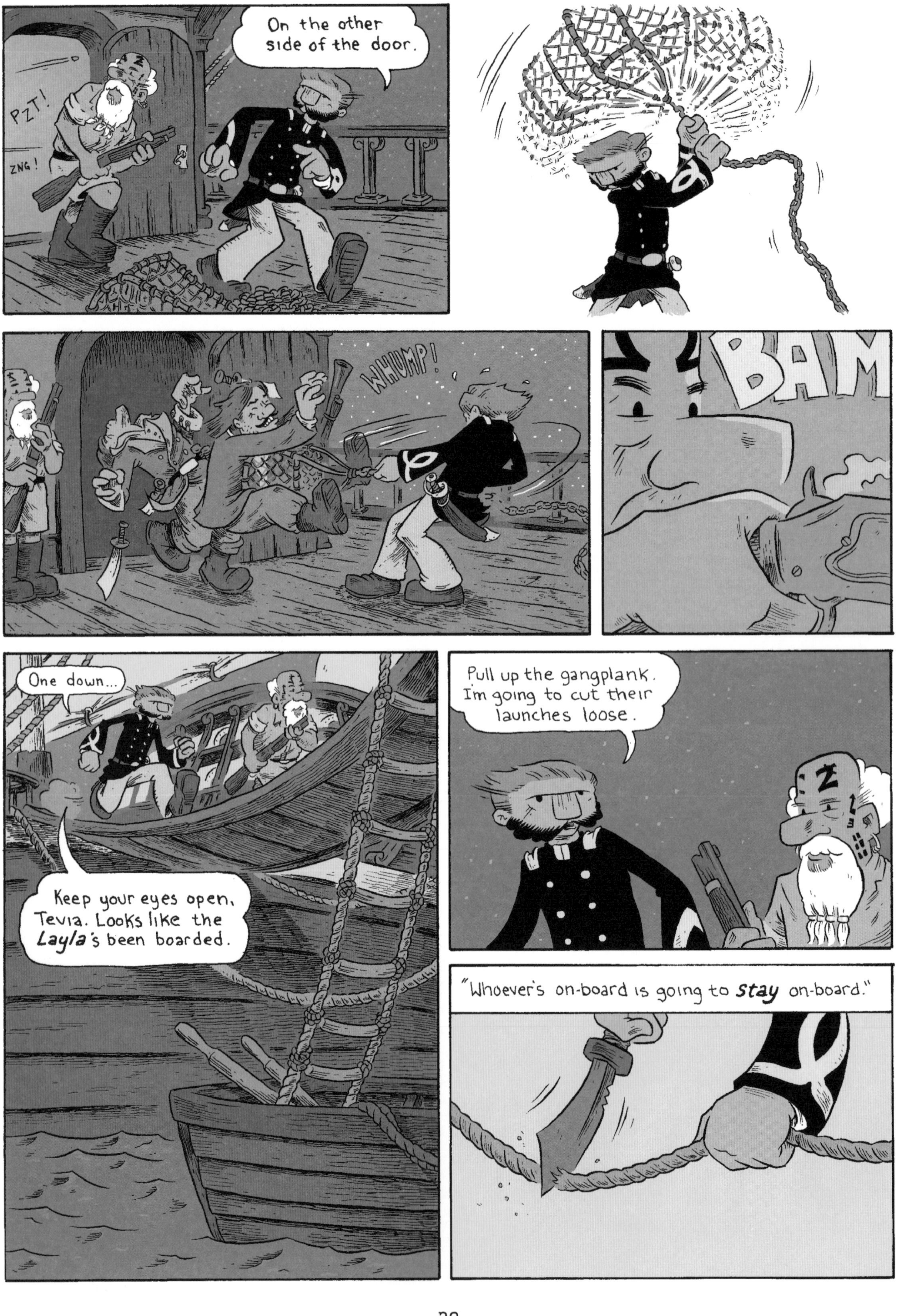
On the other side of the door.
PZT!
ZNG!
WHUMP!
BAM
One down...
Keep your eyes open, Tevia. Looks like the *Layla*'s been boarded.
Pull up the gangplank. I'm going to cut their launches loose.
"Whoever's on-board is going to **stay** on-board."

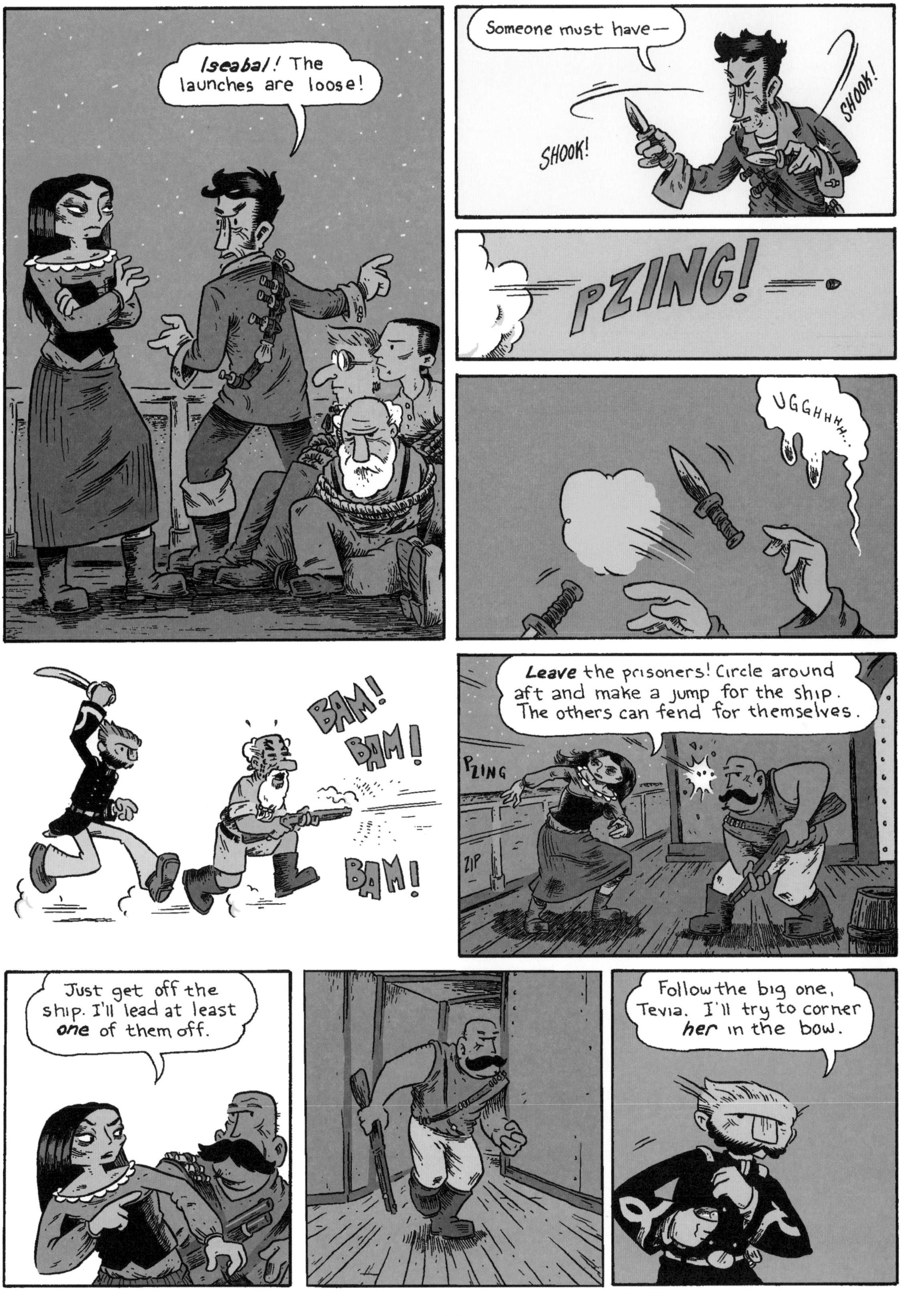

Iseabal! The launches are loose!
Someone must have—
SHOOK!
SHOOK!
PZING!
UGGHHHH...
BAM!
BAM!
BAM!
Leave the prisoners! Circle around aft and make a jump for the ship. The others can fend for themselves.
PZING
ZIP
Just get off the ship. I'll lead at least one of them off.
Follow the big one, Tevia. I'll try to corner her in the bow.

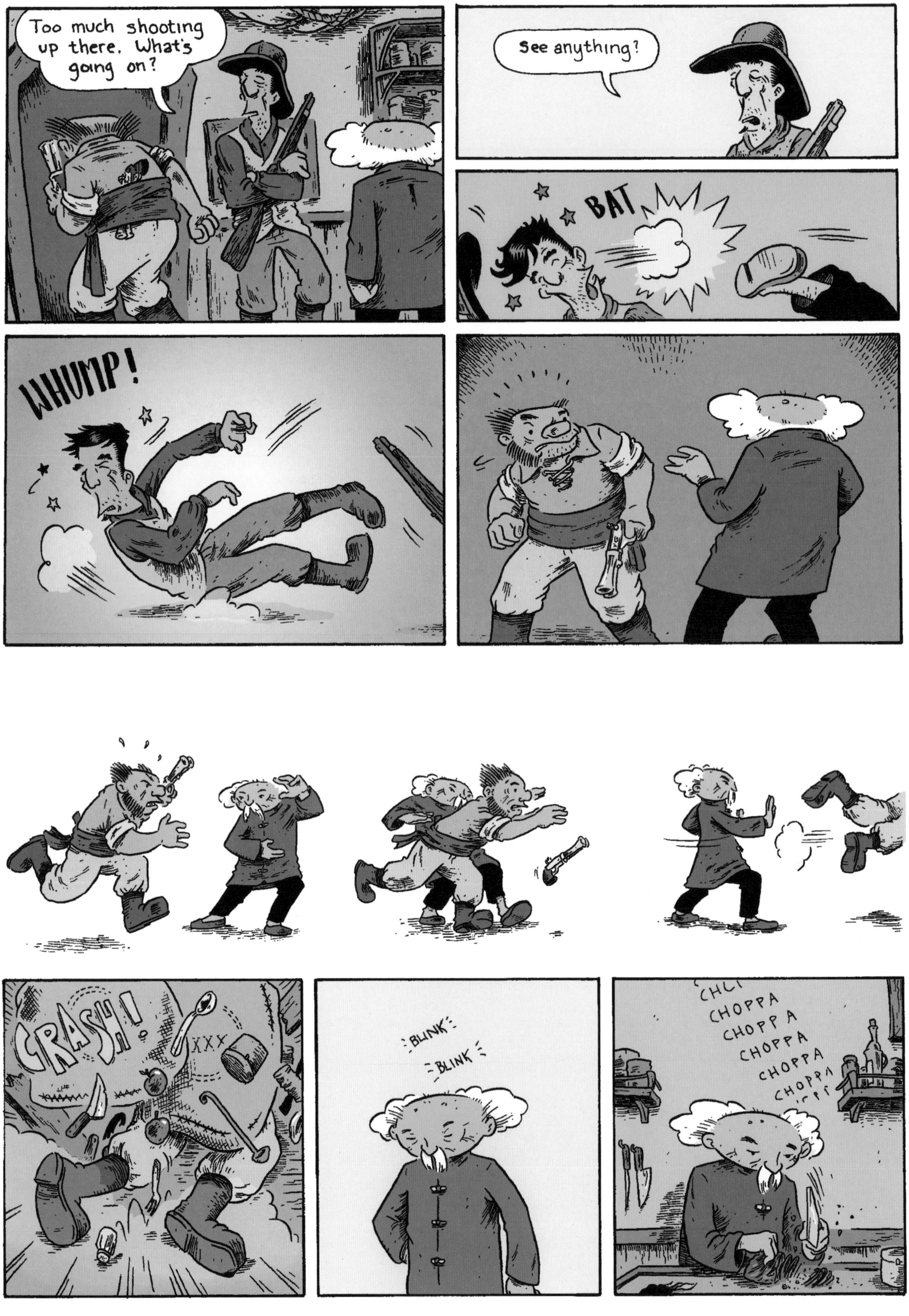
Too much shooting up there. What's going on?
See anything?
BAT
WHUMP!
CRASH!
XXX
BLINK
BLINK
CHOPPA
CHOPPA
CHOPPA
CHOPPA
CHOPPA

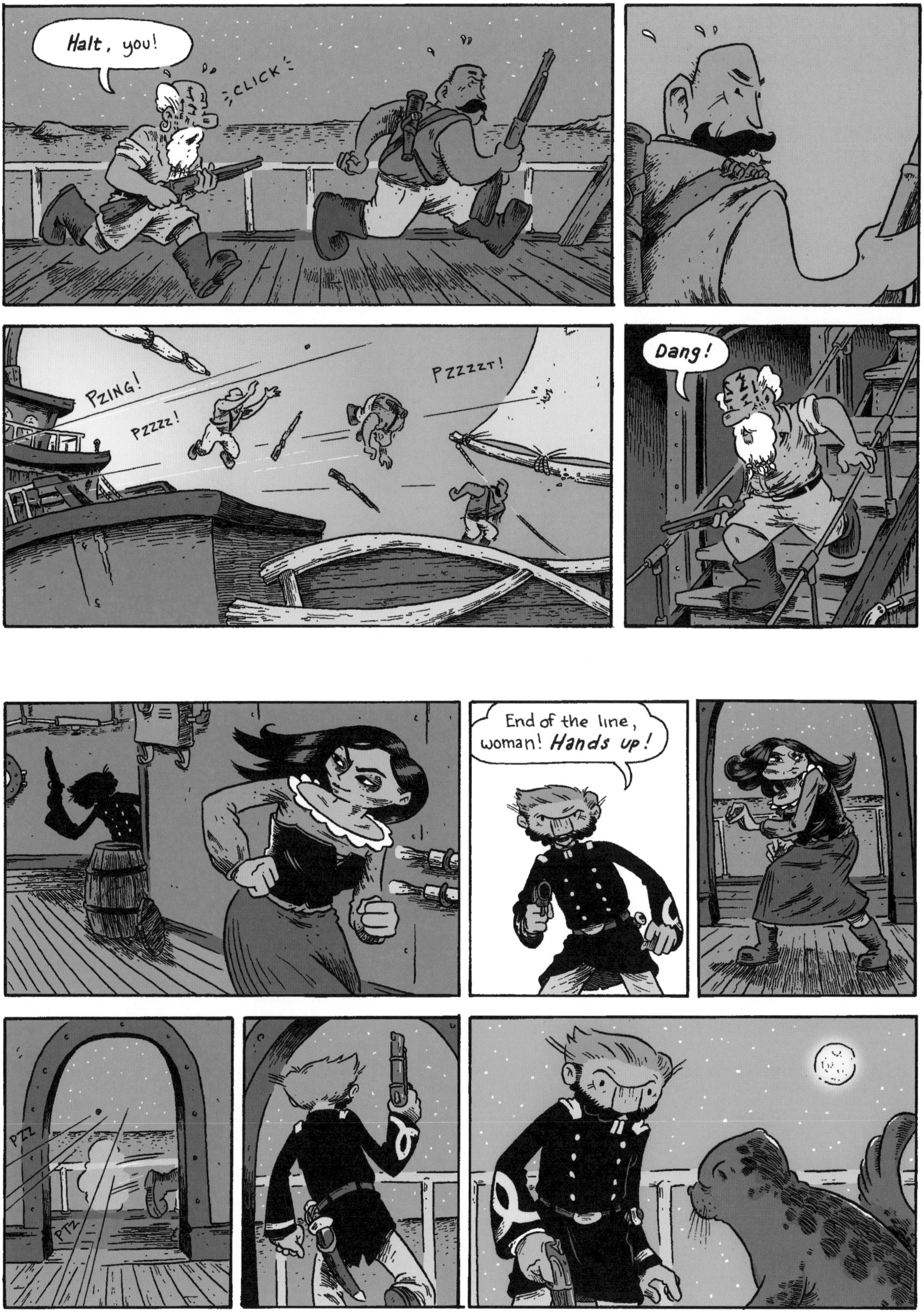

Halt, you!
CLICK
PZING!
PZZZZ!
PZZZZT!
Dang!
End of the line, woman! Hands up!
PZZ
PTZ

Curious...
SPLASH
Curious...

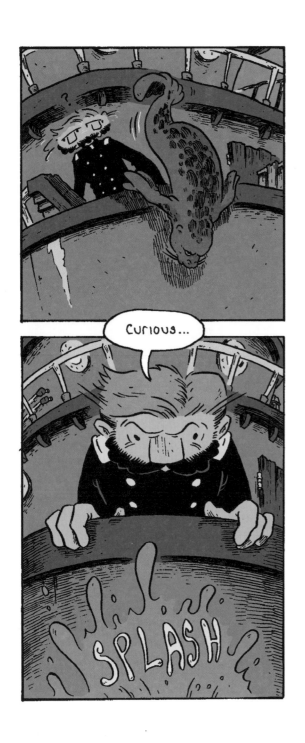

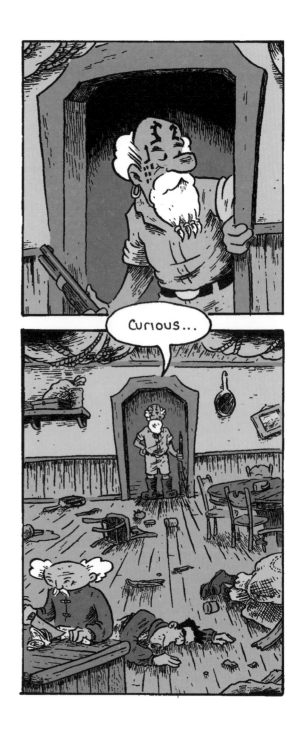

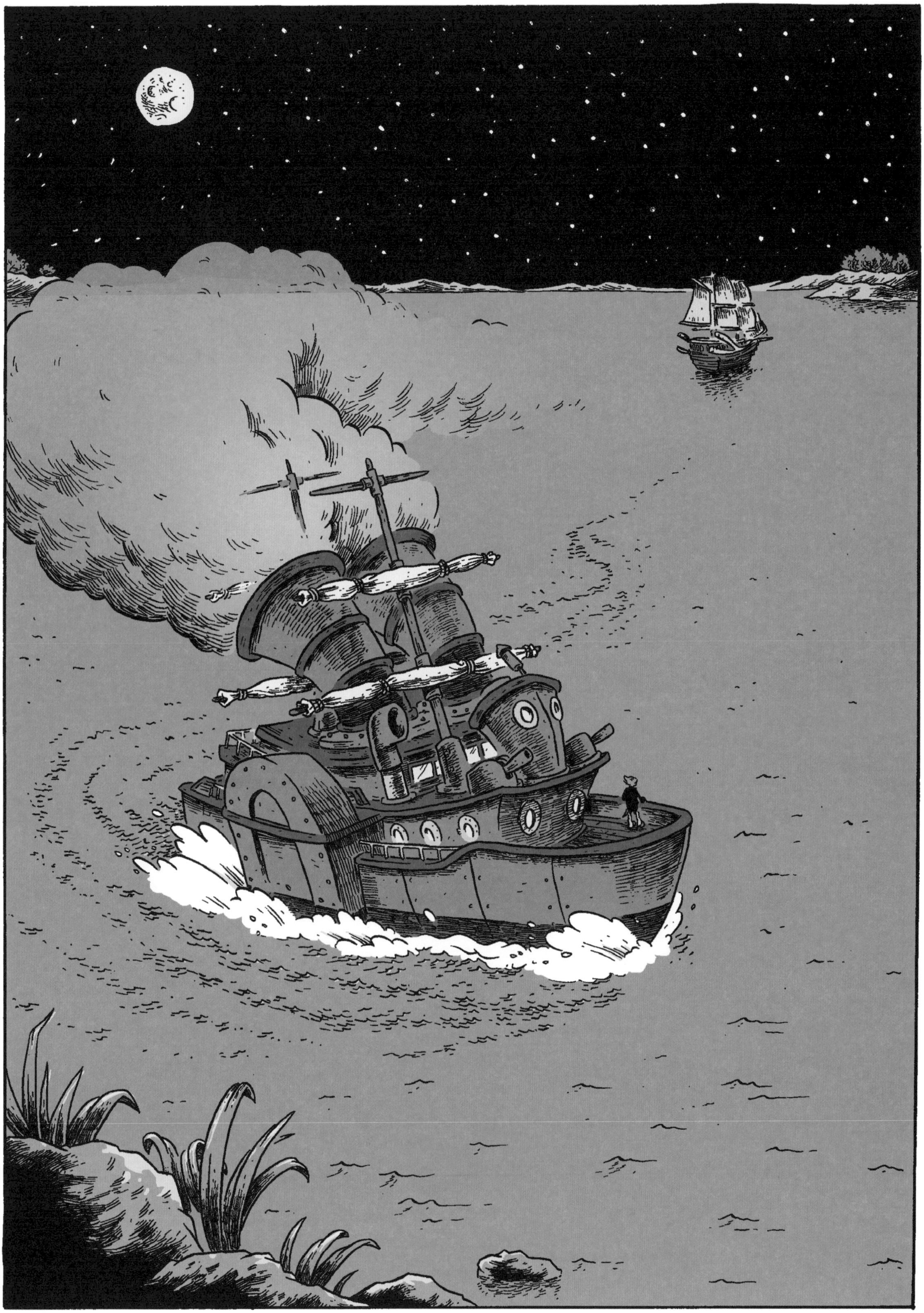

CHAPTER FOUR

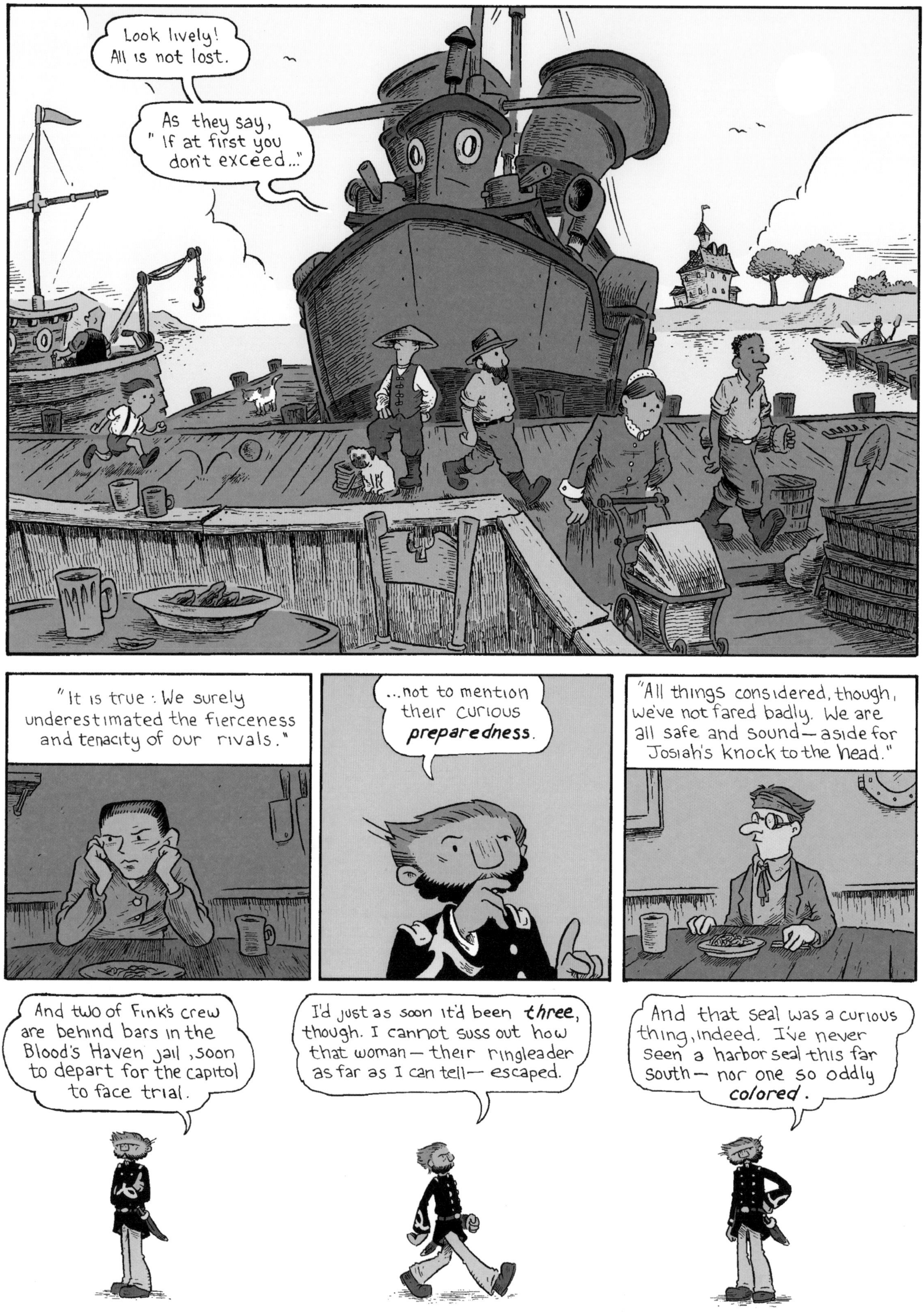
Look lively! All is not lost.
As they say, "If at first you don't exceed..."
"It is true: We surely underestimated the fierceness and tenacity of our rivals."
...not to mention their curious *preparedness*.
"All things considered, though, we've not fared badly. We are all safe and sound—aside for Josiah's knock to the head."
And two of Fink's crew are behind bars in the Blood's Haven jail, soon to depart for the capitol to face trial.
I'd just as soon it'd been *three*, though. I cannot suss out how that woman—their ringleader as far as I can tell—escaped.
And that seal was a curious thing, indeed. I've never seen a harbor seal this far south—nor one so oddly *colored*.

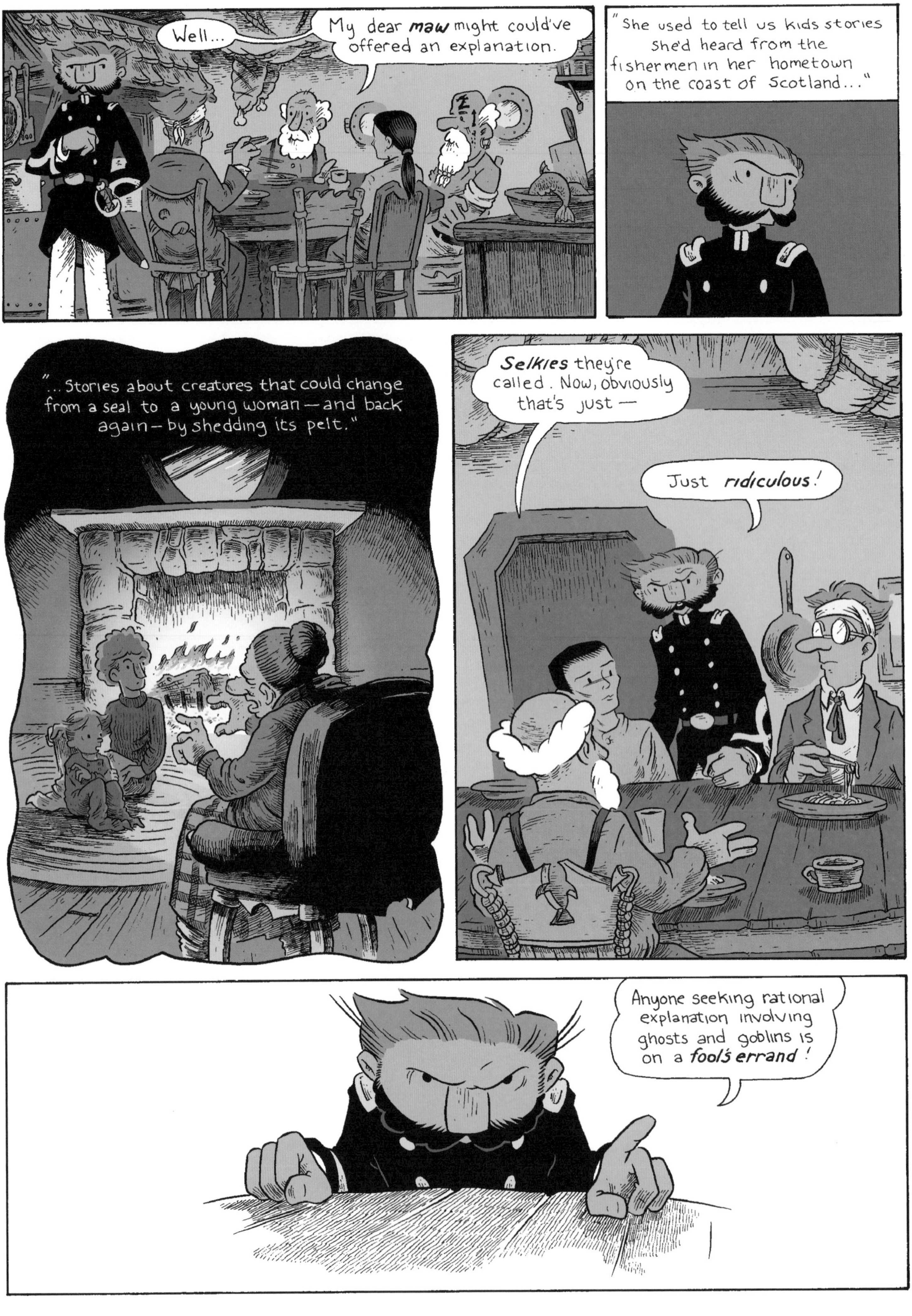
Well...
My dear maw might could've offered an explanation.
"She used to tell us kids stories she'd heard from the fishermen in her hometown on the coast of Scotland..."
"...Stories about creatures that could change from a seal to a young woman—and back again—by shedding its pelt."
Selkies they're called. Now, obviously that's just—
Just ridiculous!
Anyone seeking rational explanation involving ghosts and goblins is on a fool's errand!

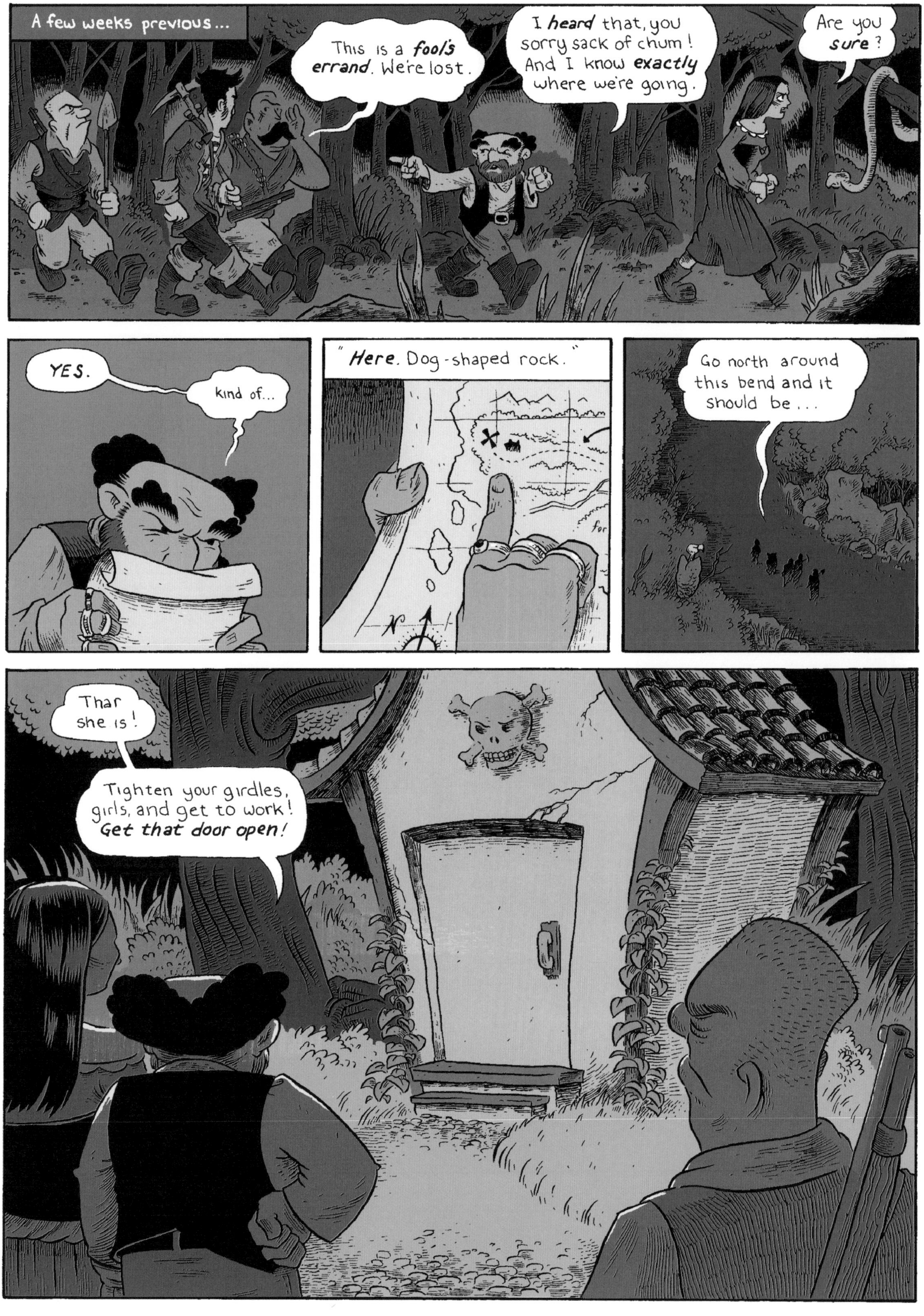
A few weeks previous...
This is a *fool's errand*. We're lost.
I *heard* that, you sorry sack of chum! And I know *exactly* where we're going.
Are you *sure*?
YES.
kind of...
"*Here*. Dog-shaped rock."
Go north around this bend and it should be...
Thar she is!
Tighten your girdles, girls, and get to work! **Get that door open!**

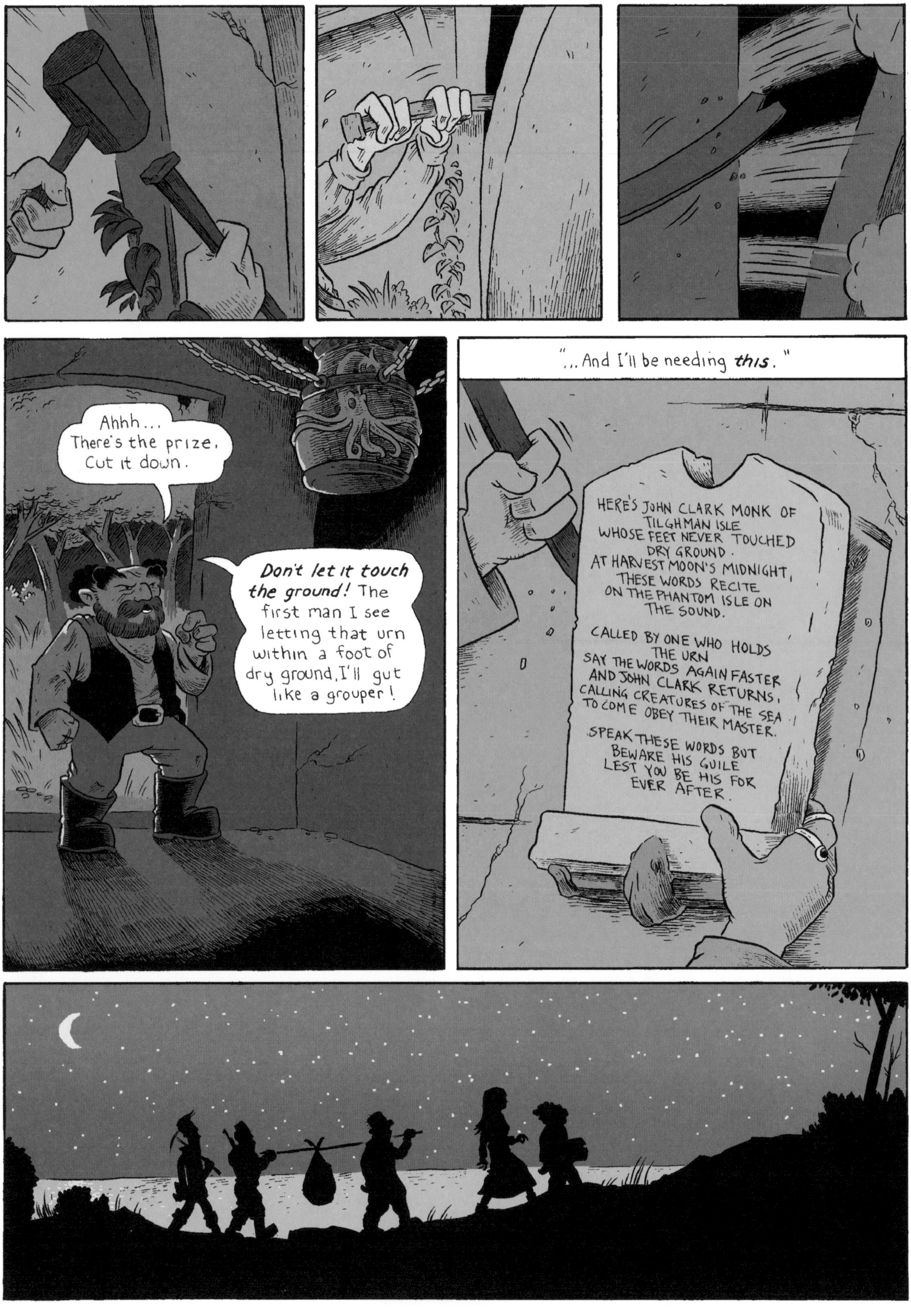
Ahhh... There's the prize. Cut it down.
Don't let it touch the ground! The first man I see letting that urn within a foot of dry ground, I'll gut like a grouper!
"... And I'll be needing this."
HERE'S JOHN CLARK MONK OF TILGHMAN ISLE WHOSE FEET NEVER TOUCHED DRY GROUND. AT HARVEST MOON'S MIDNIGHT, THESE WORDS RECITE ON THE PHANTOM ISLE ON THE SOUND.
CALLED BY ONE WHO HOLDS THE URN SAY THE WORDS AGAIN FASTER AND JOHN CLARK RETURNS, CALLING CREATURES OF THE SEA TO COME OBEY THEIR MASTER.
SPEAK THESE WORDS BUT BEWARE HIS GUILE LEST YOU BE HIS FOR EVER AFTER.

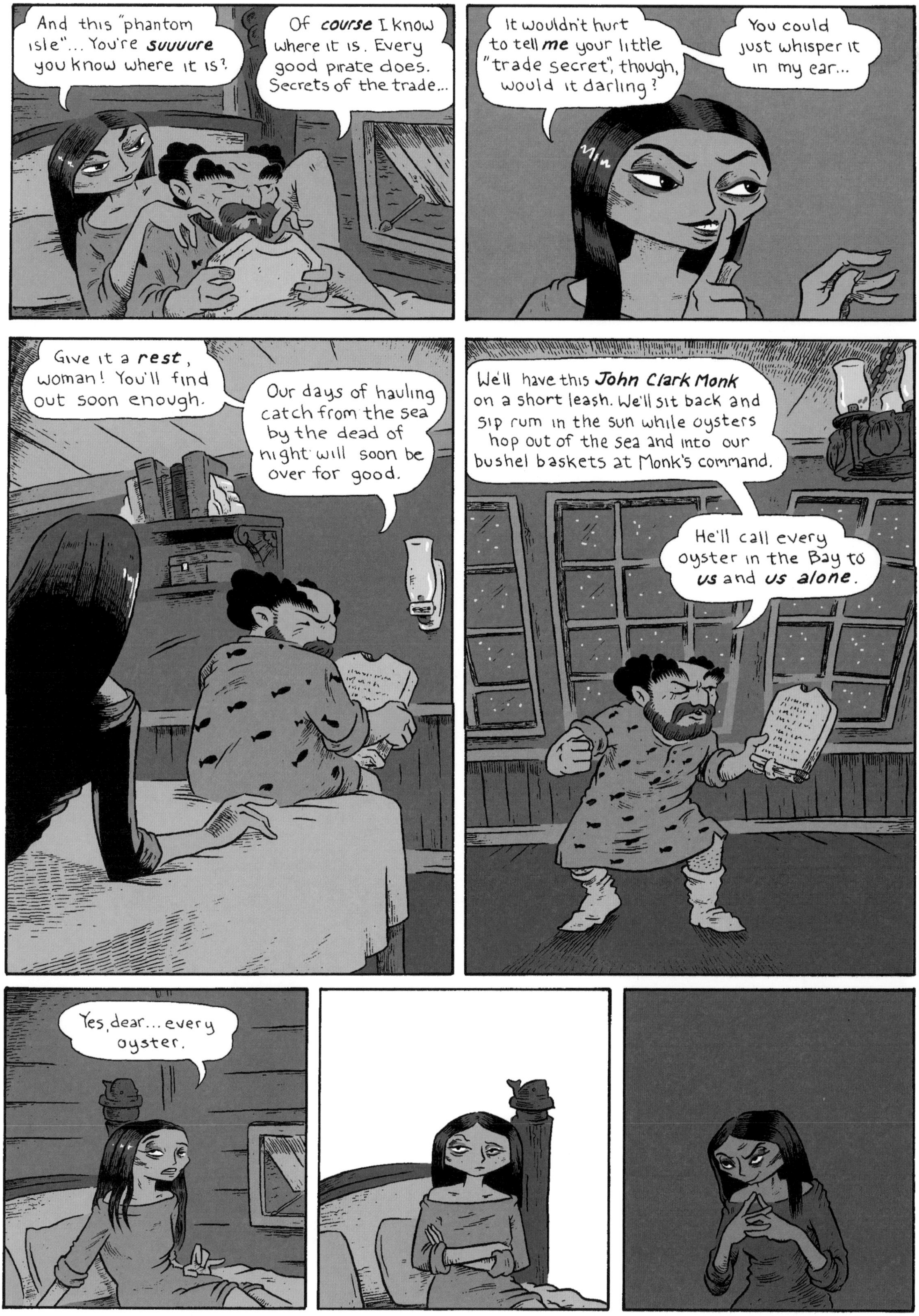

And this "phantom isle"... You're *suuuure* you know where it is?
Of *course* I know where it is. Every good pirate does. Secrets of the trade...
It wouldn't hurt to tell *me* your little "trade secret", though, would it darling?
You could just whisper it in my ear...
Give it a *rest*, woman! You'll find out soon enough.
Our days of hauling catch from the sea by the dead of night will soon be over for good.
We'll have this *John Clark Monk* on a short leash. We'll sit back and sip rum in the sun while oysters hop out of the sea and into our bushel baskets at Monk's command.
He'll call every oyster in the Bay to *us* and *us alone*.
Yes, dear... every oyster.

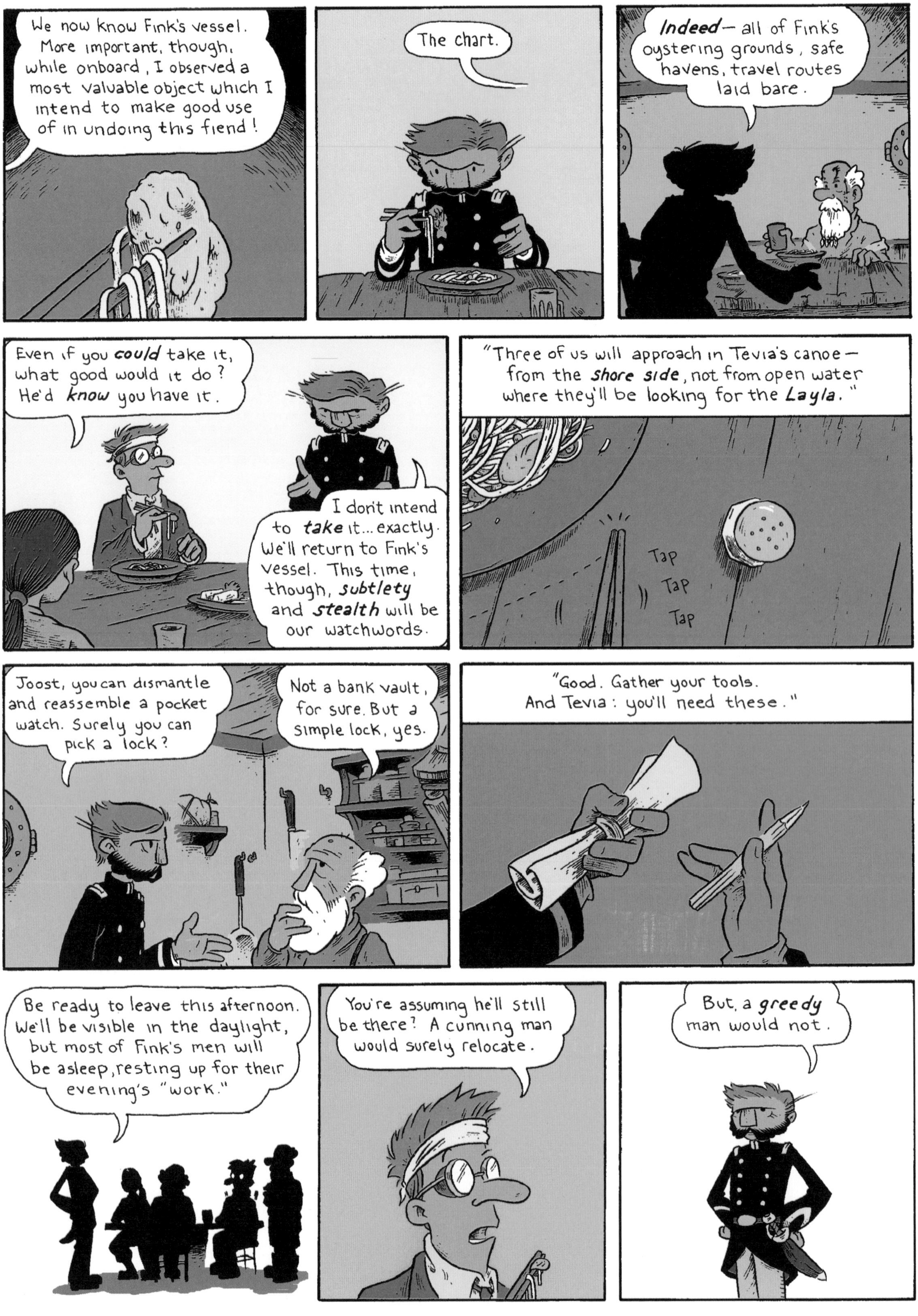

We now know Fink's vessel. More important, though, while onboard, I observed a most valuable object which I intend to make good use of in undoing this fiend!
The chart.
Indeed — all of Fink's oystering grounds, safe havens, travel routes laid bare.
Even if you could take it, what good would it do? He'd know you have it.
I don't intend to take it... exactly. We'll return to Fink's vessel. This time, though, subtlety and stealth will be our watchwords.
"Three of us will approach in Tevia's canoe — from the shore side, not from open water where they'll be looking for the Layla."
Tap
Tap
Tap
Joost, you can dismantle and reassemble a pocket watch. Surely you can pick a lock?
Not a bank vault, for sure. But a simple lock, yes.
"Good. Gather your tools. And Tevia: you'll need these."
Be ready to leave this afternoon. We'll be visible in the daylight, but most of Fink's men will be asleep, resting up for their evening's "work."
You're assuming he'll still be there? A cunning man would surely relocate.
But, a greedy man would not.

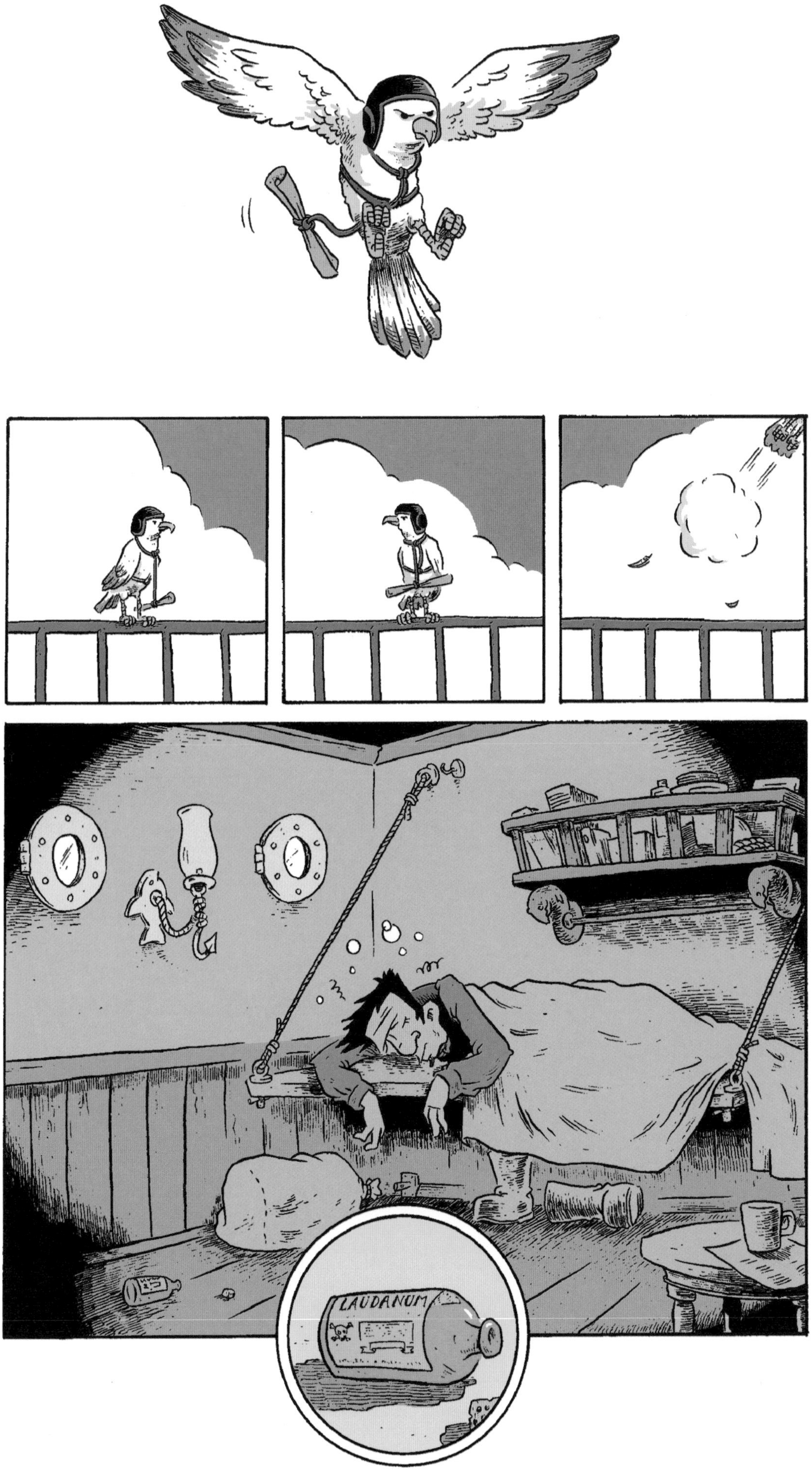
LAUDANUM

CHAPTER FIVE

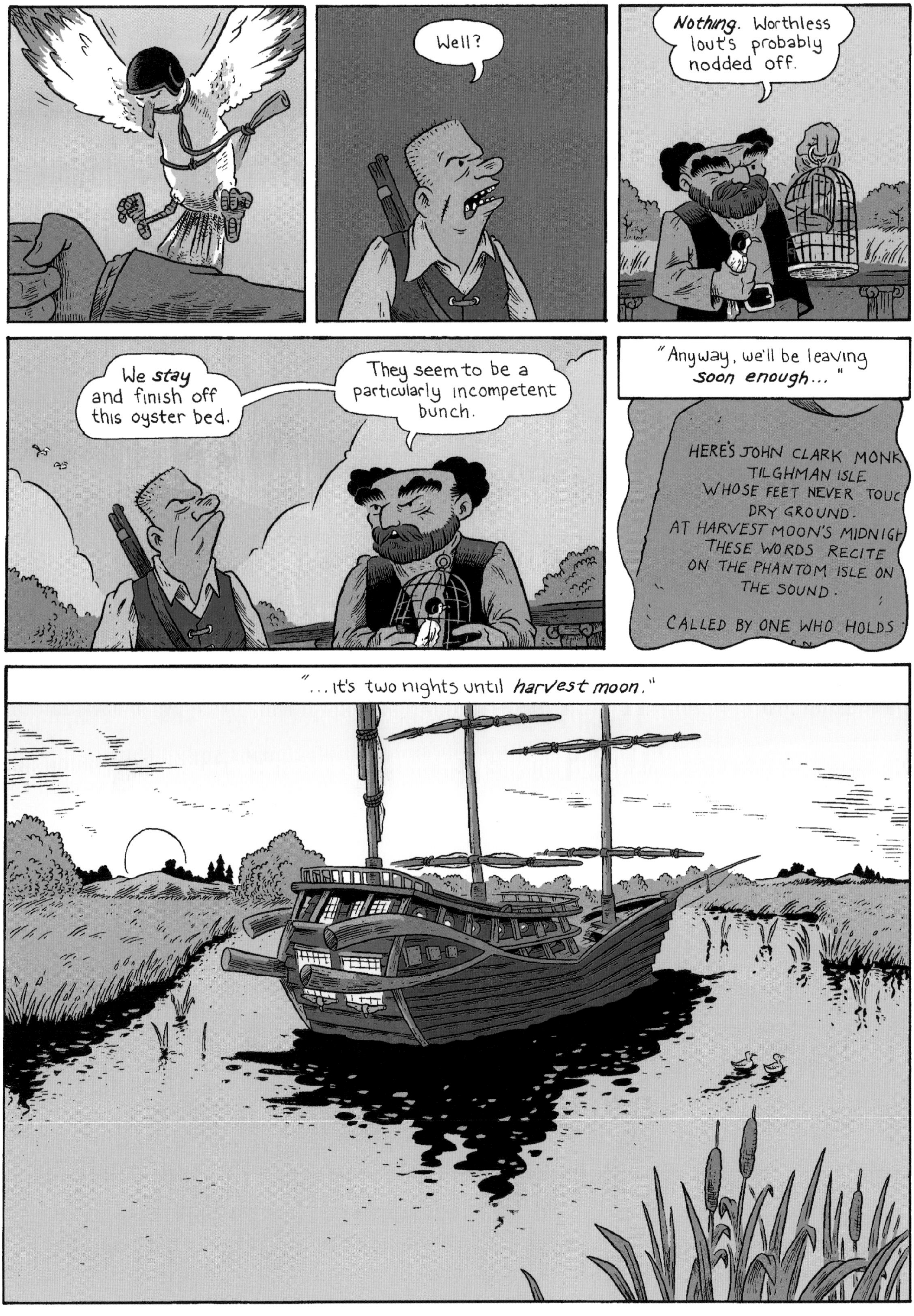

Well?
Nothing. Worthless lout's probably nodded off.
We *stay* and finish off this oyster bed.
They seem to be a particularly incompetent bunch.
"Anyway, we'll be leaving *soon enough*..."
HERE'S JOHN CLARK MONK
TILGHMAN ISLE
WHOSE FEET NEVER TOUC
DRY GROUND.
AT HARVEST MOON'S MIDNIGH
THESE WORDS RECITE
ON THE PHANTOM ISLE ON
THE SOUND.
CALLED BY ONE WHO HOLDS
"...it's two nights until *harvest moon*."

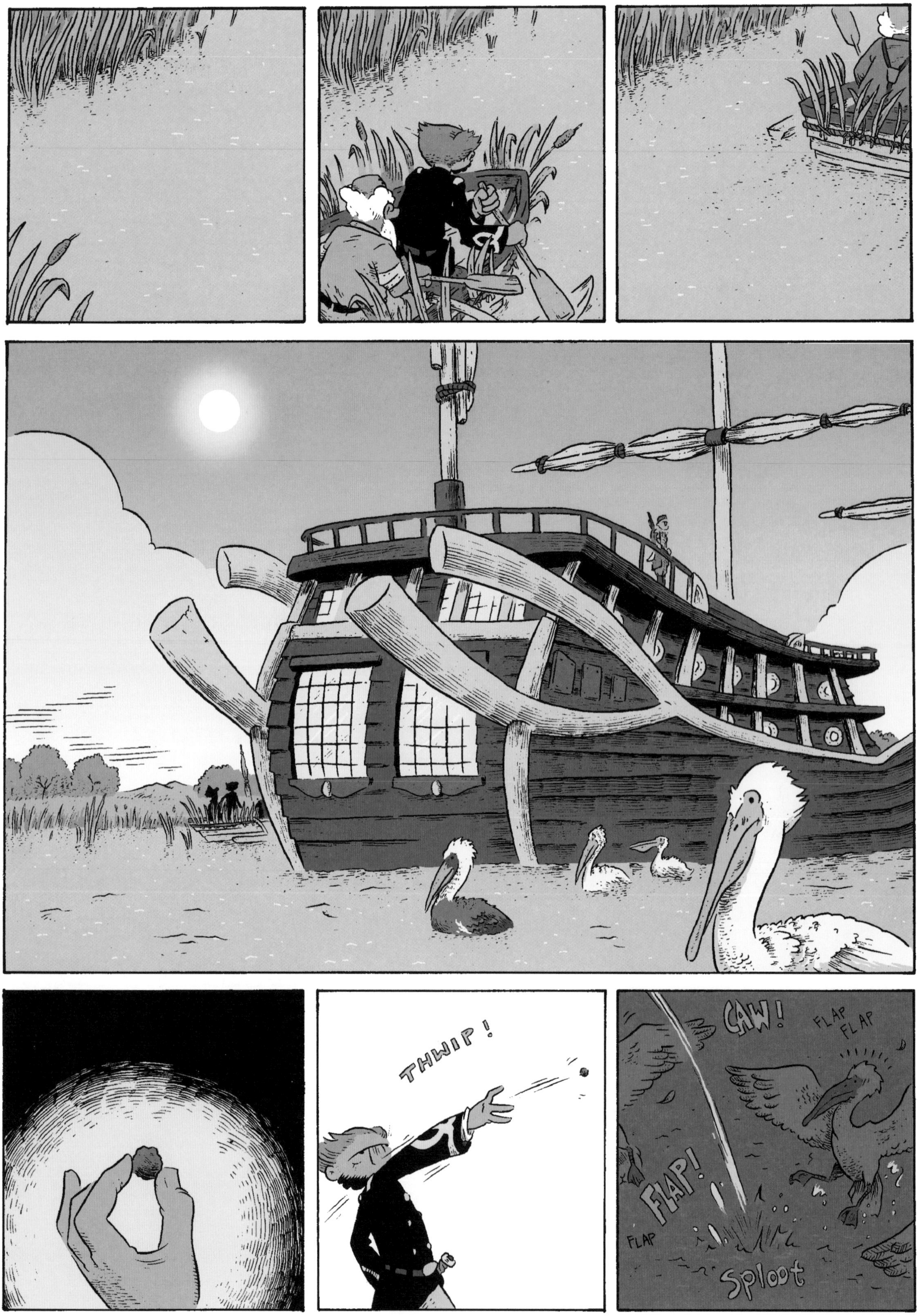
THWIP!
CAW!
FLAP FLAP
FLAP!
FLAP
Sploot

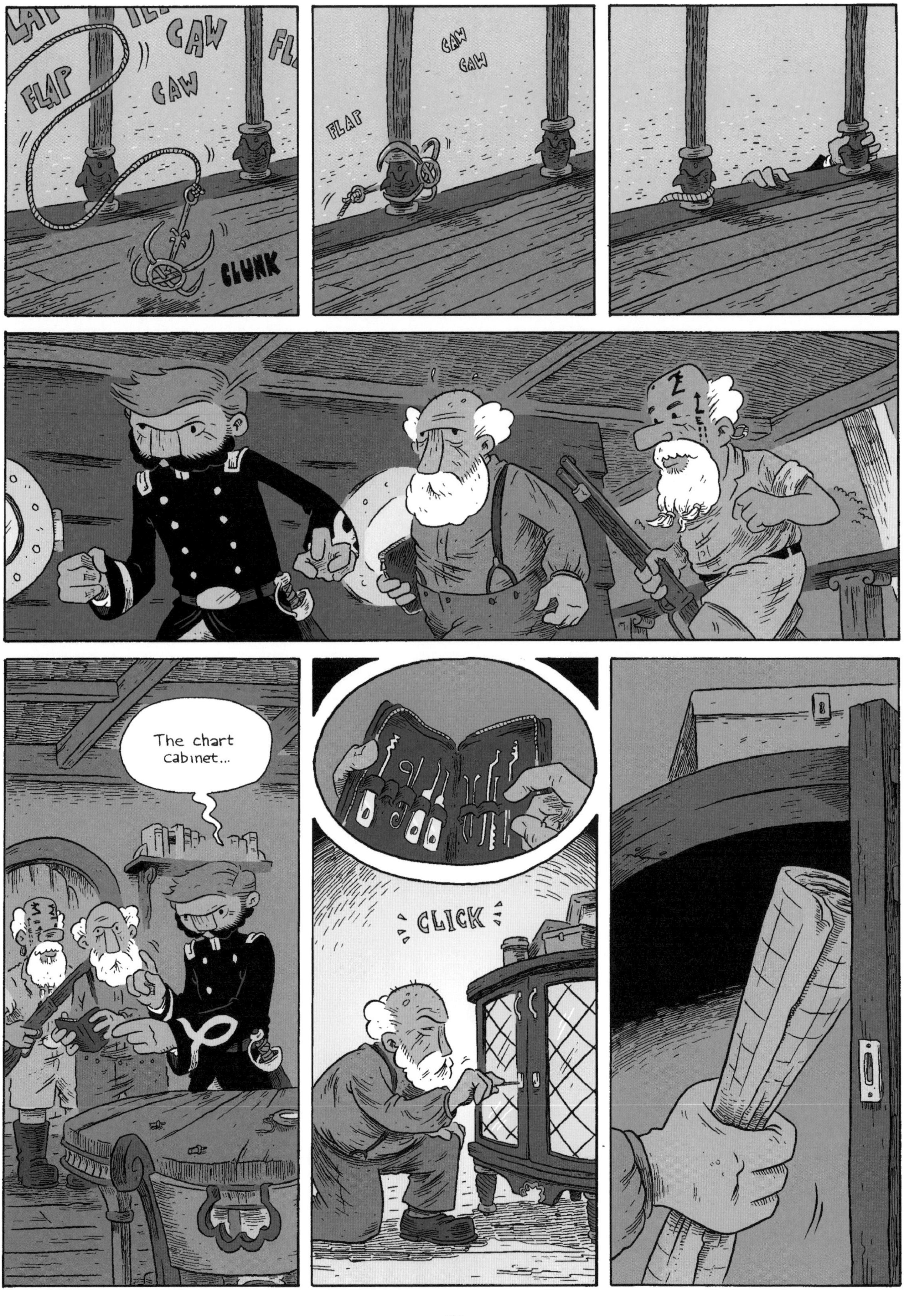
FLAP
CAW
CAW
CLUNK
FLAP
CAW
CAW
The chart cabinet...
CLICK

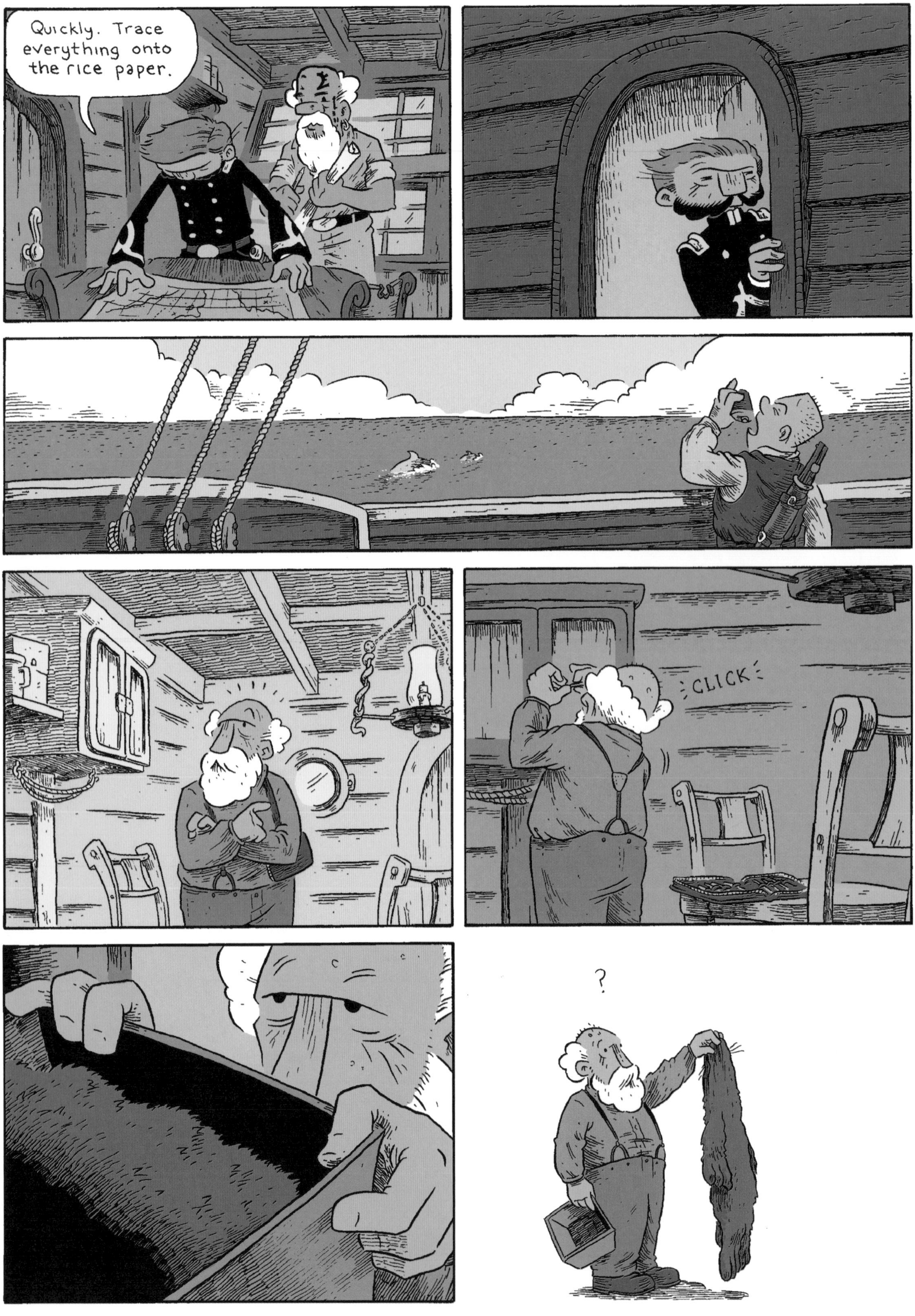
Quickly. Trace everything onto the rice paper.
CLICK
?

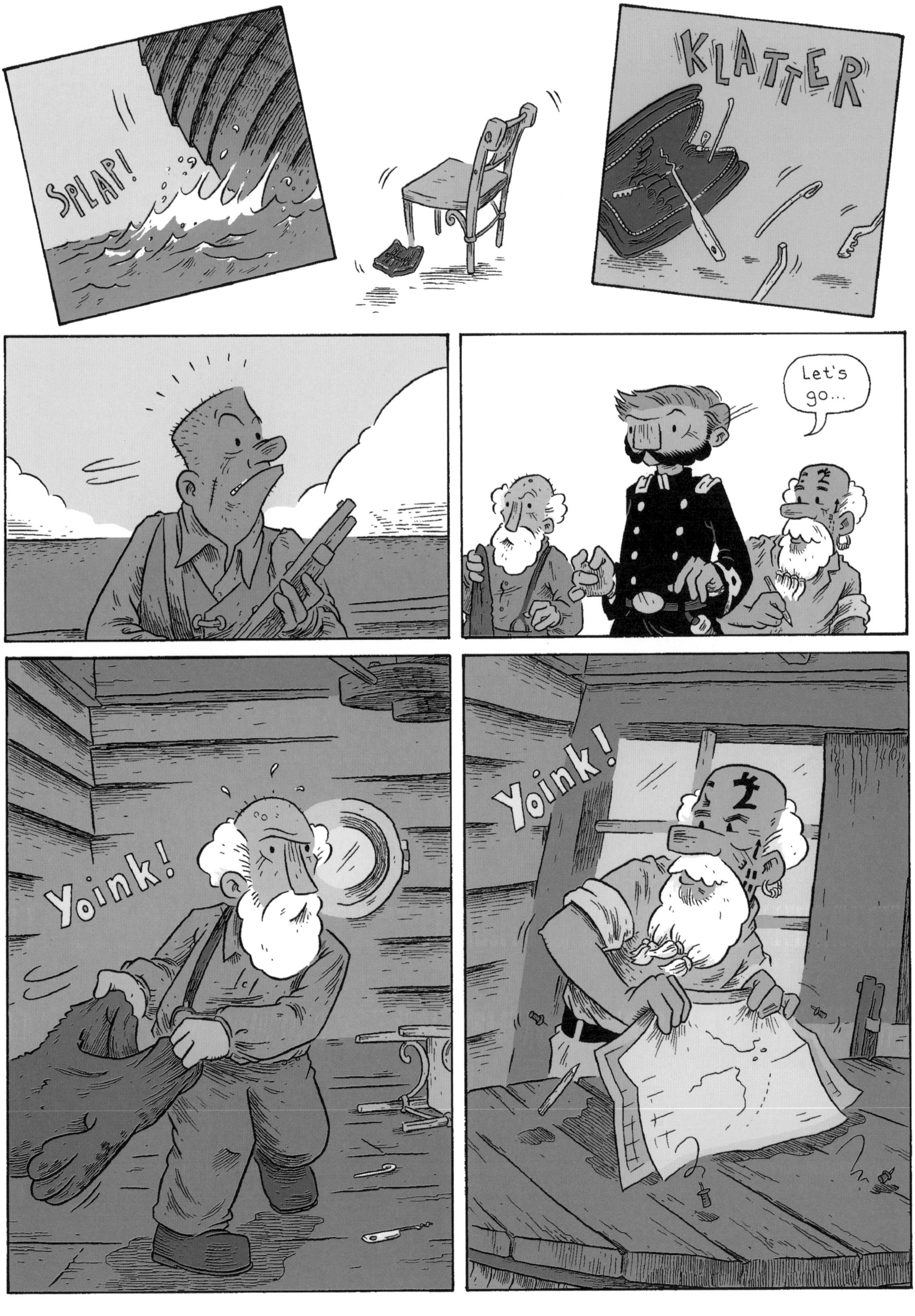
SPLAP!
KLATTER
Let's go...
Yoink!
Yoink!

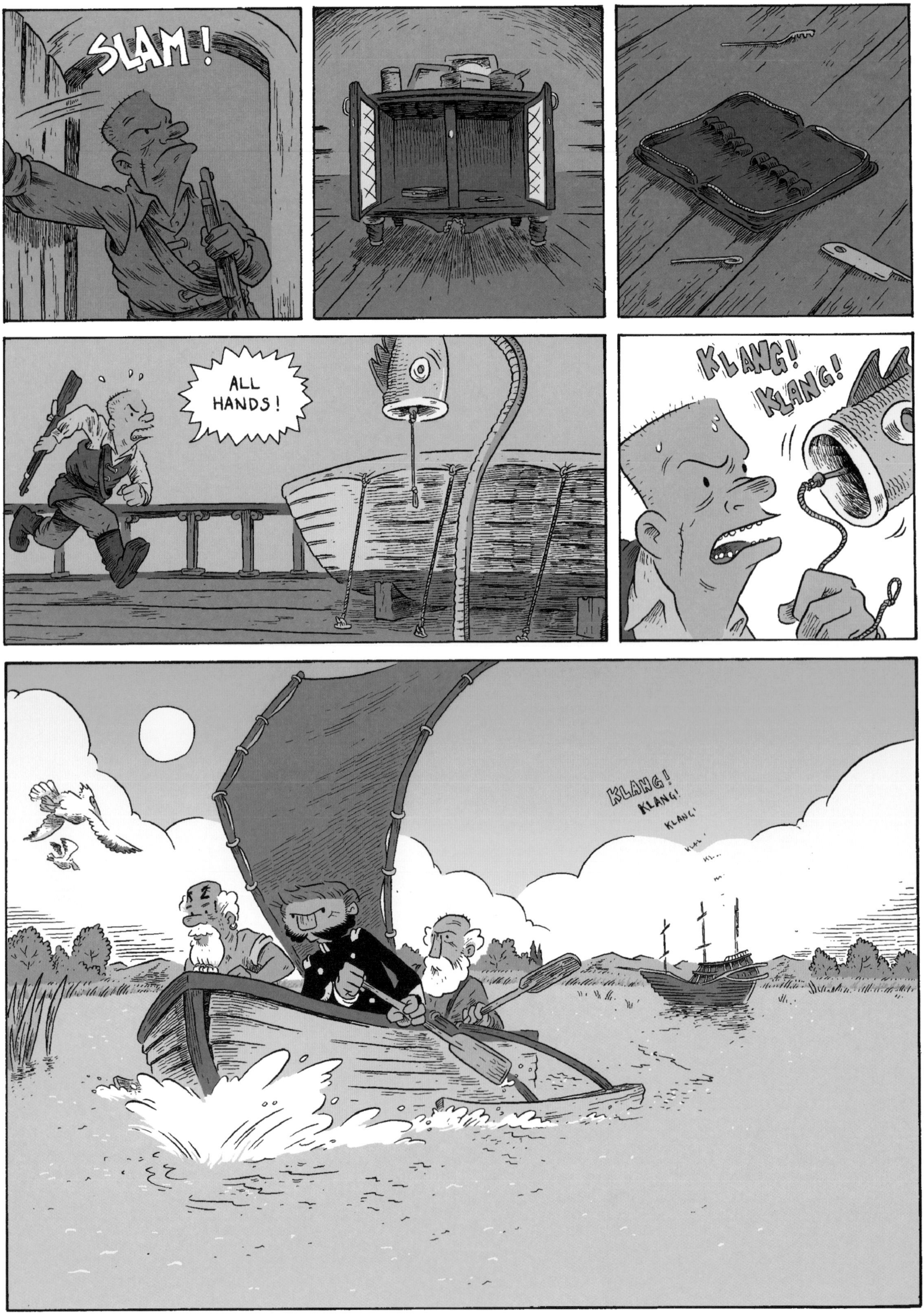
SLAM!
ALL HANDS!
KLANG! KLANG!
KLANG!
KLANG!
KLANG!

CHAPTER SIX

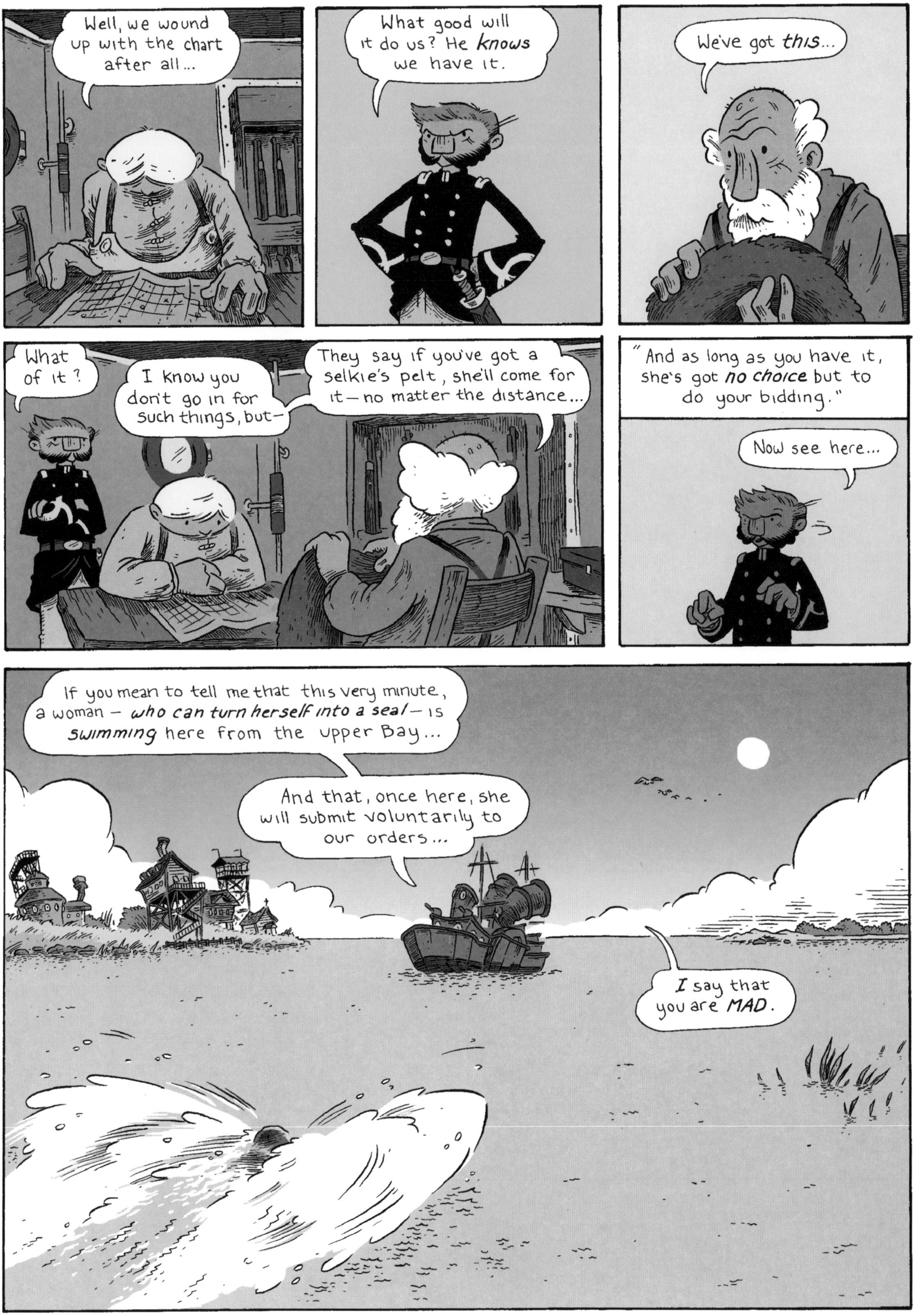
Well, we wound up with the chart after all...
What good will it do us? He *knows* we have it.
We've got *this*...
What of it?
I know you don't go in for such things, but-
They say if you've got a selkie's pelt, she'll come for it—no matter the distance...
"And as long as you have it, she's got *no choice* but to do your bidding."
Now see here...
If you mean to tell me that this very minute, a woman — *who can turn herself into a seal* — is *swimming* here from the upper Bay...
And that, once here, she will submit voluntarily to our orders...
I say that you are *MAD*.

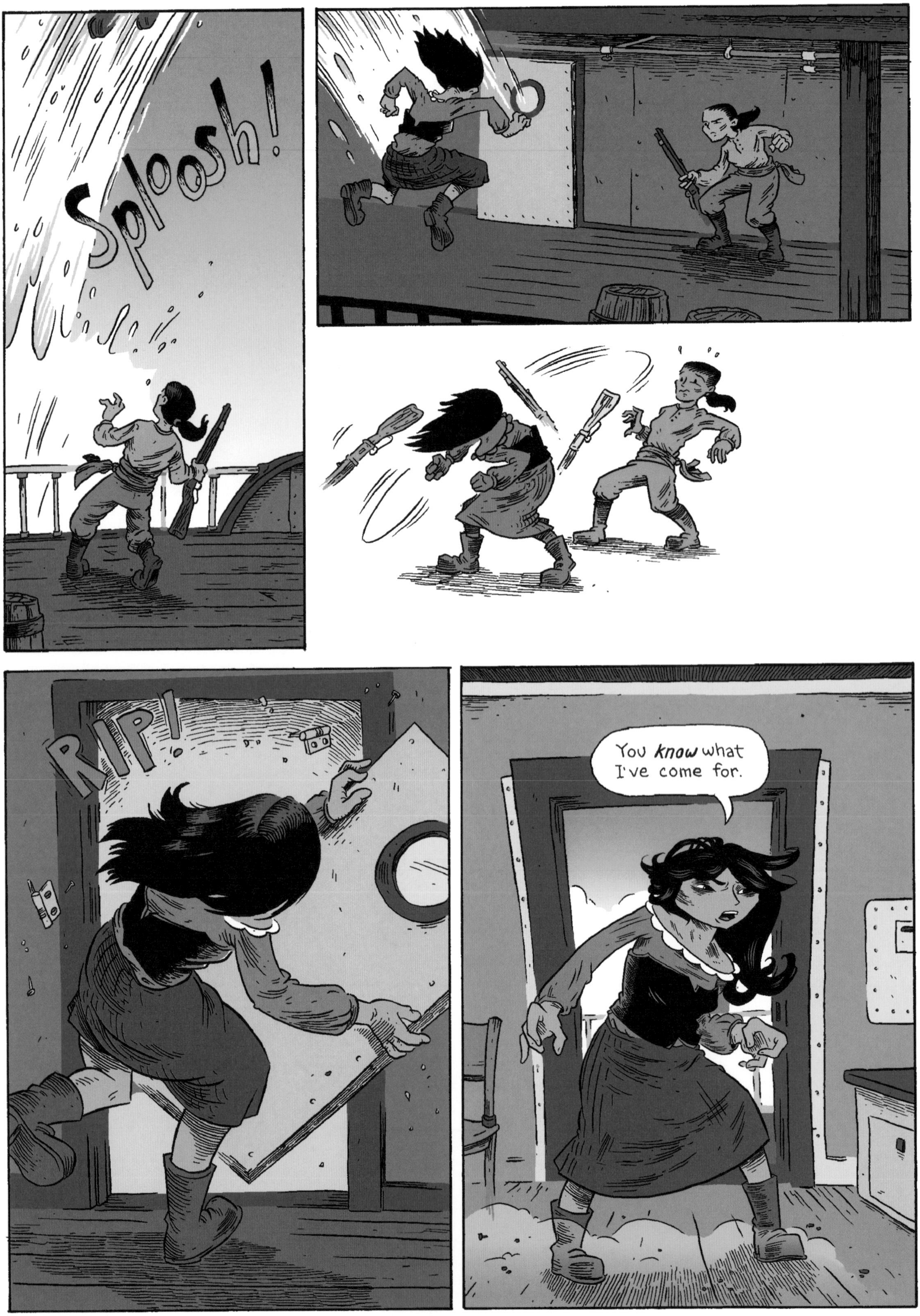
Sploosh!
RIP!
You *know* what I've come for.

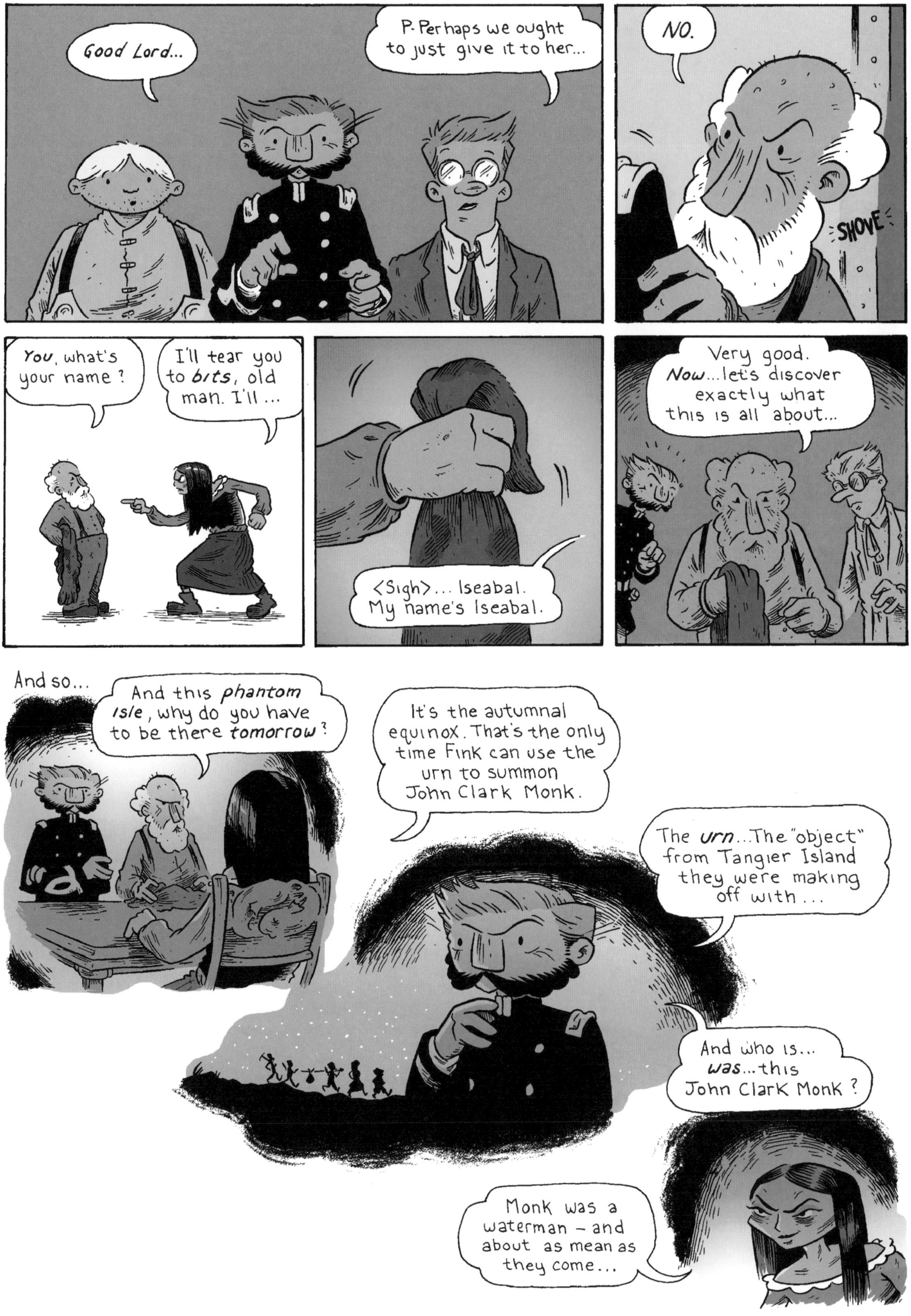
Good Lord...
P-Perhaps we ought to just give it to her...
NO.
SHOVE
You, what's your name?
I'll tear you to bits, old man. I'll...
<Sigh>... Iseabal. My name's Iseabal.
Very good. Now... let's discover exactly what this is all about...
And so...
And this phantom isle, why do you have to be there tomorrow?
It's the autumnal equinox. That's the only time Fink can use the urn to summon John Clark Monk.
The urn... The "object" from Tangier Island they were making off with...
And who is... was... this John Clark Monk?
Monk was a waterman – and about as mean as they come...

One winter he'd been abandoned in his dory off the coast of Newfoundland in a terrible storm...

"His schooner long gone, he'd been left for dead. Any other man'd have given up. But Monk was too filled with hate to die.

"He grabbed the oars and plunged his hands into the freezing water, then held them there until they froze together.

"Monk swore revenge on the captain who left him to drift. He vowed to keep rowing 'till he got to shore – or rowed clean through to the bone."

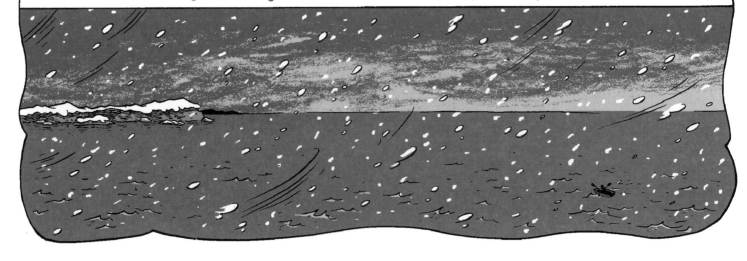

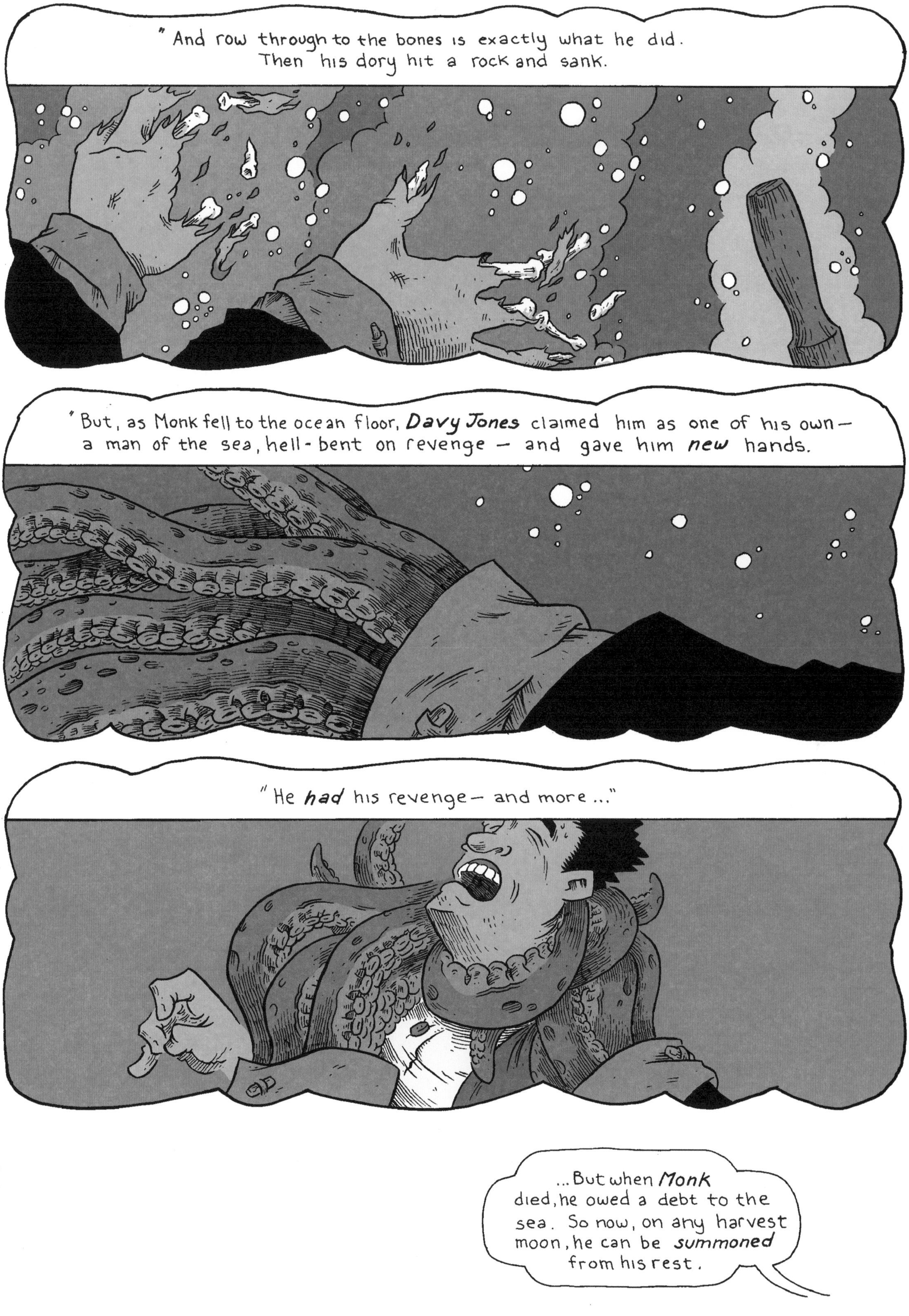
"And row through to the bones is exactly what he did. Then his dory hit a rock and sank.
"But, as Monk fell to the ocean floor, **Davy Jones** claimed him as one of his own— a man of the sea, hell-bent on revenge — and gave him ***new*** hands.
"He ***had*** his revenge— and more..."
...But when *Monk* died, he owed a debt to the sea. So now, on any harvest moon, he can be *summoned* from his rest.

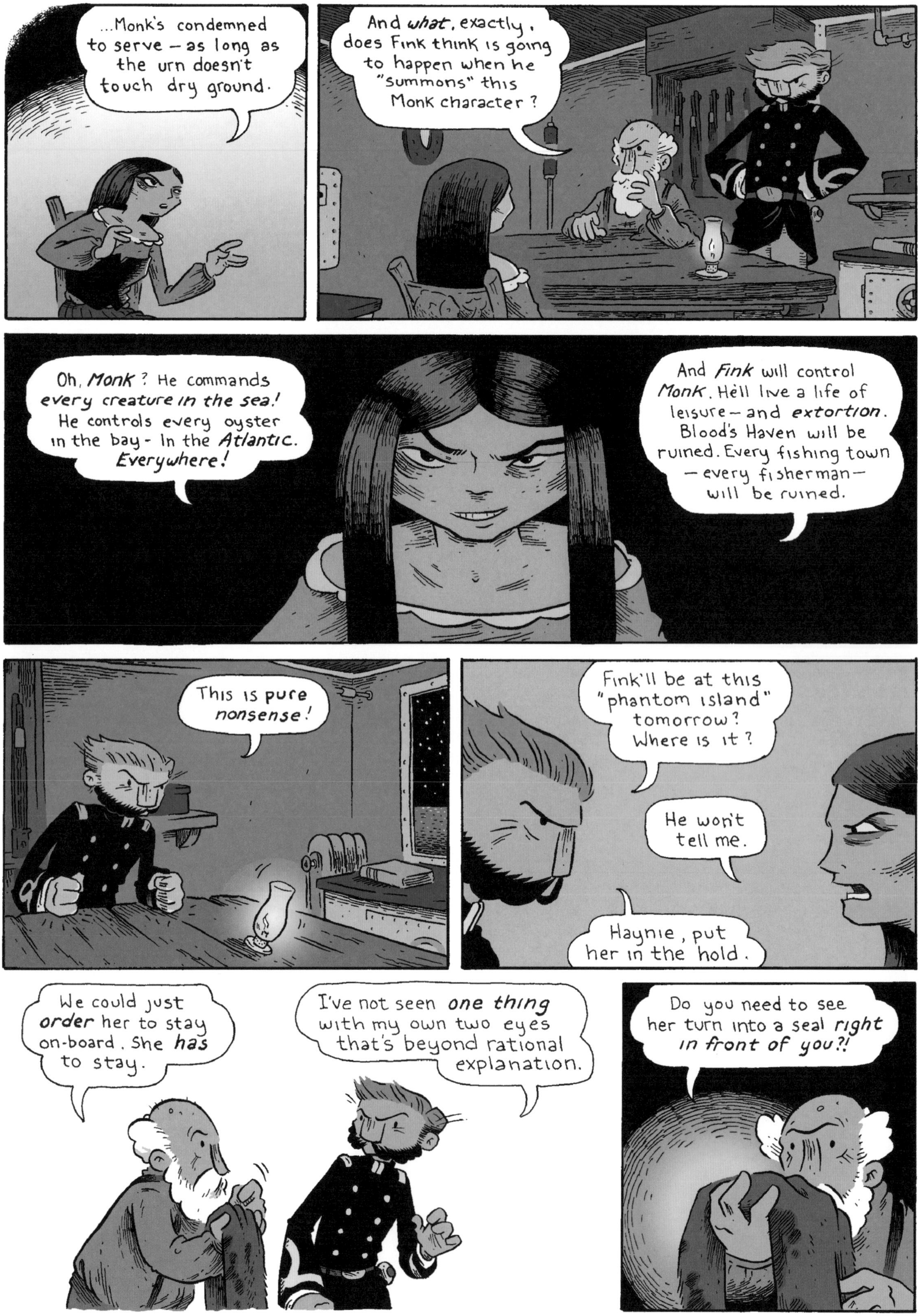
...Monk's condemned to serve – as long as the urn doesn't touch dry ground.
And what, exactly, does Fink think is going to happen when he "summons" this Monk character?
Oh, Monk? He commands every creature in the sea! He controls every oyster in the bay - In the Atlantic. Everywhere!
And Fink will control Monk. He'll live a life of leisure – and extortion. Blood's Haven will be ruined. Every fishing town – every fisherman – will be ruined.
This is pure nonsense!
Fink'll be at this "phantom island" tomorrow? Where is it?
He won't tell me.
Haynie, put her in the hold.
We could just order her to stay on-board. She has to stay.
I've not seen one thing with my own two eyes that's beyond rational explanation.
Do you need to see her turn into a seal right in front of you?!

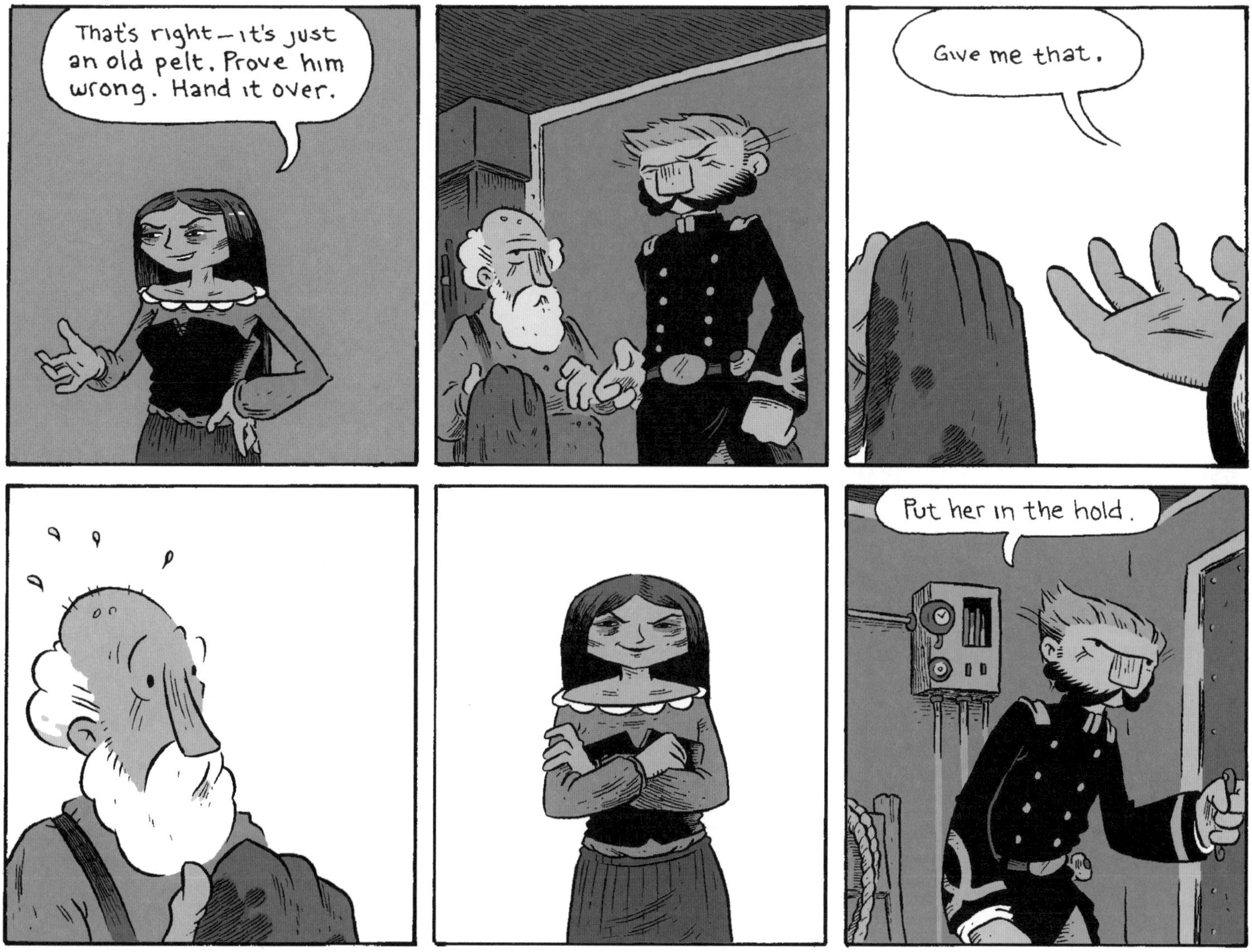
That's right—it's just an old pelt. Prove him wrong. Hand it over.
Give me that.
Put her in the hold.

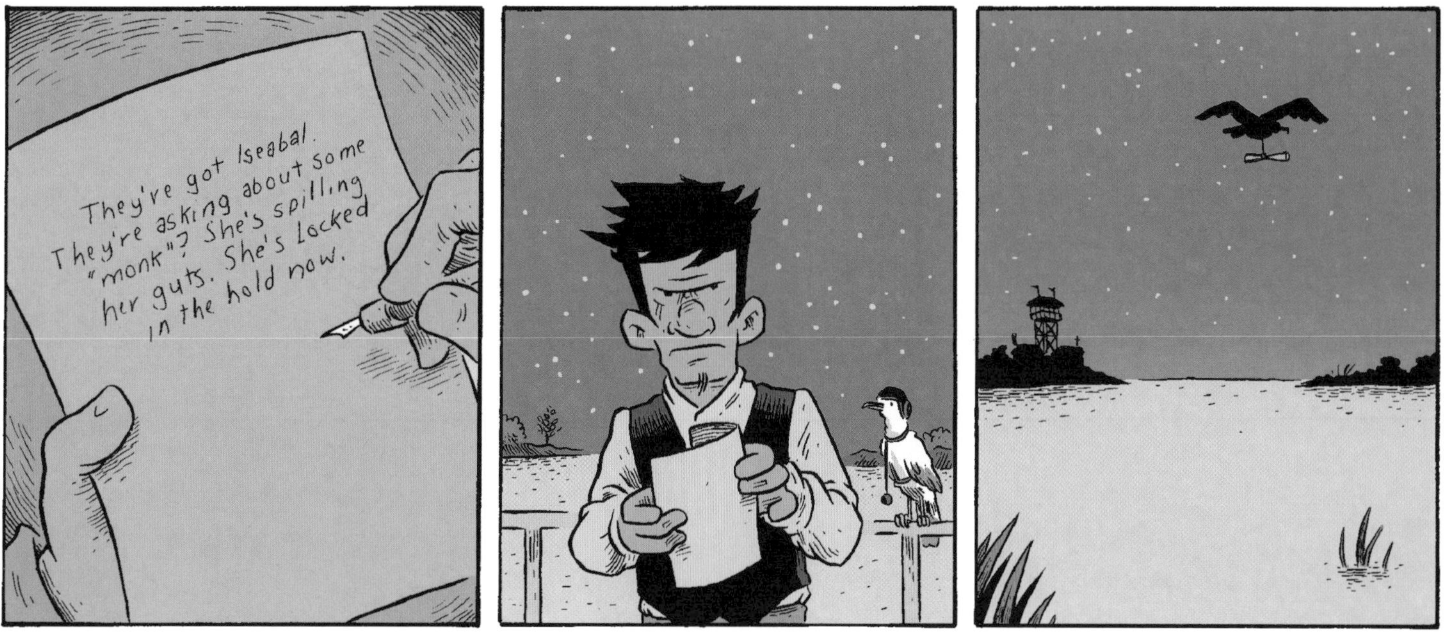
They're got Iseabal. They're asking about some "monk"? She's spilling her guts. She's locked in the hold now.

CHAPTER SEVEN

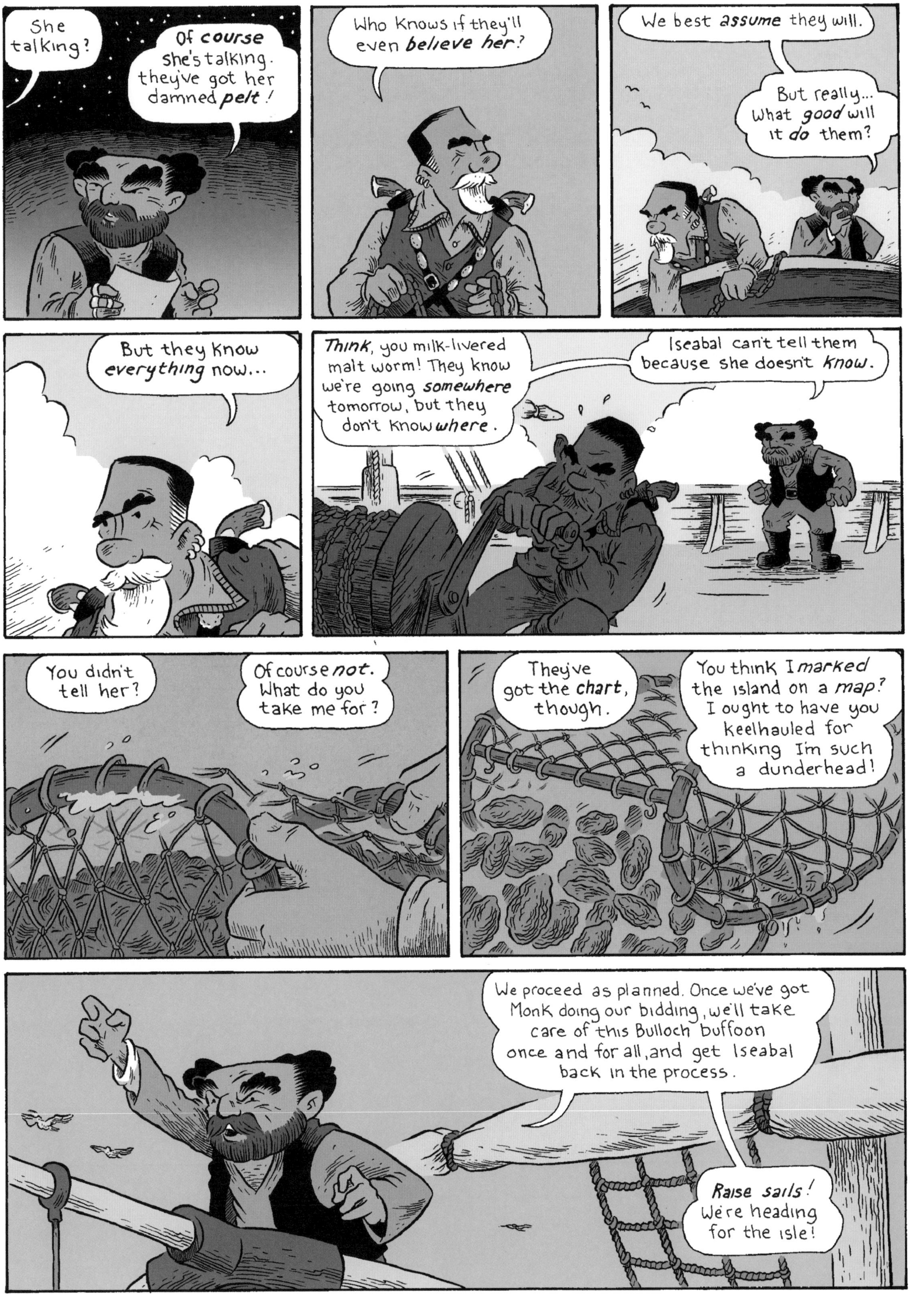
She talking?
Of course she's talking. they've got her damned pelt!
Who knows if they'll even believe her?
We best assume they will.
But really... What good will it do them?
But they know everything now...
Think, you milk-livered malt worm! They know we're going somewhere tomorrow, but they don't know where.
Iseabal can't tell them because she doesn't know.
You didn't tell her?
Of course not. What do you take me for?
They've got the chart, though.
You think I marked the island on a map? I ought to have you keelhauled for thinking I'm such a dunderhead!
We proceed as planned. Once we've got Monk doing our bidding, we'll take care of this Bulloch buffoon once and for all, and get Iseabal back in the process.
Raise sails! We're heading for the isle!

Meanwhile...

This "magical sailor" nonsense aside, it's clear they're heading for *some* island in the lower bay. We can ambush them tonight if we can find it.

I don't see anything unusual marked on the chart...

What's that there?

Oh, that's *Chessie* — a sea serpent! Watermen say she's as long as—

It'd take us a *month* to search the bay for some unmarked island...

?

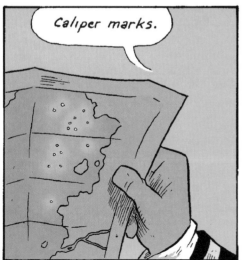

Caliper marks.

Marks from the points of the navigator's calipers. They're all over the oyster beds and ports... but *here*, too, where there's *nothing* marked.

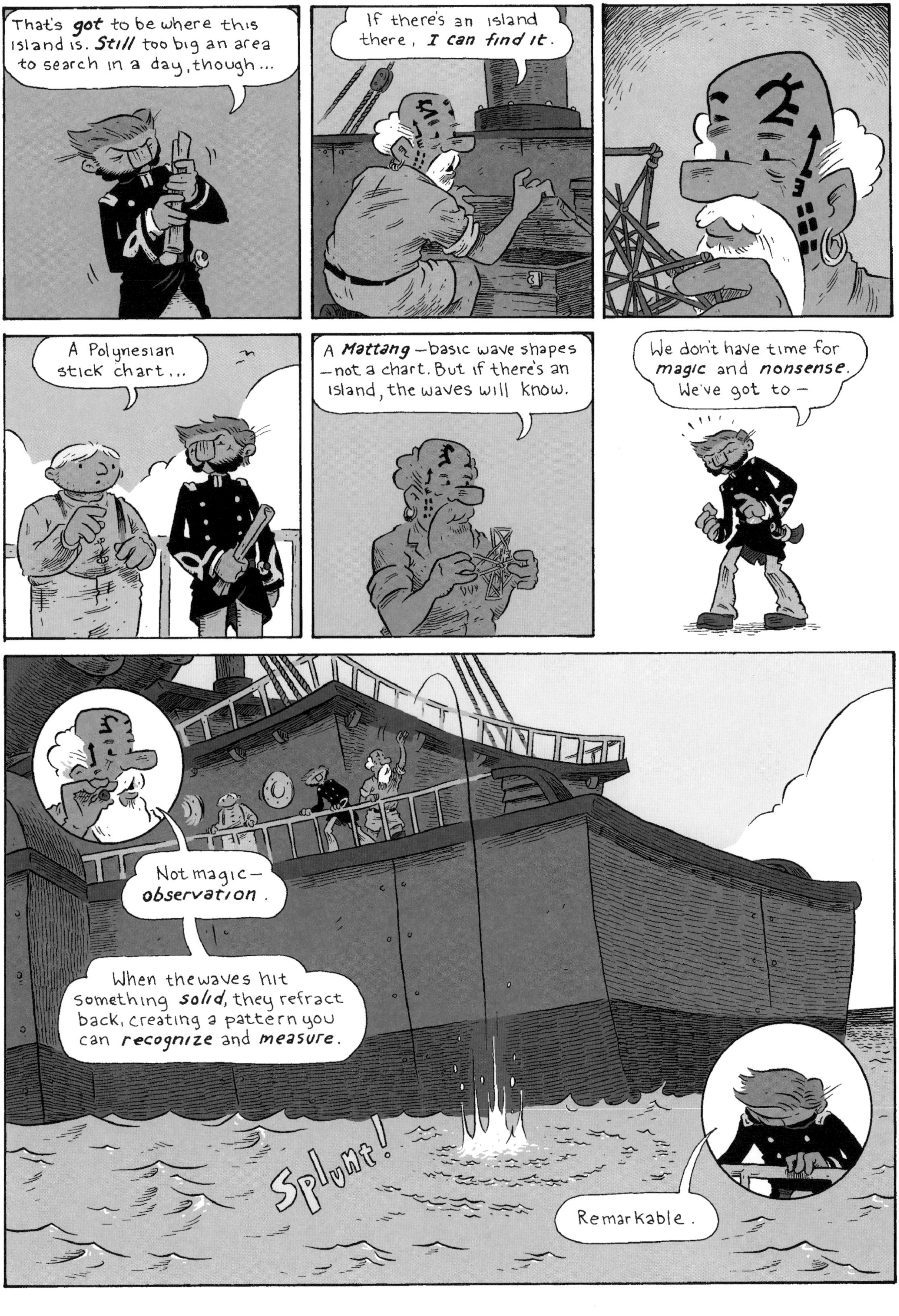
That's got to be where this island is. Still too big an area to search in a day, though...
If there's an island there, I can find it.
A Polynesian stick chart...
A Mattang — basic wave shapes — not a chart. But if there's an island, the waves will know.
We don't have time for magic and nonsense. We've got to —
Not magic — observation.
When the waves hit something solid, they refract back, creating a pattern you can recognize and measure.
Splunt!
Remarkable.

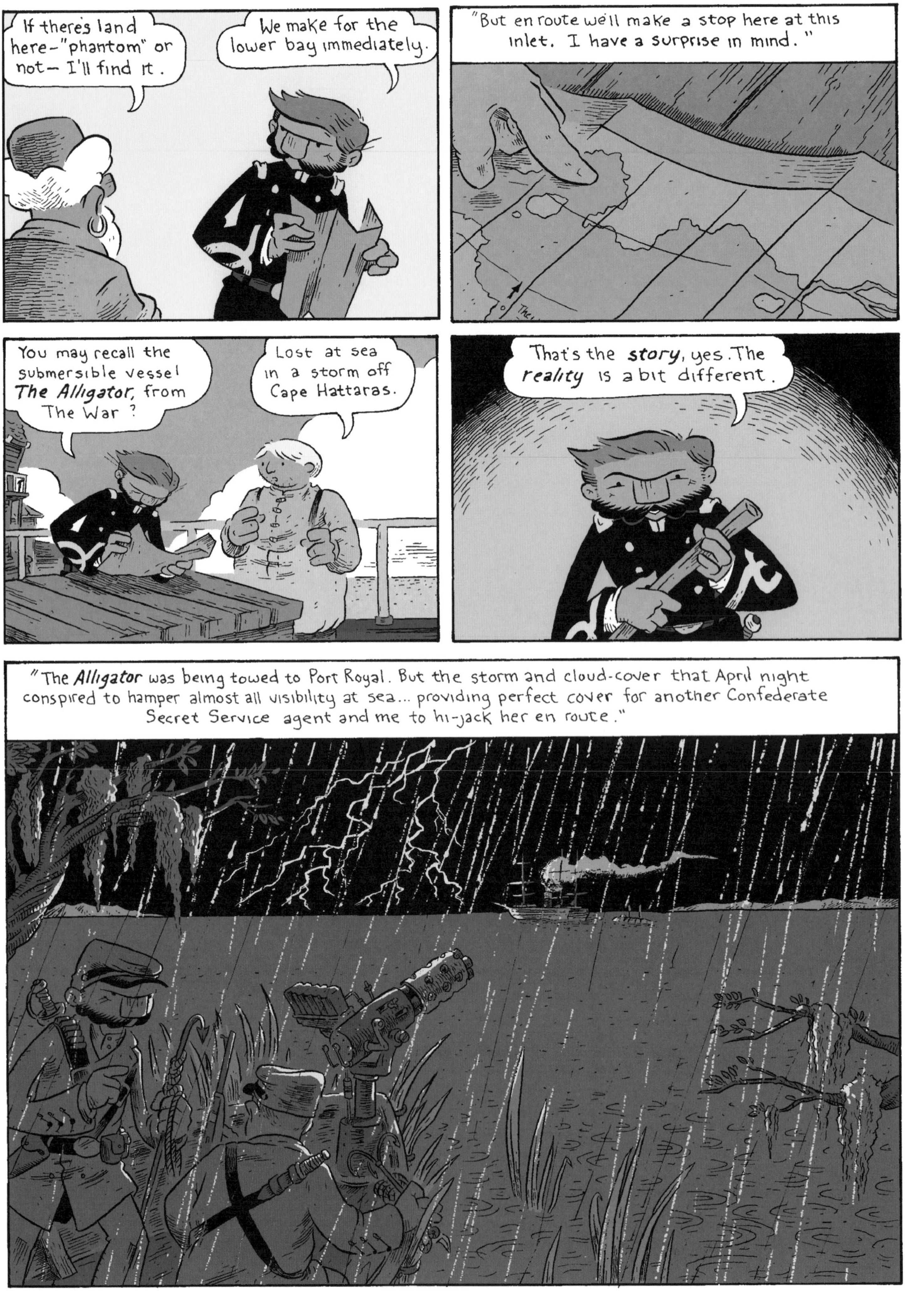
If there's land here-"phantom" or not- I'll find it.
We make for the lower bay immediately.
"But en route we'll make a stop here at this inlet. I have a surprise in mind."
You may recall the submersible vessel *The Alligator*, from The War?
Lost at sea in a storm off Cape Hattaras.
That's the *story*, yes. The *reality* is a bit different.
"The *Alligator* was being towed to Port Royal. But the storm and cloud-cover that April night conspired to hamper almost all visibility at sea... providing perfect cover for another Confederate Secret Service agent and me to hi-jack her en route."

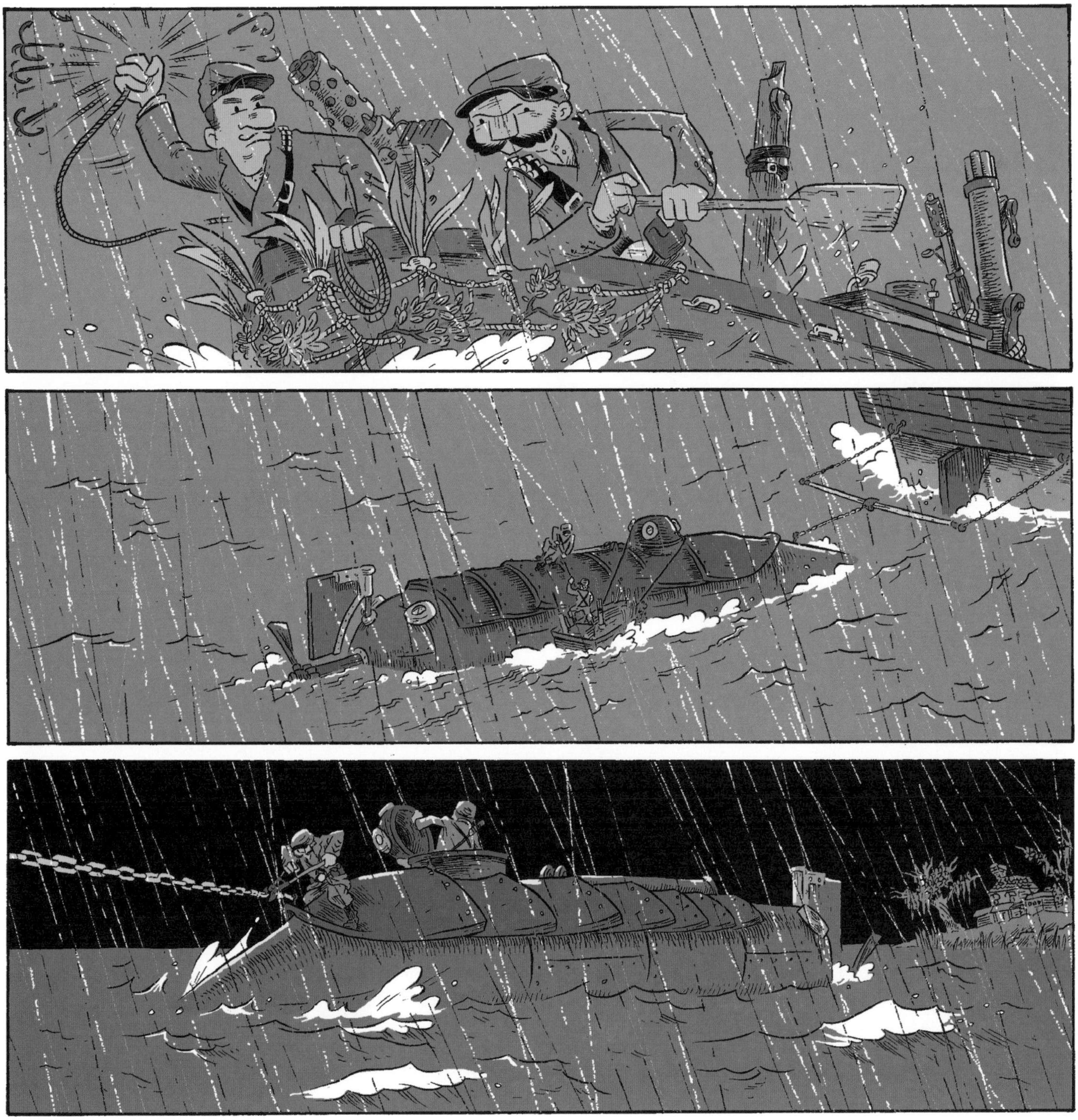

"We boarded her, cut her loose, and were away before the crew of ***The Sumter*** knew what happened."

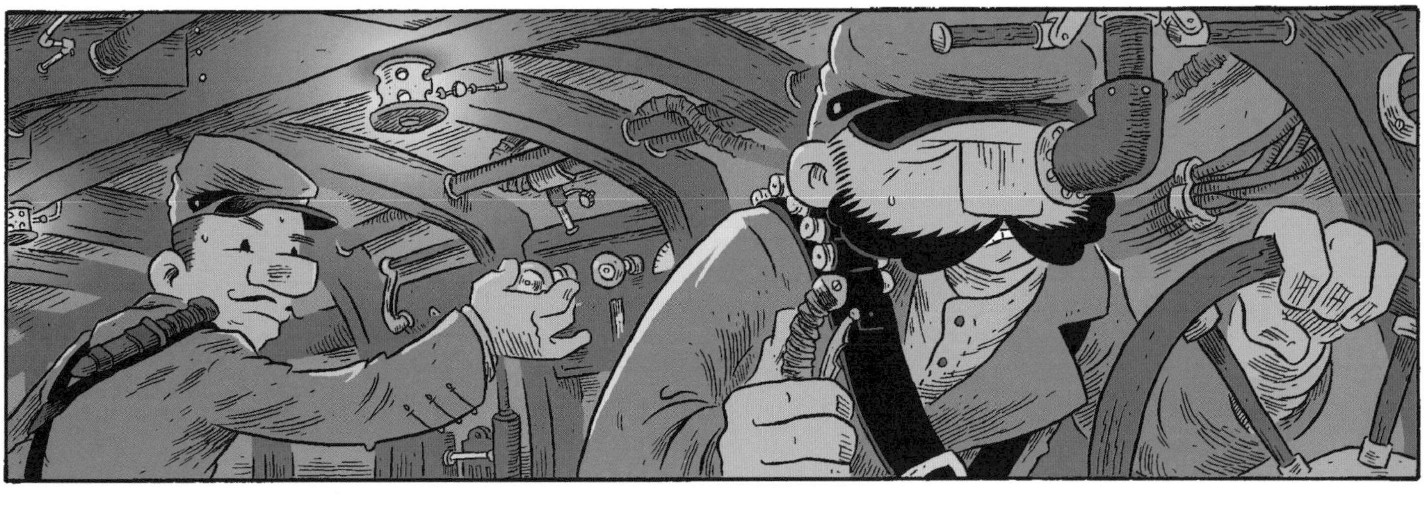

We rigged her for dive and left her submerged in this cove, thinking we'd use her later.

But the war ended and there she sits.

All on-duty crew, prepare to get under-way!

All off-duty crew, get rested below decks!

We'll need all our strength to haul up *The Alligator* as quickly as possible.

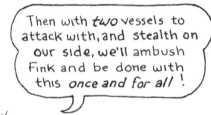
Then with *two* vessels to attack with, and stealth on our side, we'll ambush Fink and be done with this *once and for all*!

As the great sailor, John Paul Jones remarked," whoever can surprise well must concur."

"Conquer."

That's the spirit! *Conquer!*

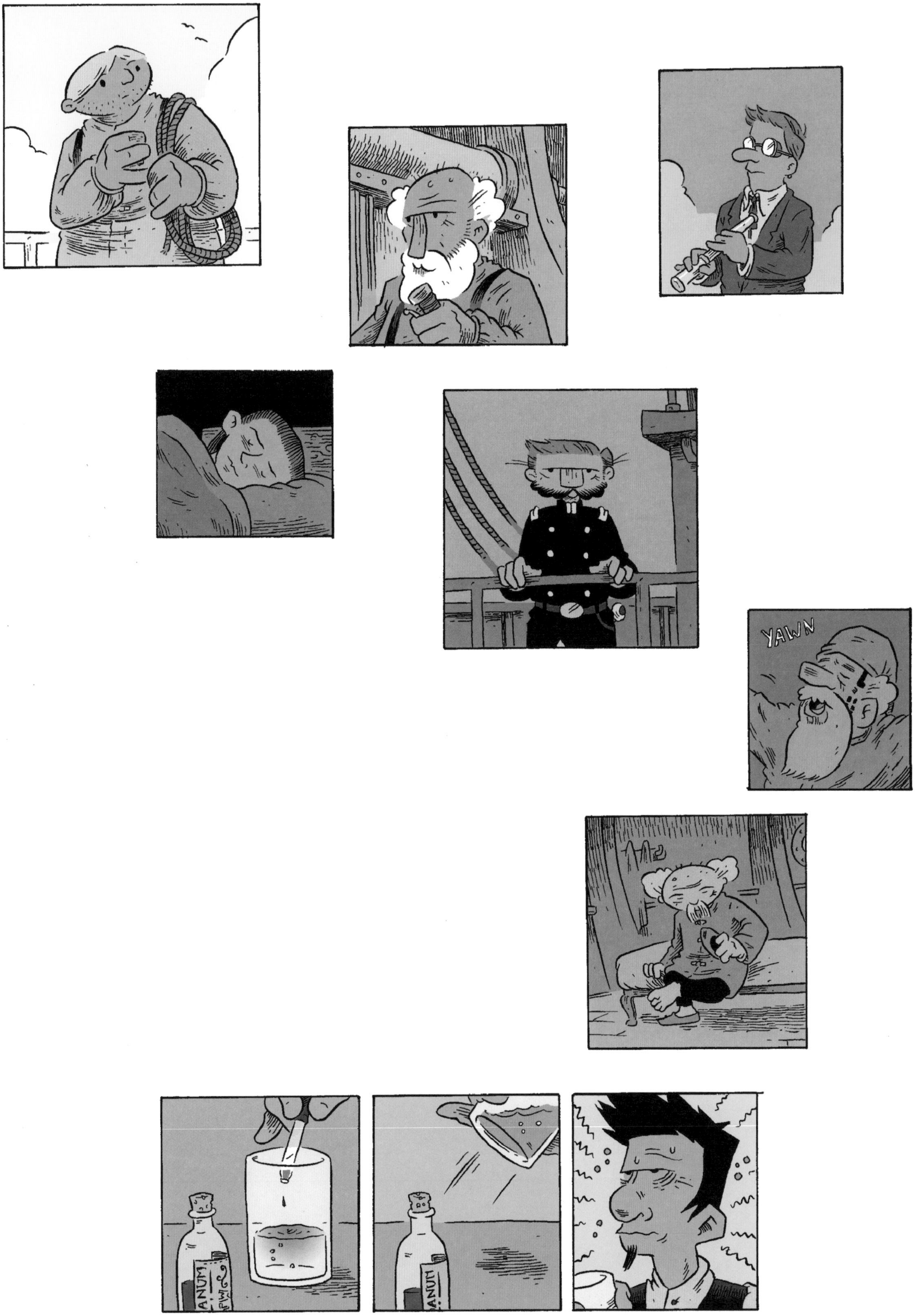
YAWN

CHAPTER EIGHT

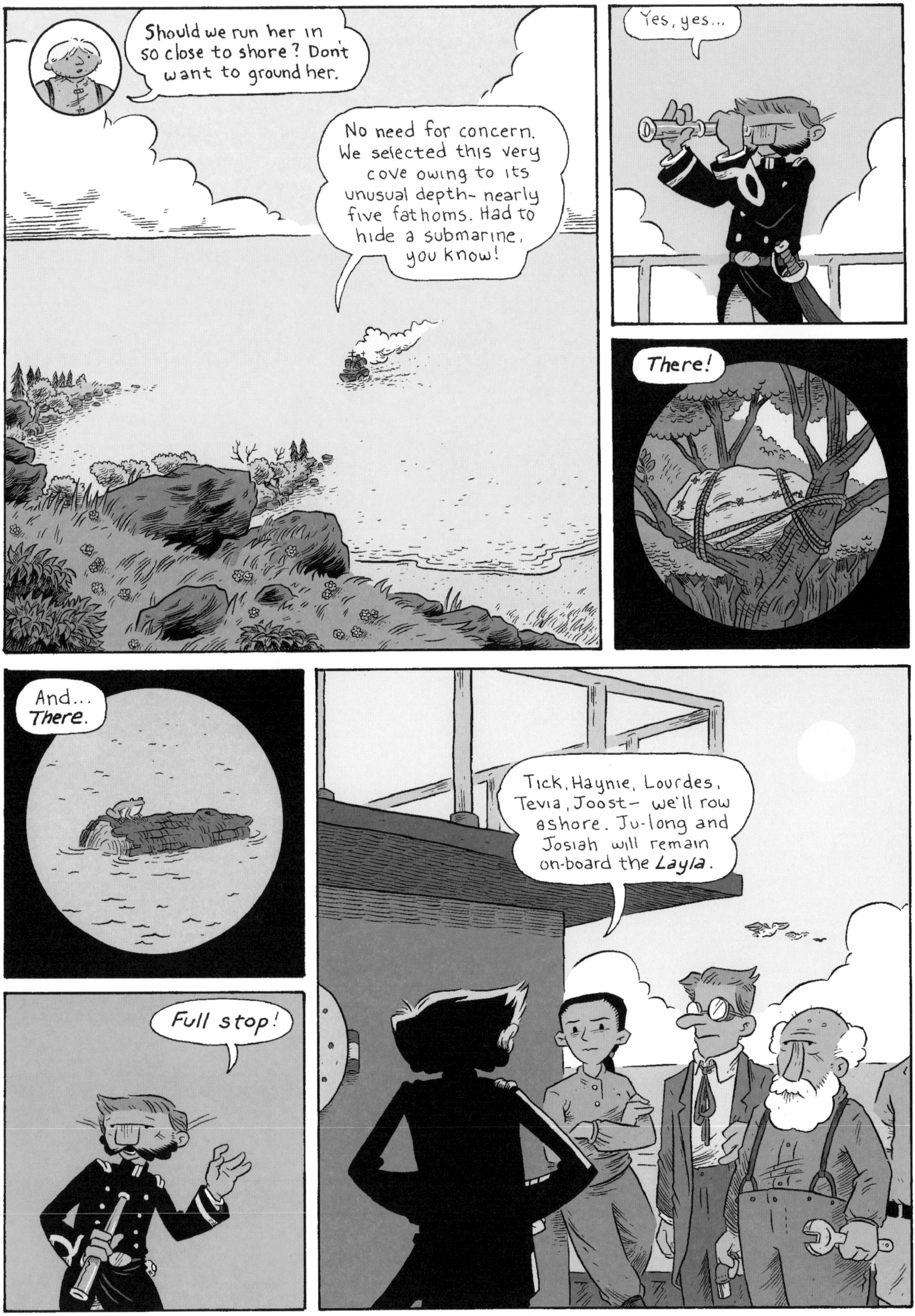
Should we run her in so close to shore? Don't want to ground her.
No need for concern. We selected this very cove owing to its unusual depth- nearly five fathoms. Had to hide a submarine, you know!
Yes, yes...
There!
And... There.
Full stop!
Tick, Haynie, Lourdes, Tevia, Joost- we'll row ashore. Ju-long and Josiah will remain on-board the Layla.

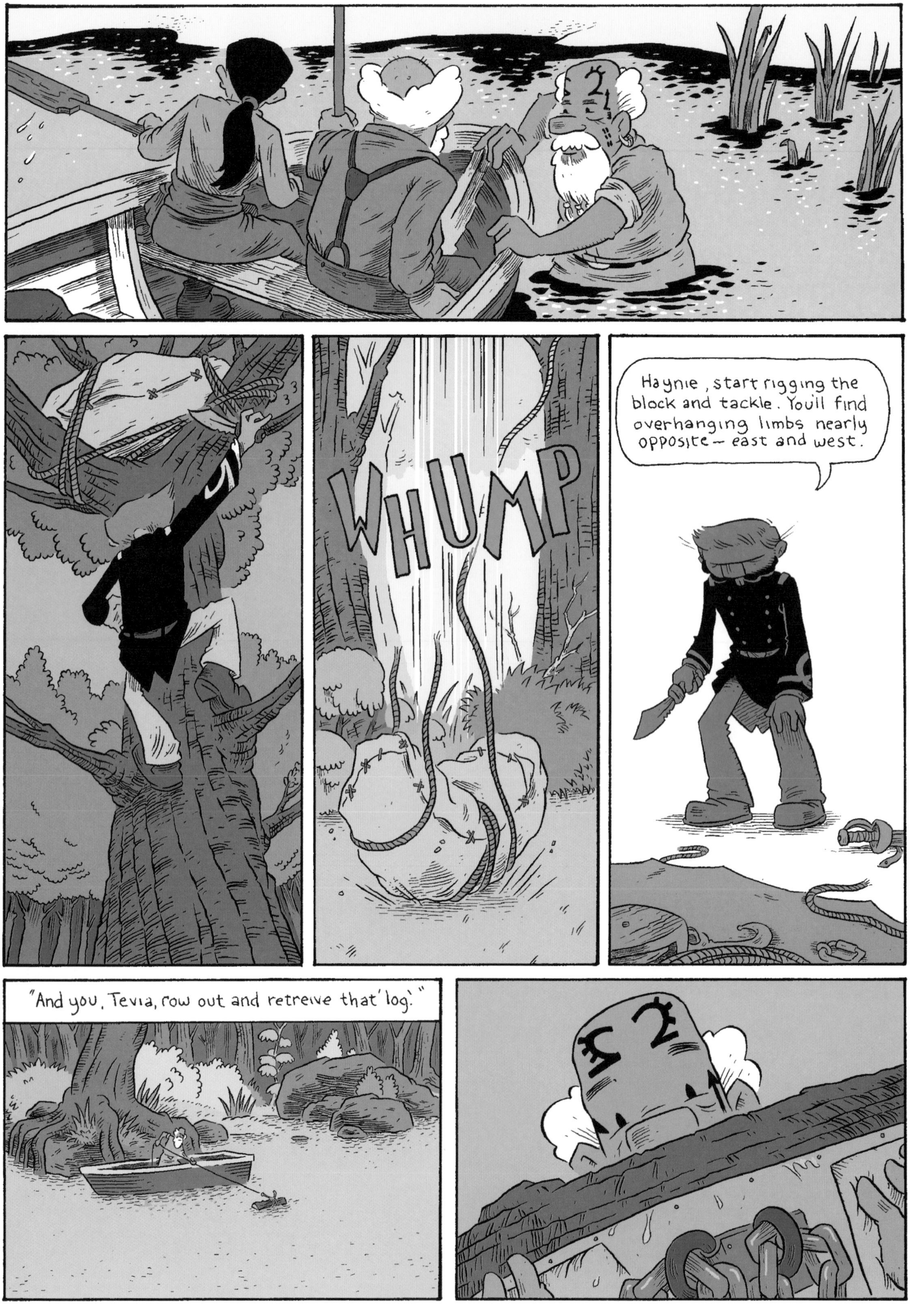
WHUMP
Haynie, start rigging the block and tackle. You'll find overhanging limbs nearly opposite — east and west.
"And you, Tevia, row out and retrieve that log."

Soon...

Everyone, grab the rope and on the count of three, *pull!*

Well, except you, Lourdes.

"...This isn't a task for the, ah, fairer sex."

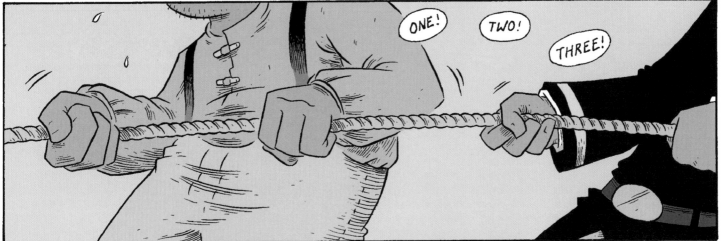

ONE!

TWO!

THREE!

It's slipping!

OK, everyone let go — and *clear!*

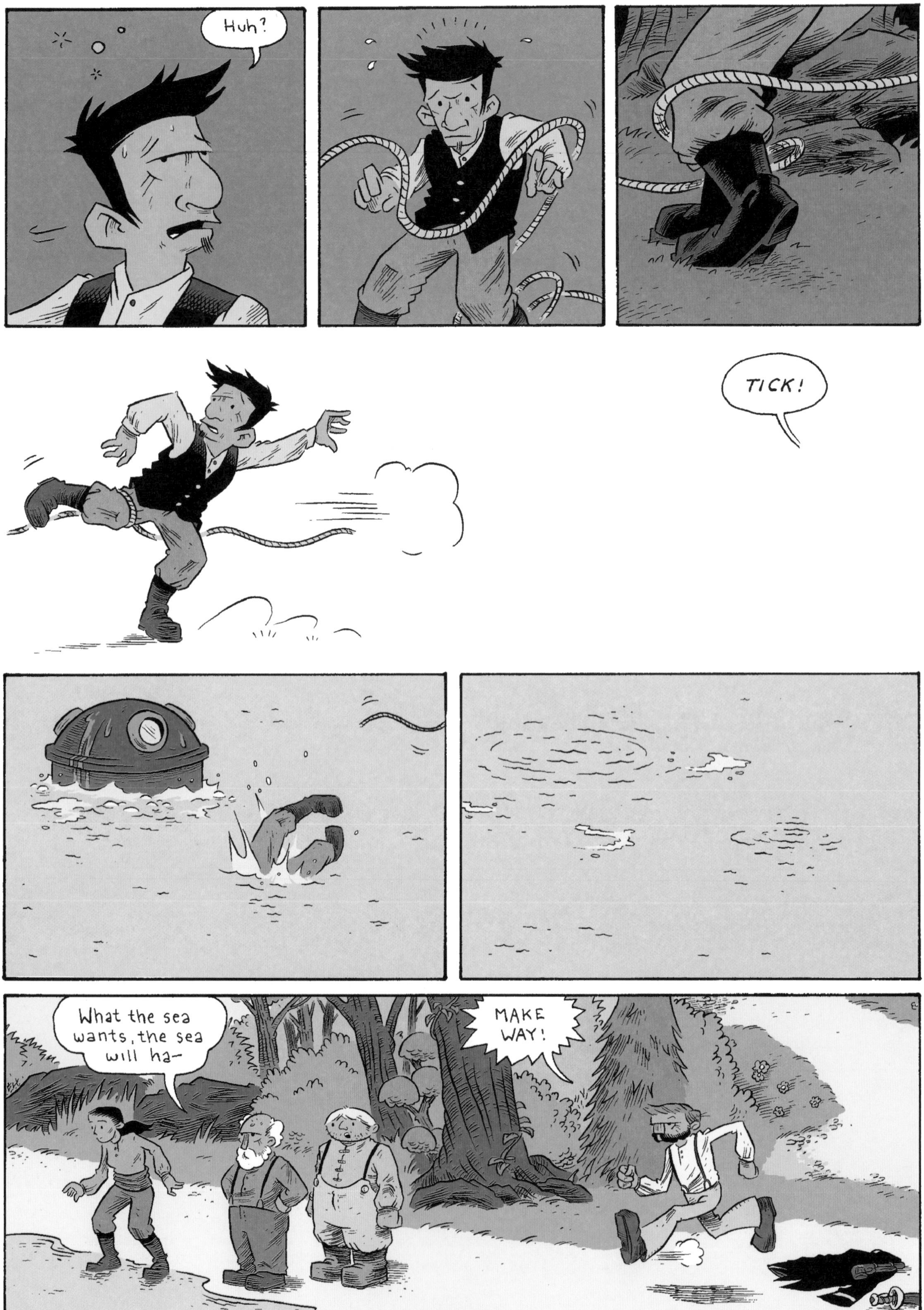
Huh?
TICK!
What the sea wants, the sea will ha-
MAKE WAY!

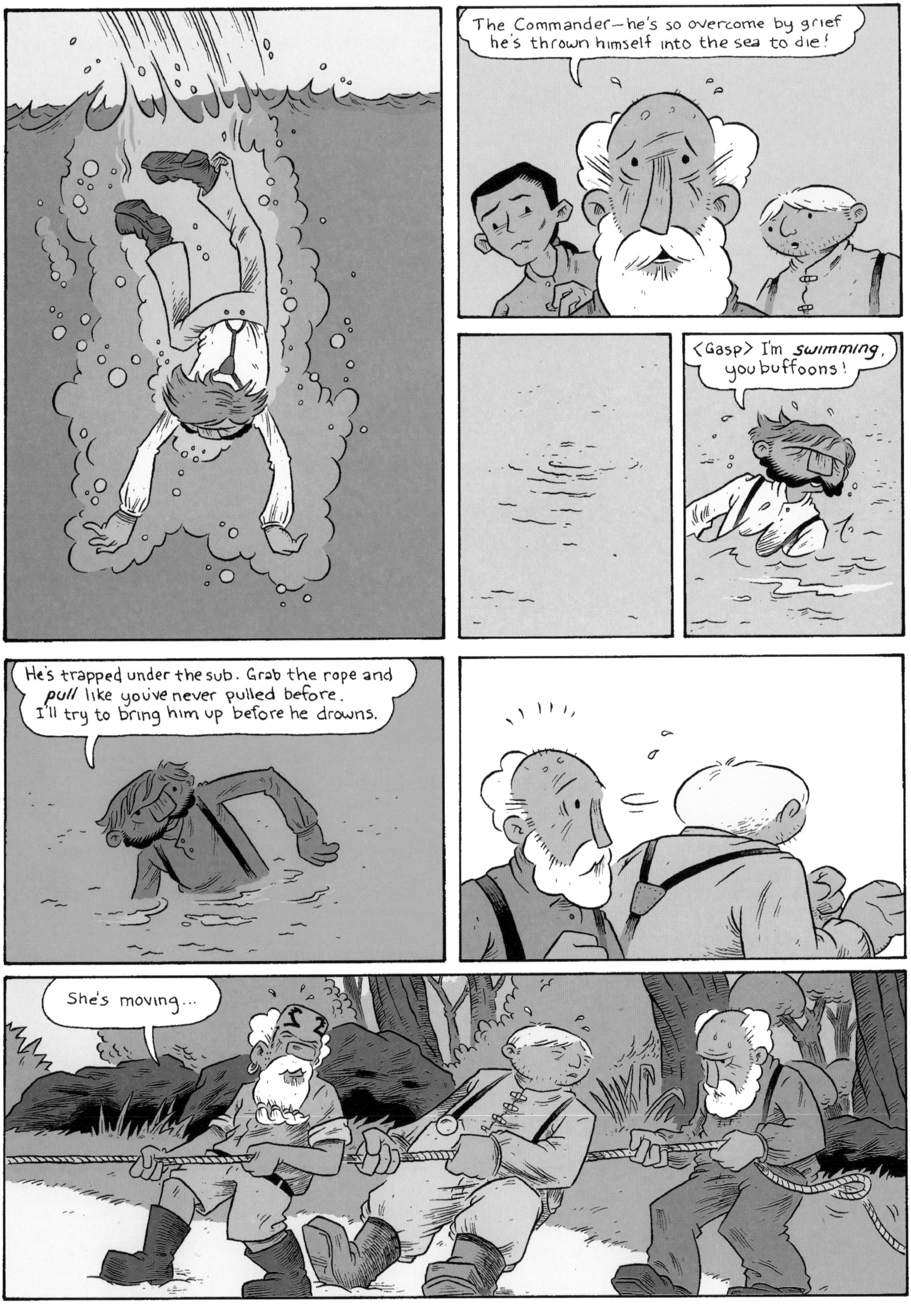

The Commander—he's so overcome by grief he's thrown himself into the sea to die!
<Gasp> I'm *swimming*, you buffoons!
He's trapped under the sub. Grab the rope and *pull* like you've never pulled before. I'll try to bring him up before he drowns.
She's moving...

Oh, for Pete's sake...

That's it. Here she comes!

She's up! Tie her off!

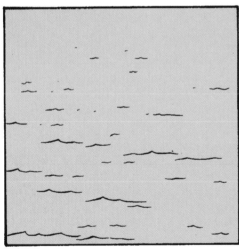

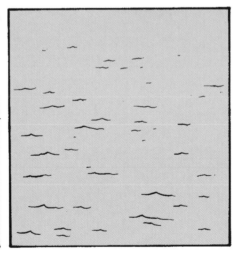

SPLOOSH

He's unconscious, but he's OK. I've got to drain the ballast tanks on the *Alligator* or she'll snap those lines.

Haynie, Tevia, get that rigging down and use it to tether the *Alligator* to the *Layla*.

The rest of you, prepare to steam for the lower bay.

94

Now, for you...

My arm...

It's just out of its socket. I'll pop it back in. On the count of five. *One*...*Two*...

Look! A *goblin*!

HUH?

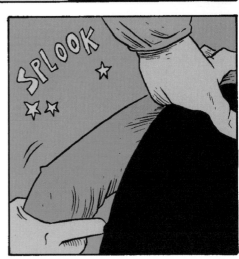

SPLOOK

That was just downright *mean*!

Oh, hey...that's better.

I can't believe you saved my life. I'd be dead for sure. Thank you...*Thank you*.

No further thanks are necessary. As the Roman philosopher Cicero said, "Gratitude is not only the greatest of virtues, but the parent of all otters."

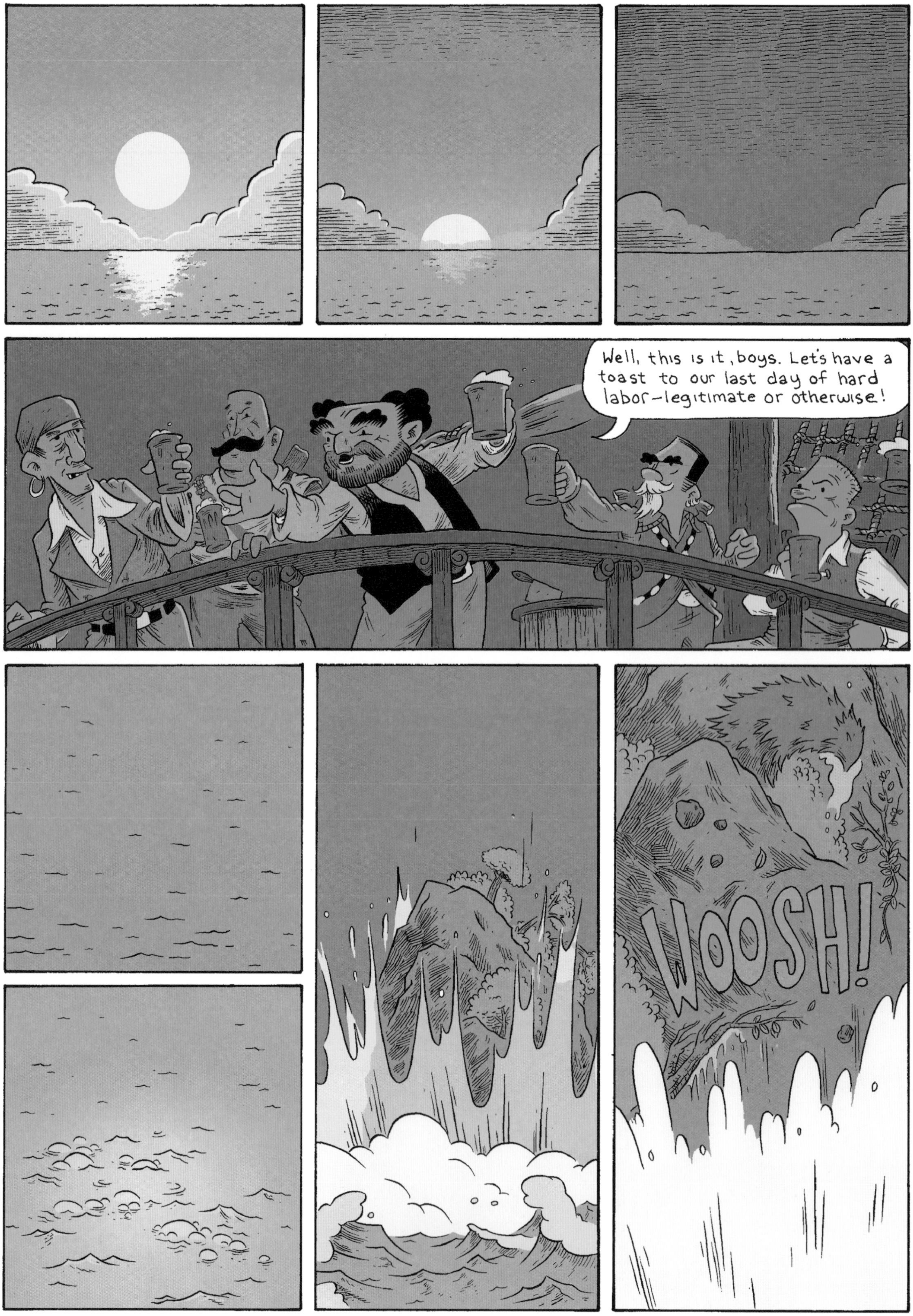
Well, this is it, boys. Let's have a toast to our last day of hard labor—legitimate or otherwise!
WOOSH!

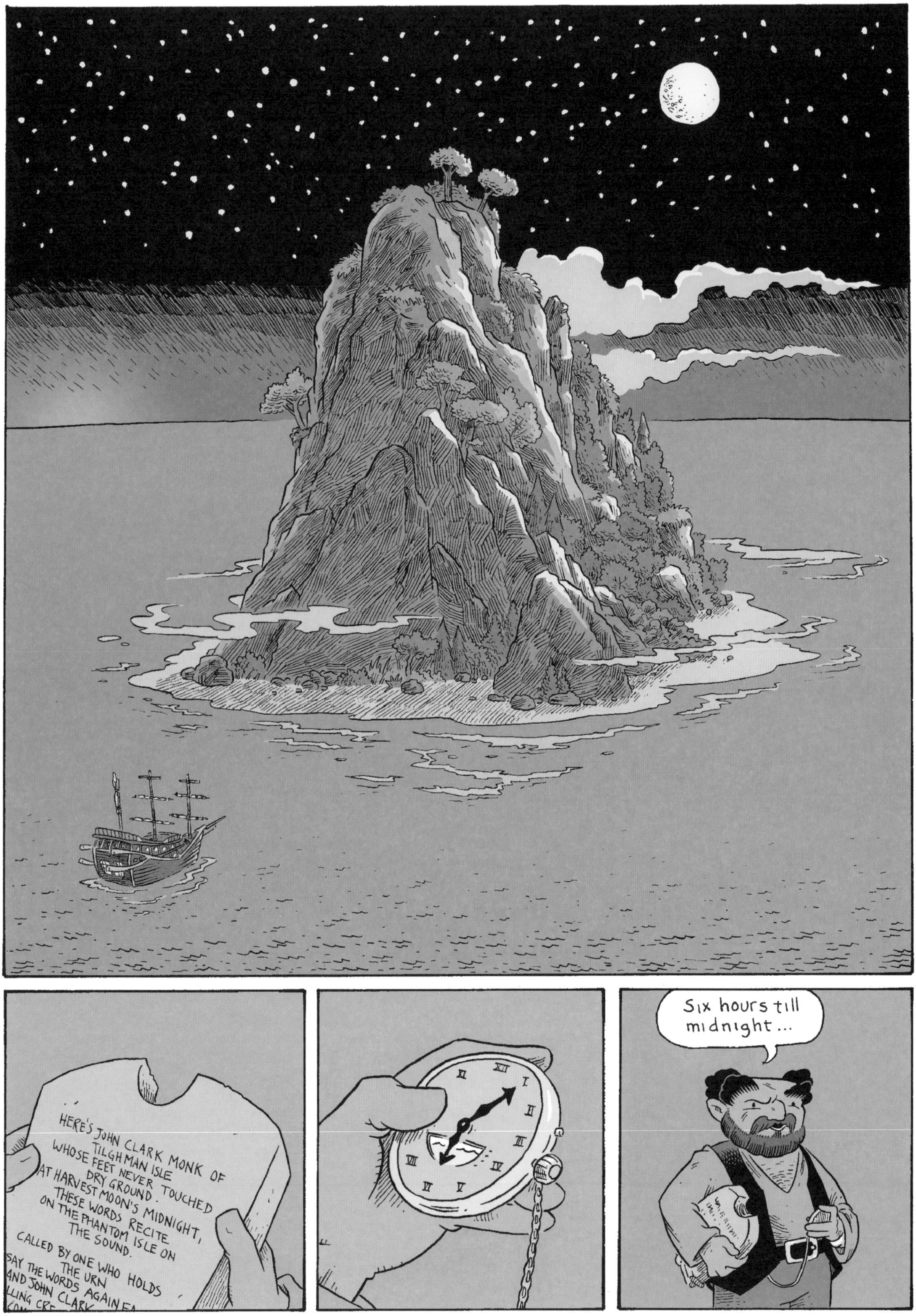
HERE'S JOHN CLARK MONK OF TILGHMAN ISLE
WHOSE FEET NEVER TOUCHED DRY GROUND.
AT HARVEST MOON'S MIDNIGHT, THESE WORDS RECITE ON THE PHANTOM ISLE ON THE SOUND.
CALLED BY ONE WHO HOLDS THE URN
SAY THE WORDS AGAIN
AND JOHN CLARK
Six hours till midnight...

CHAPTER NINE

Bungdockerik swell...

Kaelib swell?

Well...

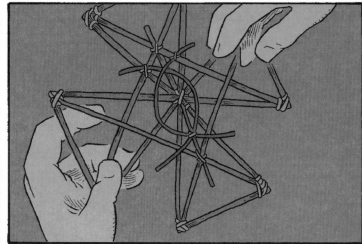

Due southeast - about three leagues - there's a land mass. Small, but it's there.

Remarkable. Back to the *Layla*.

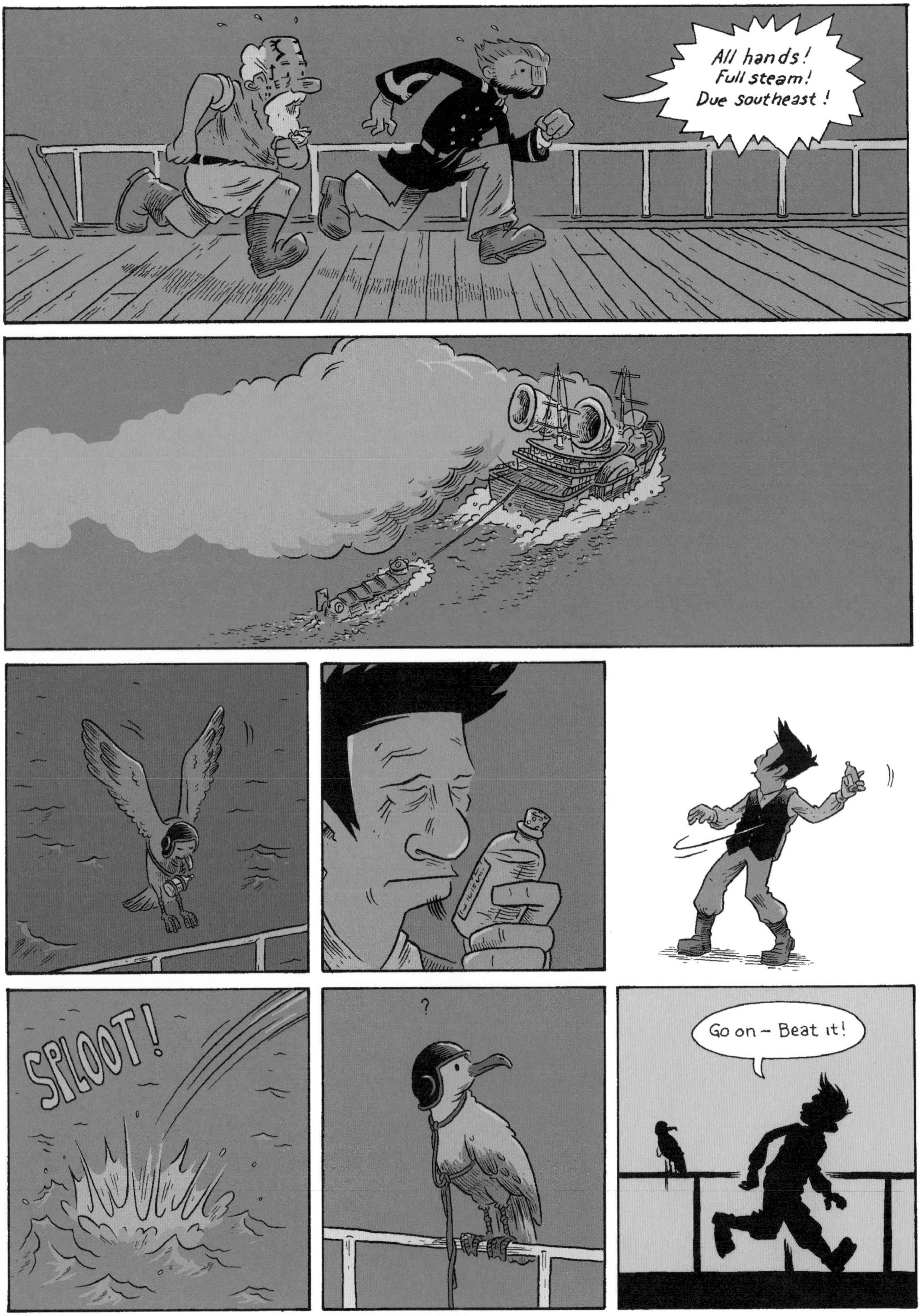
All hands! Full steam! Due southeast!
SPLOOT!
?
Go on – Beat it!

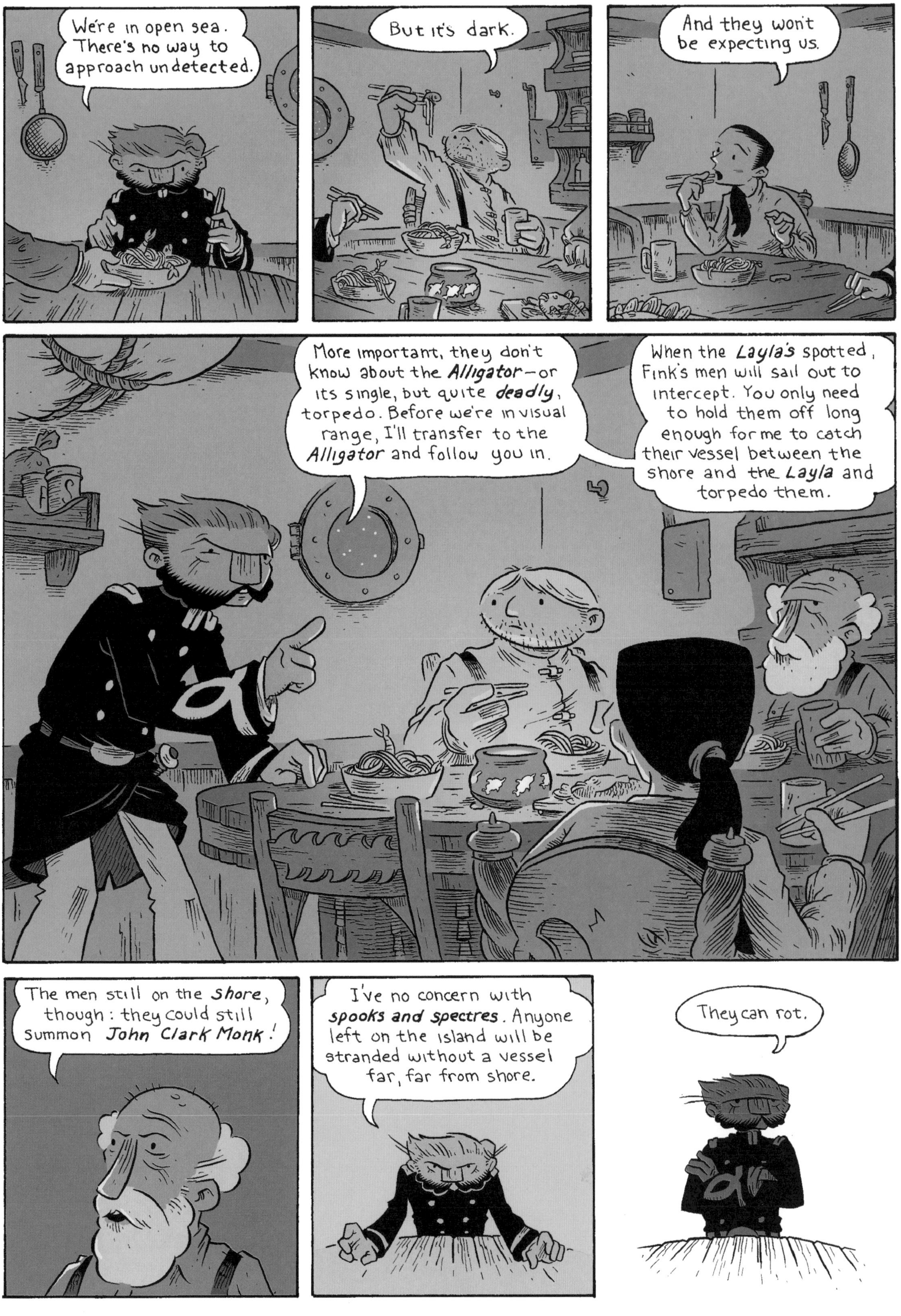
We're in open sea. There's no way to approach undetected.
But it's dark.
And they won't be expecting us.
More important, they don't know about the *Alligator*—or its single, but quite *deadly*, torpedo. Before we're in visual range, I'll transfer to the *Alligator* and follow you in.
When the *Layla's* spotted, Fink's men will sail out to intercept. You only need to hold them off long enough for me to catch their vessel between the shore and the *Layla* and torpedo them.
The men still on the *shore*, though: they could still summon *John Clark Monk*!
I've no concern with *spooks and spectres*. Anyone left on the island will be stranded without a vessel far, far from shore.
They can rot.

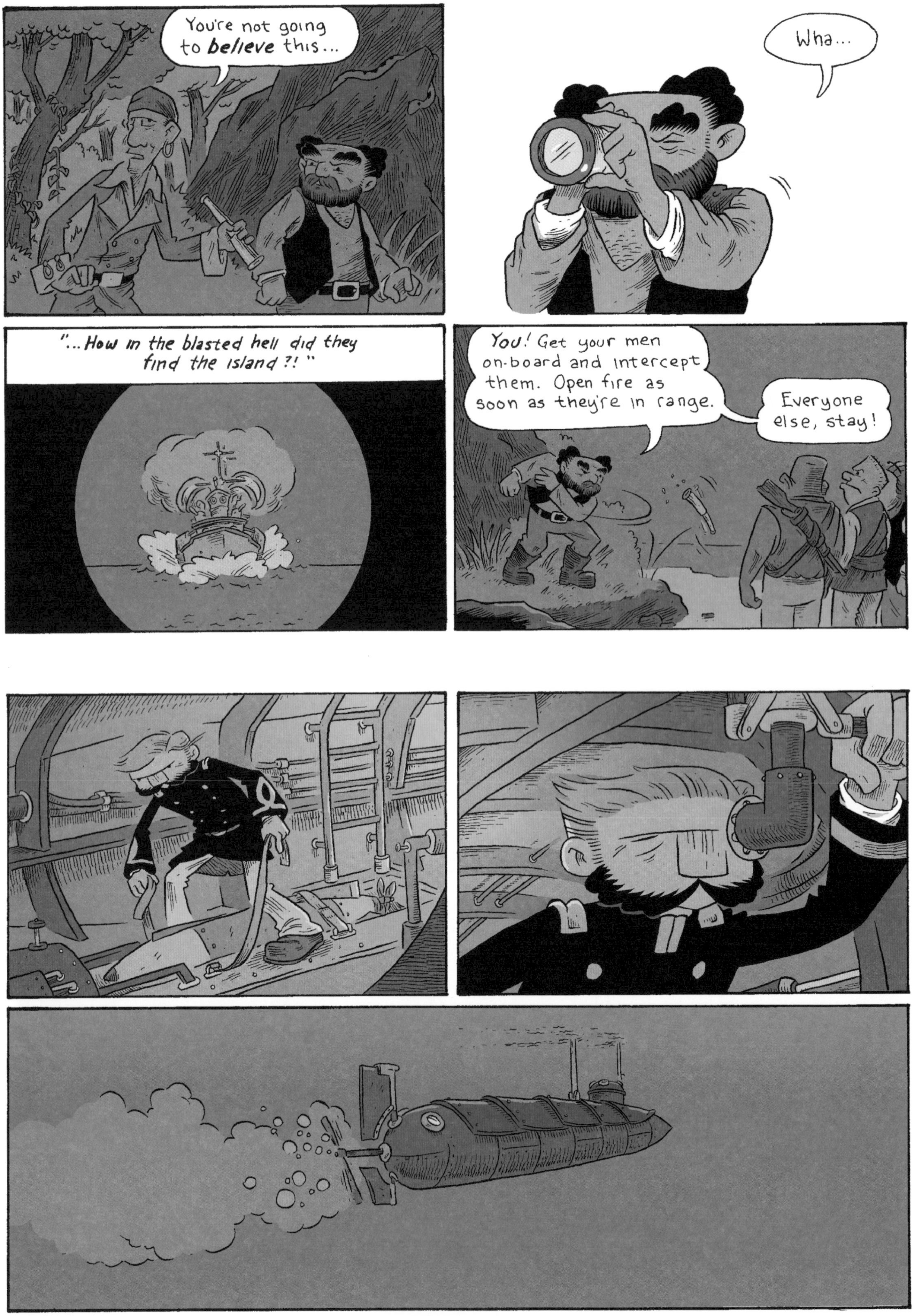
You're not going to believe this...
Wha...
"...How in the blasted hell did they find the island?!"
You! Get your men on-board and intercept them. Open fire as soon as they're in range.
Everyone else, stay!

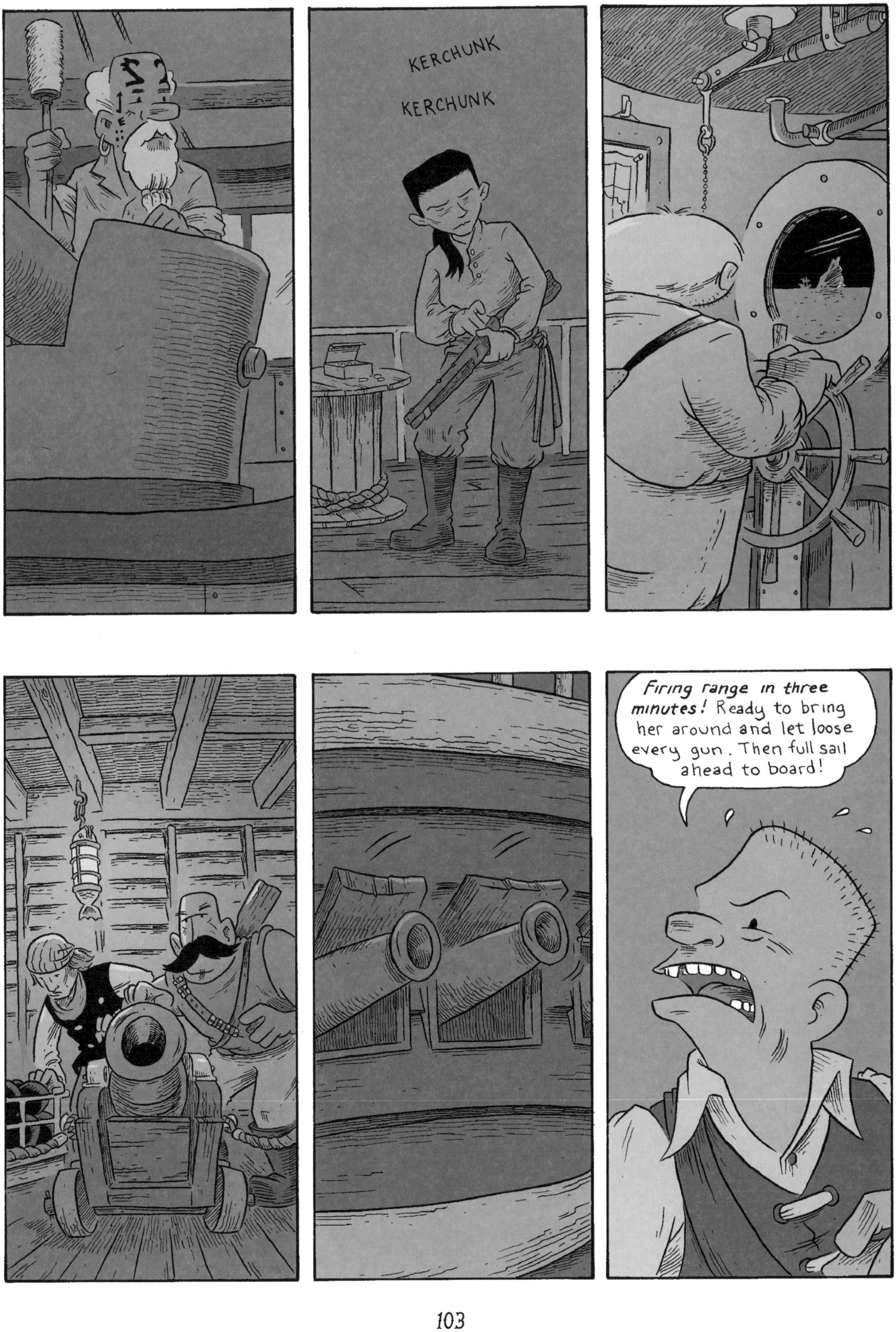
KERCHUNK
KERCHUNK
Firing range in three minutes! Ready to bring her around and let loose every gun. Then full sail ahead to board!

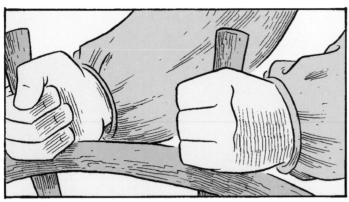

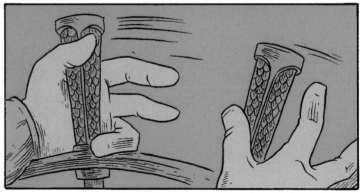

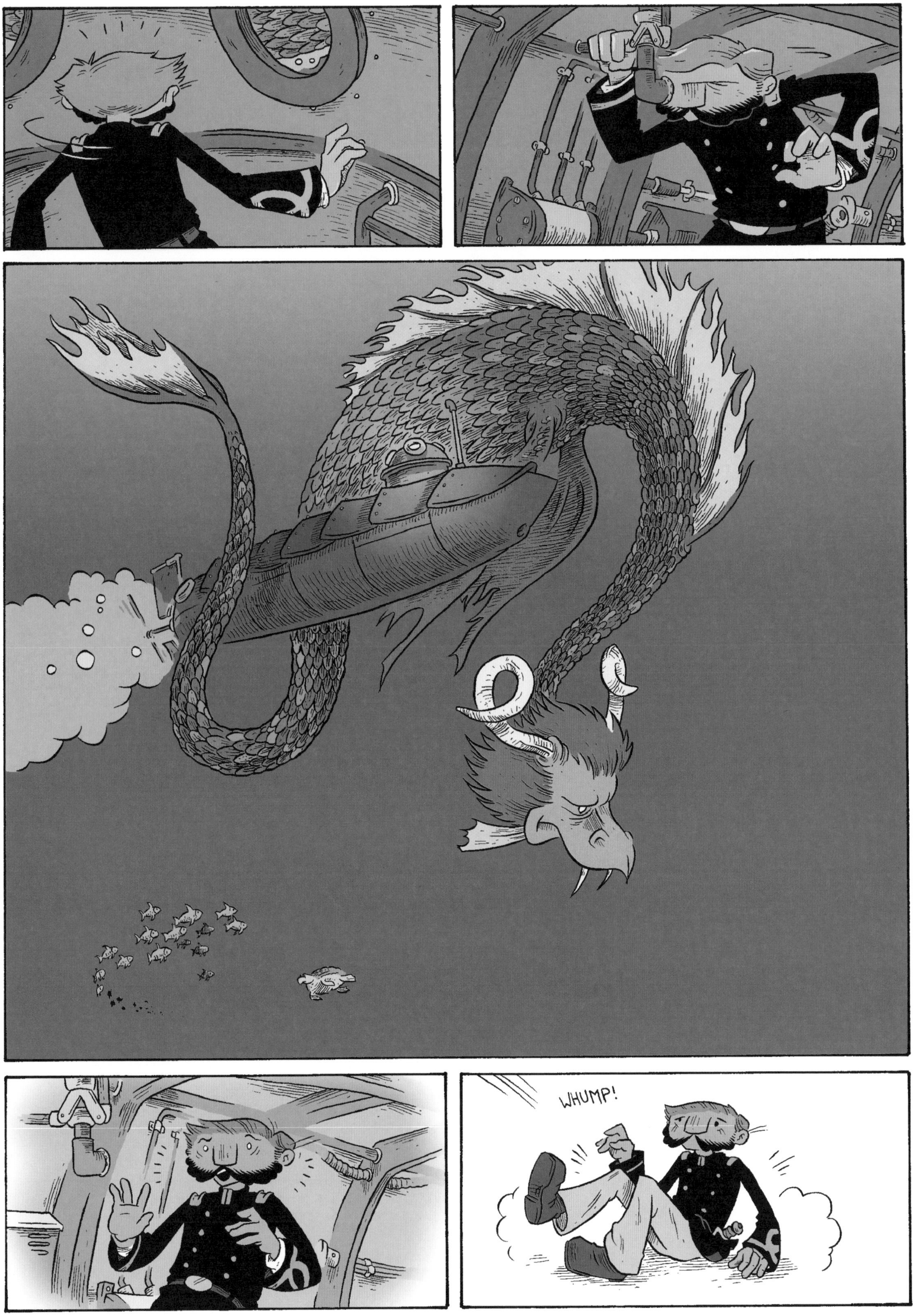
WHUMP!

CHAPTER TEN

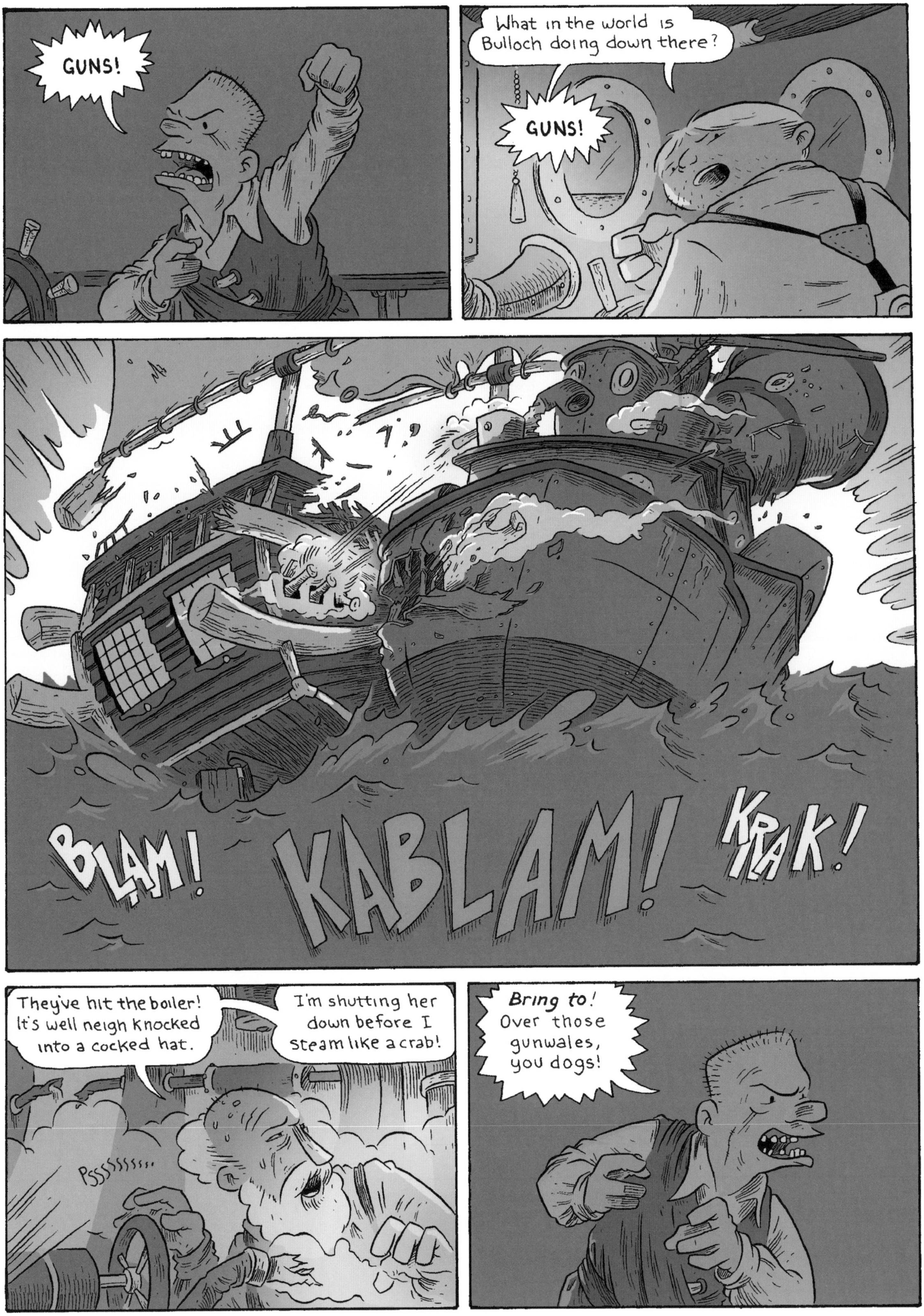

GUNS!
What in the world is Bulloch doing down there?
GUNS!
BLAM!
KABLAM!
KRAK!
They've hit the boiler! It's well neigh knocked into a cocked hat.
I'm shutting her down before I steam like a crab!
PSSSSSSSS...
Bring to! Over those gunwales, you dogs!

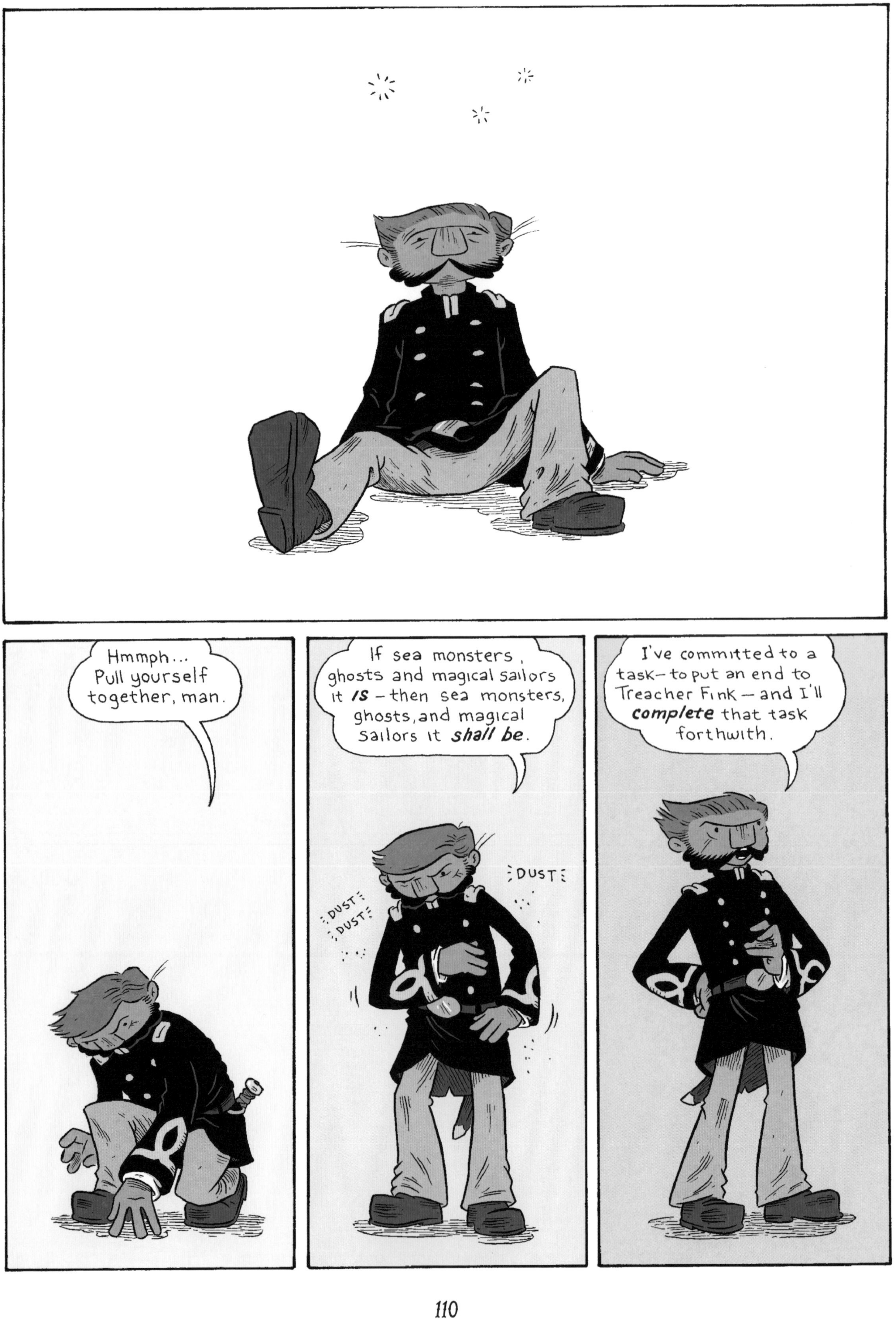
Hmmph...
Pull yourself together, man.
If sea monsters, ghosts and magical sailors it *IS* – then sea monsters, ghosts, and magical sailors it *shall be*.
DUST
DUST
DUST
I've committed to a task – to put an end to Treacher Fink – and I'll *complete* that task forthwith.

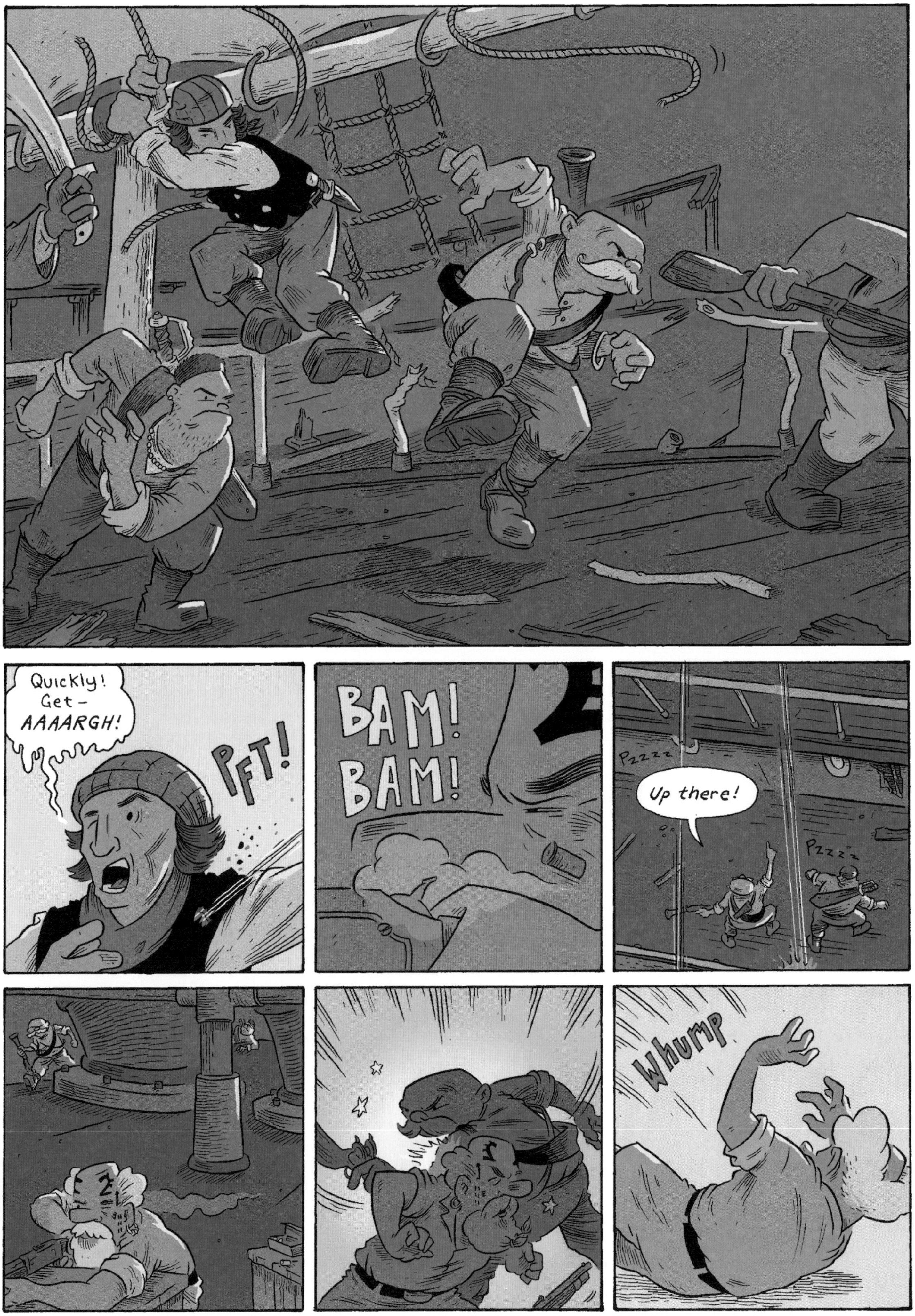
Quickly! Get - AAAARGH!
PFT!
BAM! BAM!
Pzzzz
Up there!
Pzzzz
Whump

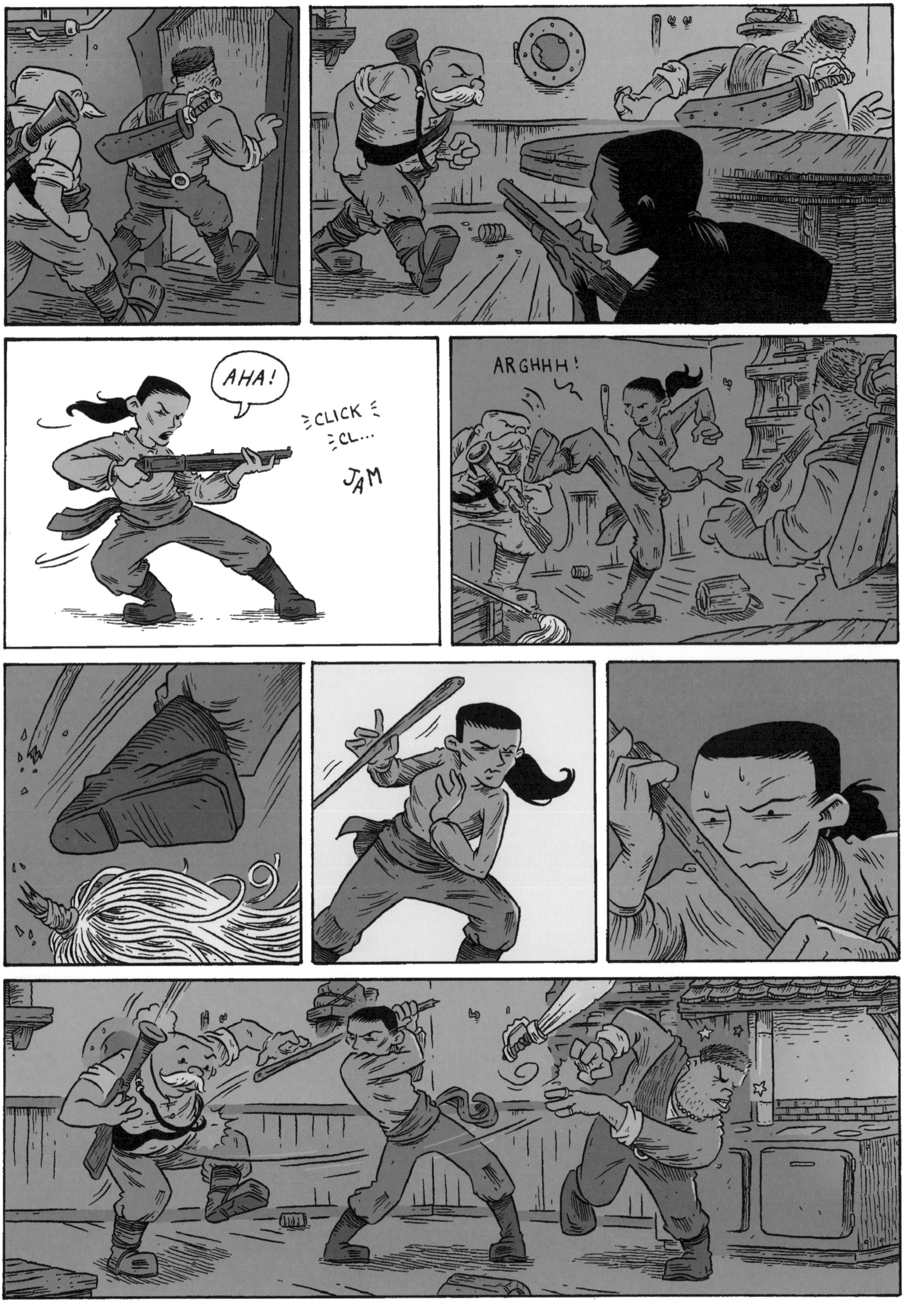
AHA!
CLICK
CL...
JAM
ARGHHH!

I need a hand in here. She's gone crazy as a loon!

It's called Jogo do Pau! Come back in here and I'll show you how it works, you lummox!

Meanwhile:

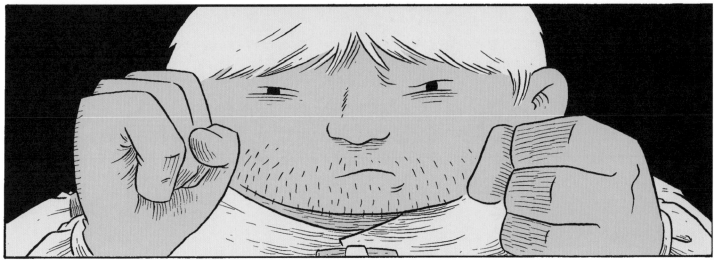

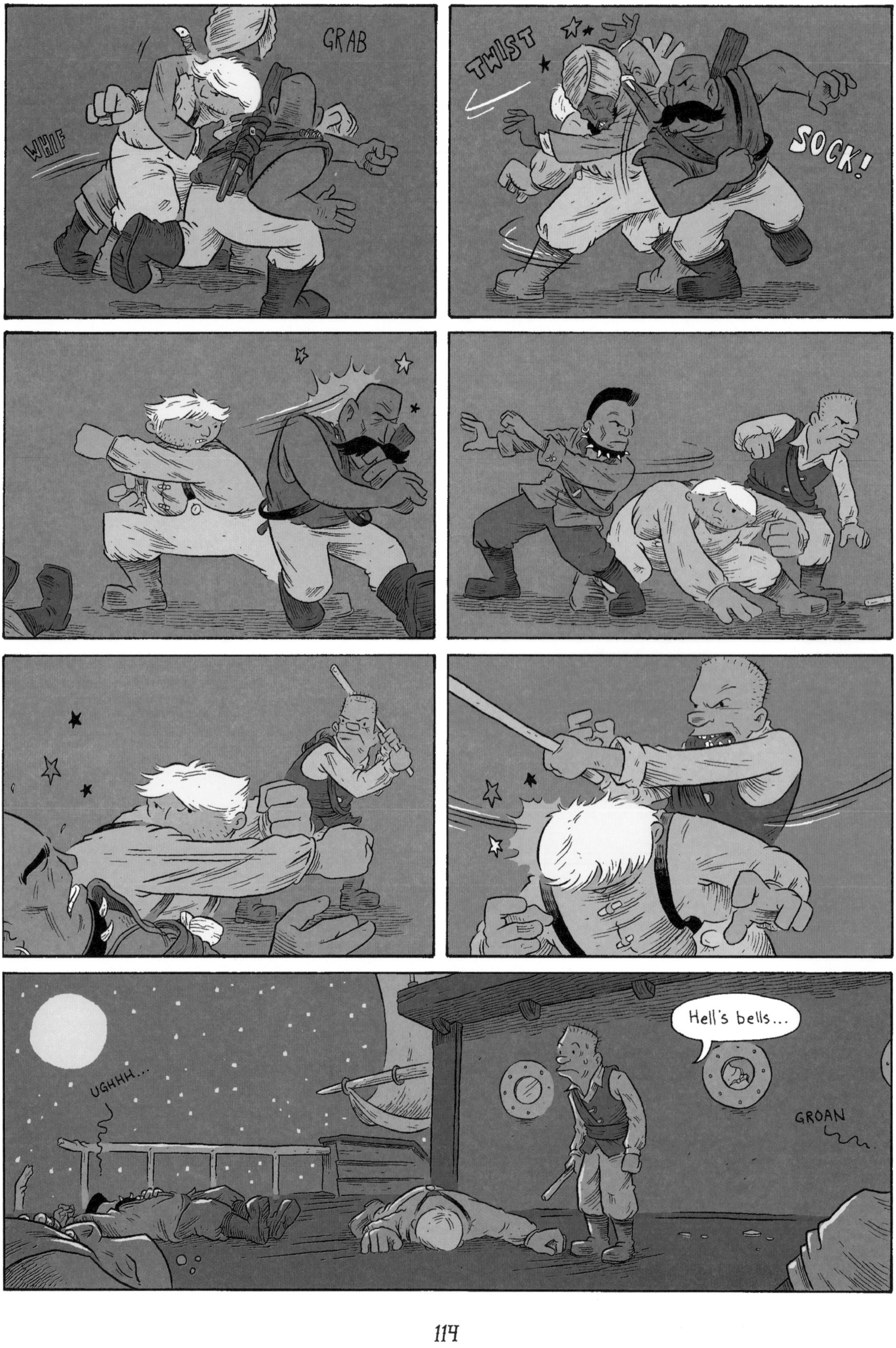
GRAB
WHIF
TWIST
SOCK!
UGHHH...
Hell's bells...
GROAN

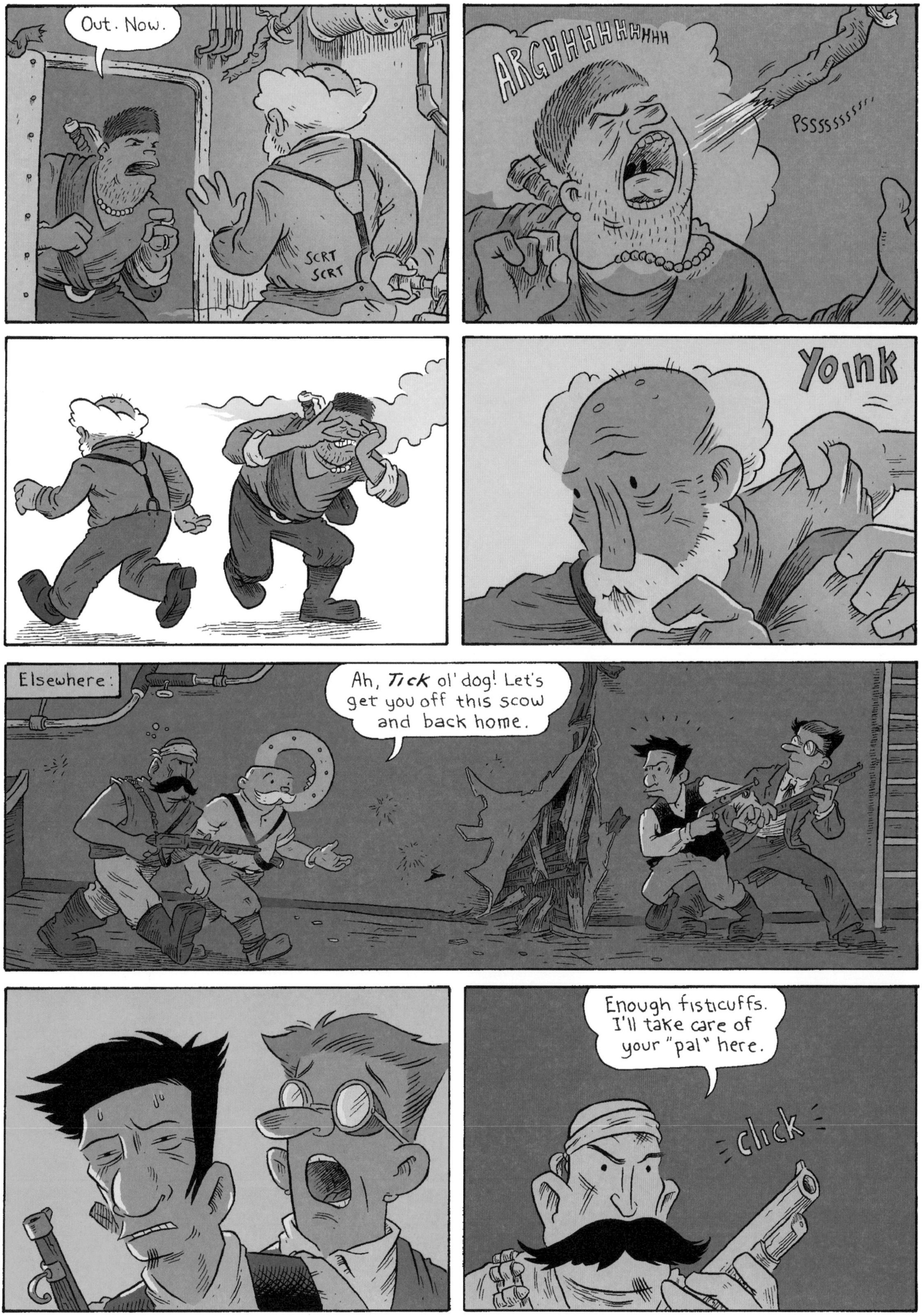
Out. Now.
SCRT SCRT
ARGHHHHHHHHH
PSSSSSSSSS
YOINK
Elsewhere:
Ah, *Tick* ol' dog! Let's get you off this scow and back home.
Enough fisticuffs. I'll take care of your "pal" here.
click

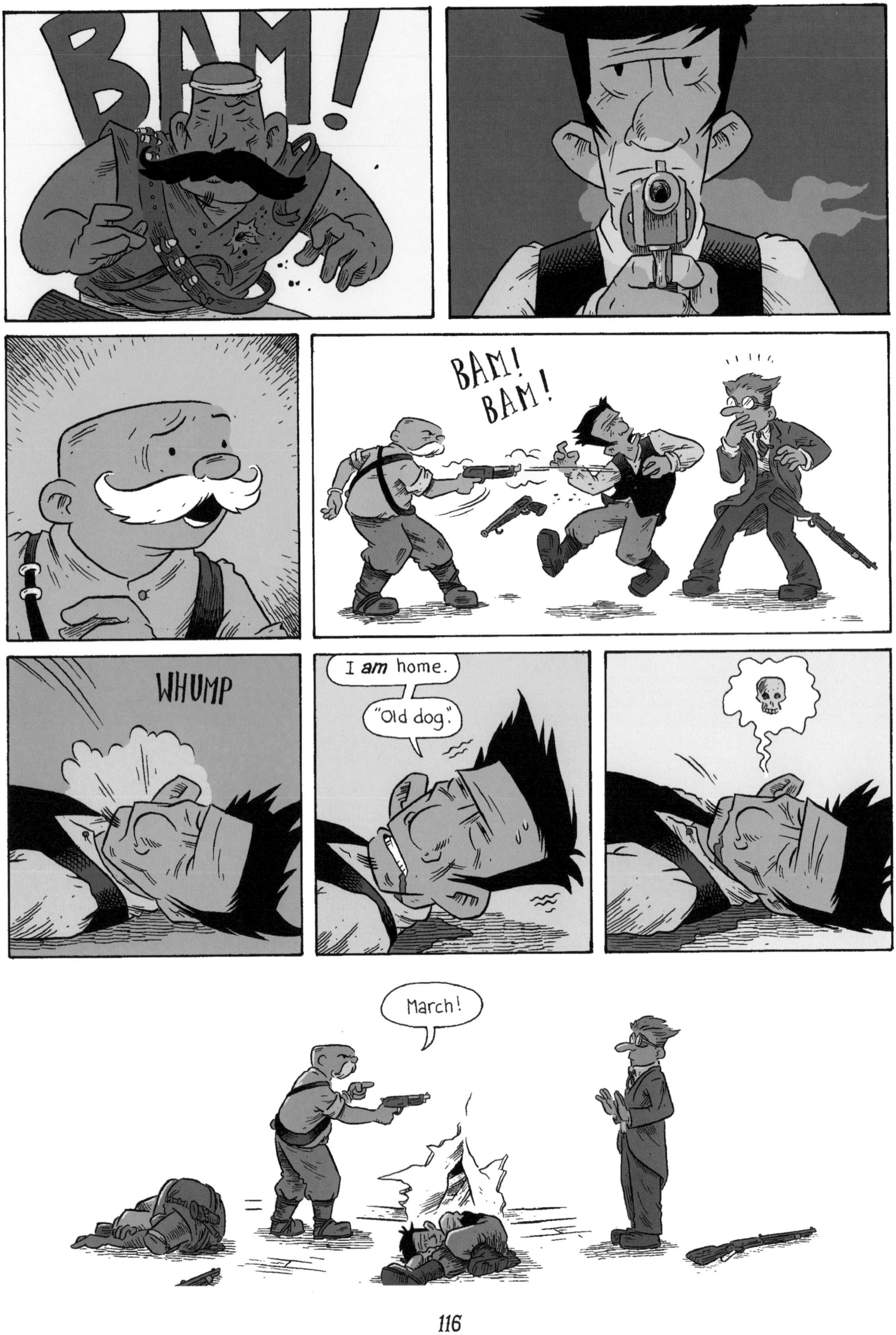
BAM!
BAM!
BAM!
WHUMP
I am home.
"Old dog."
March!

Found it.

THROW!

GRAB!

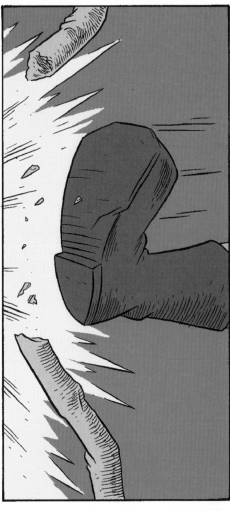

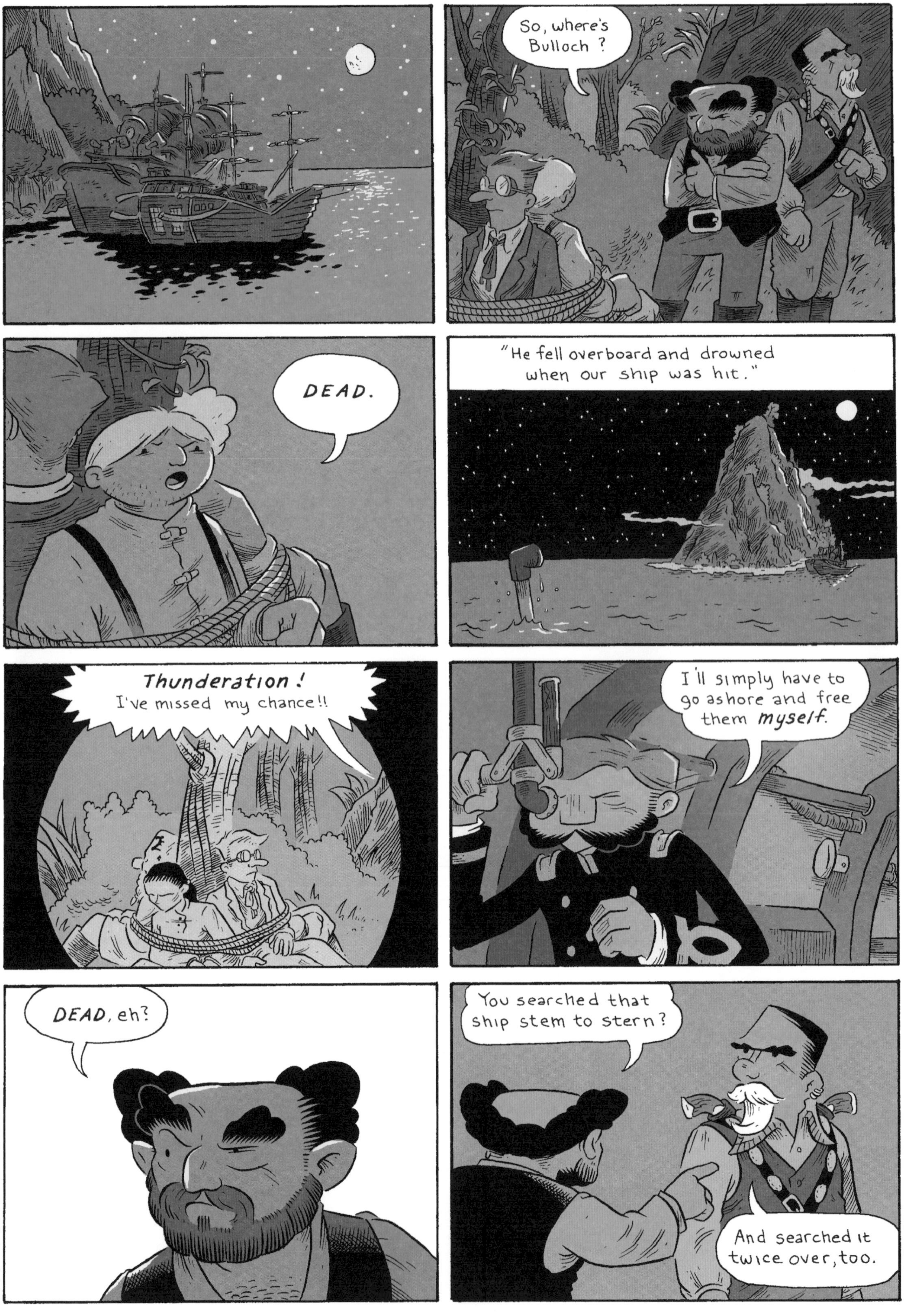

So, where's Bulloch ?
DEAD.
"He fell overboard and drowned when our ship was hit."
Thunderation ! I've missed my chance!!
I'll simply have to go ashore and free them myself.
DEAD, eh?
You searched that ship stem to stern ?
And searched it twice over, too.

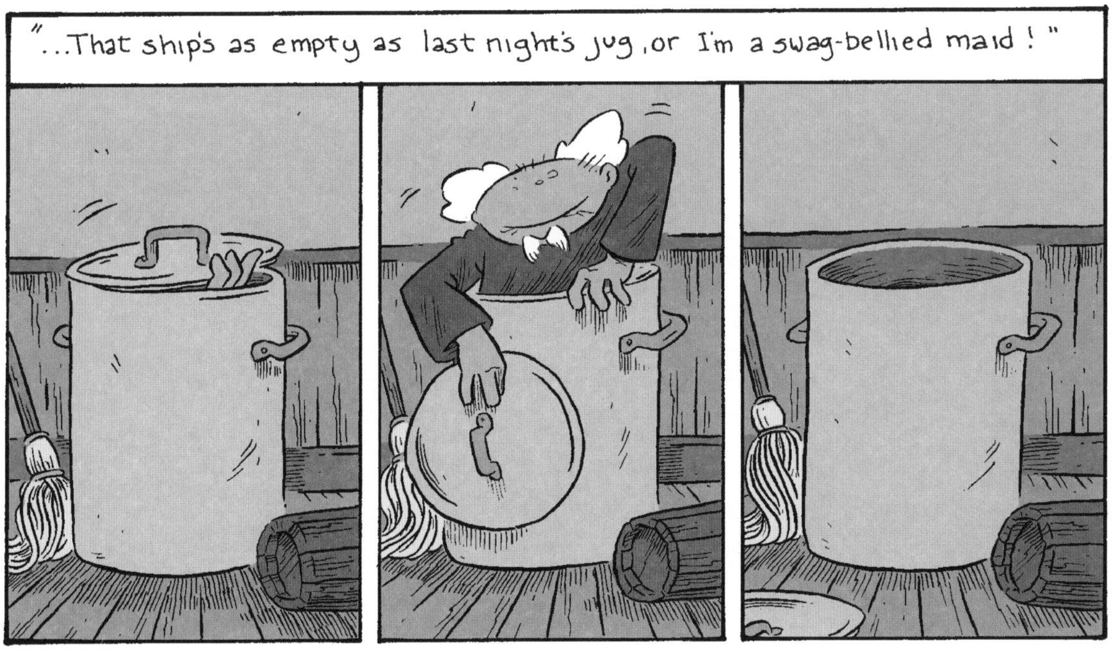
"...That ship's as empty as last night's jug, or I'm a swag-bellied maid!"

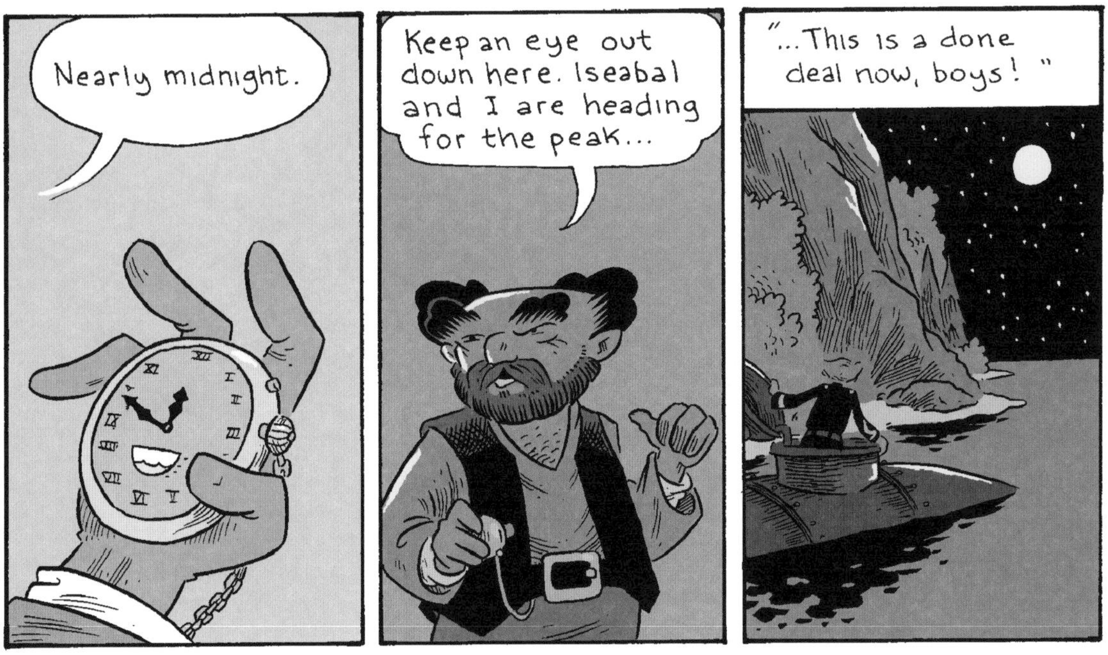
Nearly midnight.
Keep an eye out down here. Iseabal and I are heading for the peak...
"...This is a done deal now, boys!"

CHAPTER ELEVEN

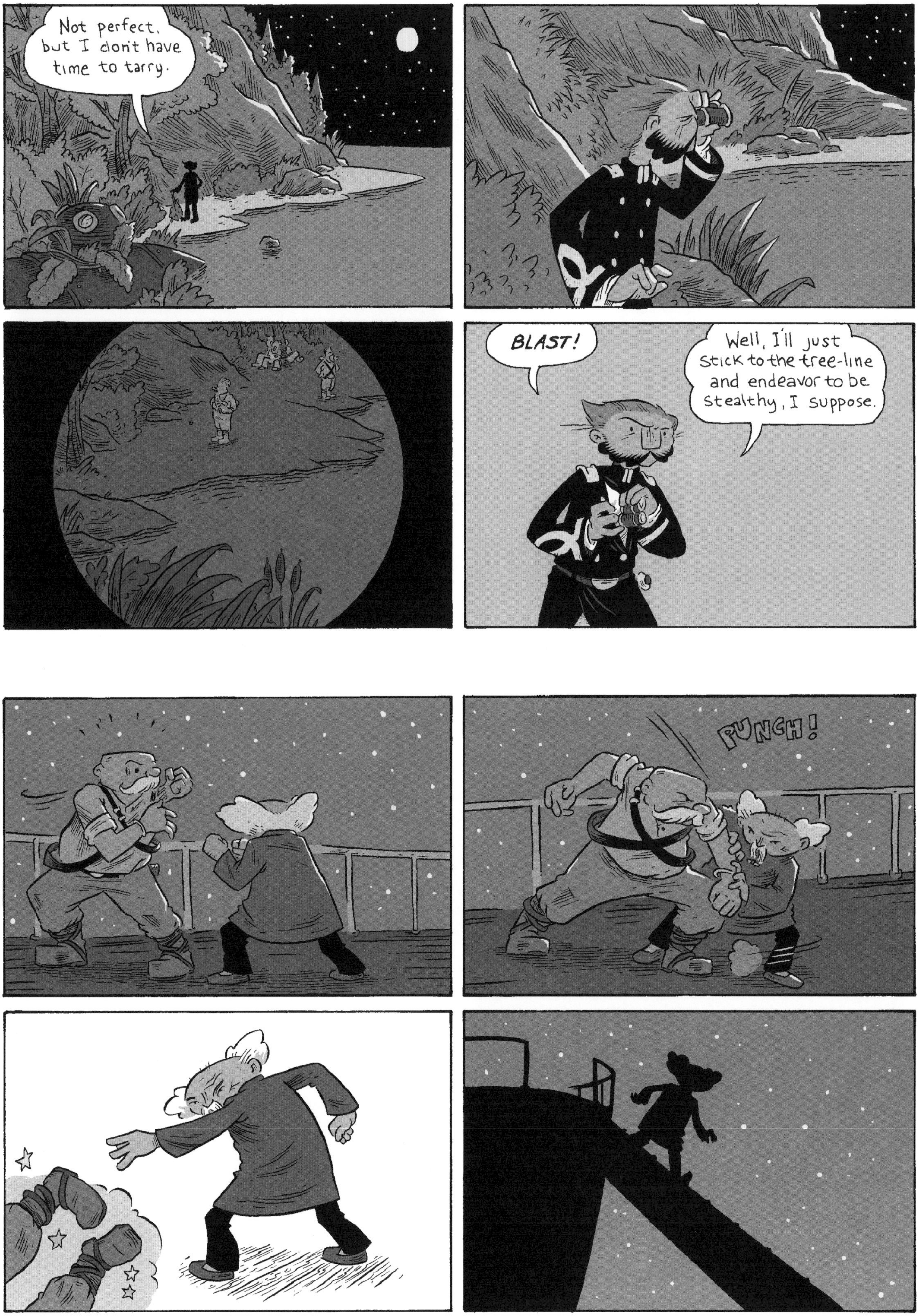
Not perfect, but I don't have time to tarry.
BLAST!
Well, I'll just stick to the tree-line and endeavor to be stealthy, I suppose.
PUNCH!

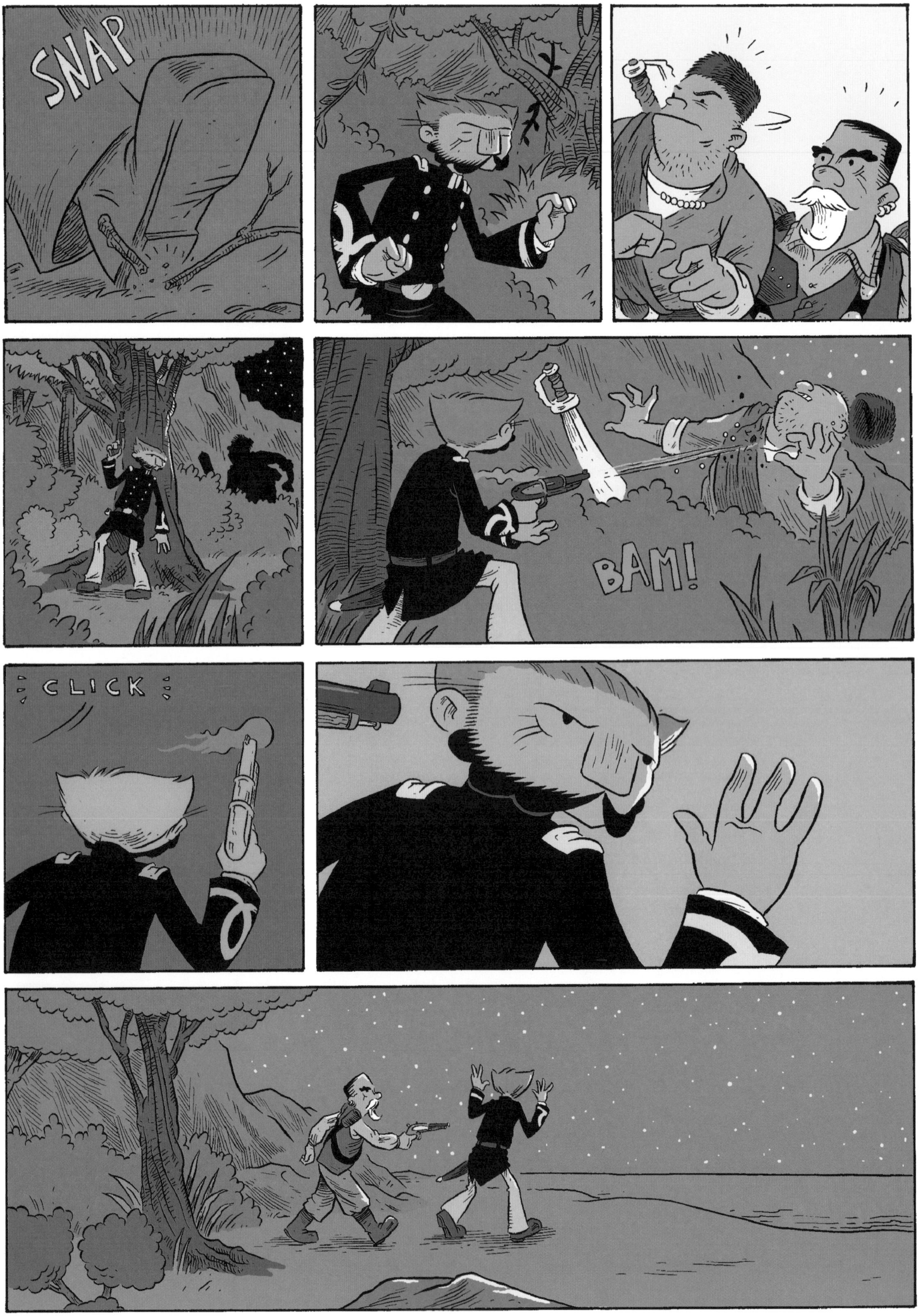
SNAP
BAM!
CLICK

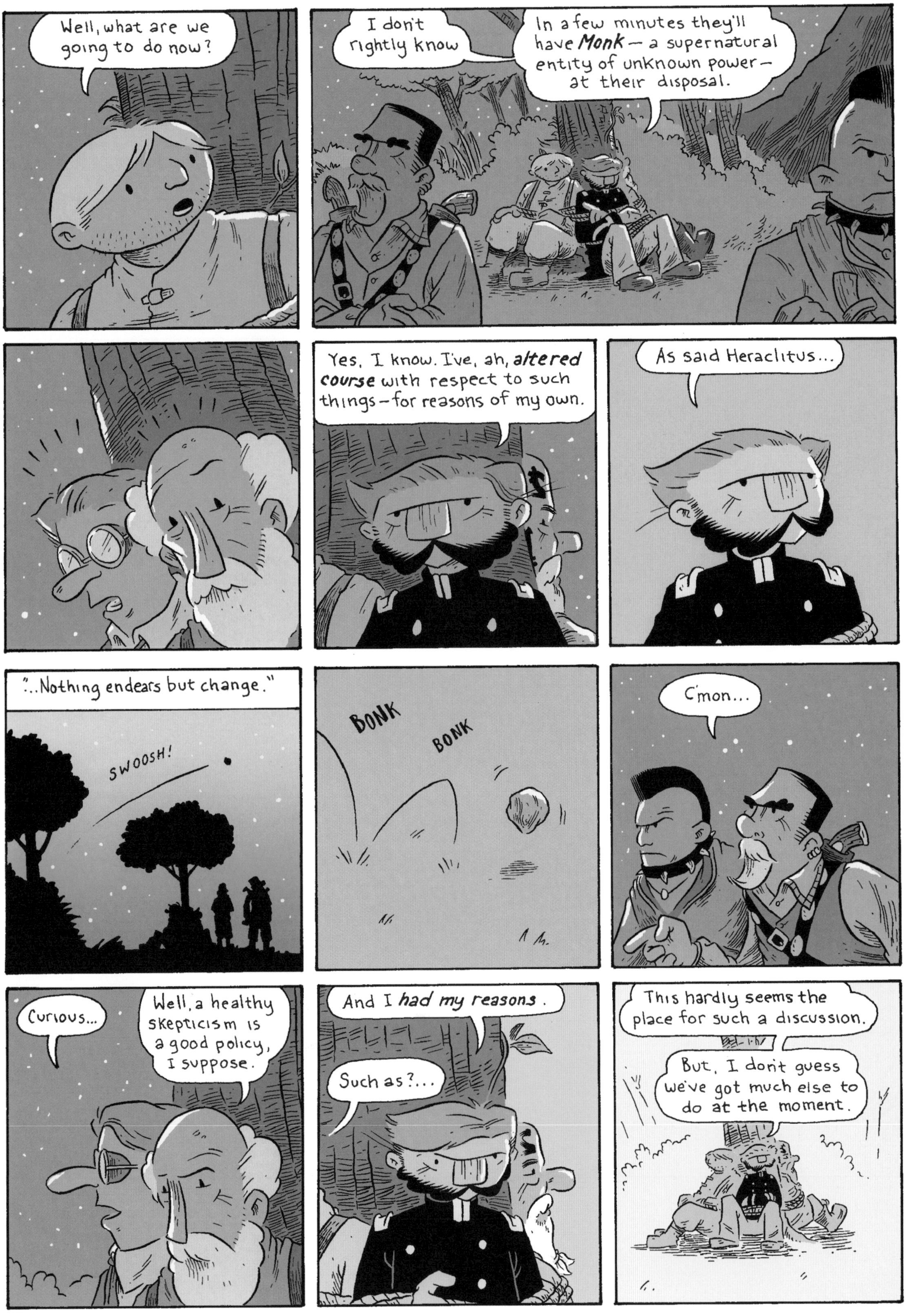
Well, what are we going to do now?
I don't rightly know
In a few minutes they'll have Monk — a supernatural entity of unknown power — at their disposal.
Yes, I know. I've, ah, altered course with respect to such things — for reasons of my own.
As said Heraclitus...
"...Nothing endears but change."
SWOOSH!
BONK
BONK
C'mon...
Curious...
Well, a healthy skepticism is a good policy, I suppose.
And I had my reasons.
Such as?...
This hardly seems the place for such a discussion.
But, I don't guess we've got much else to do at the moment.

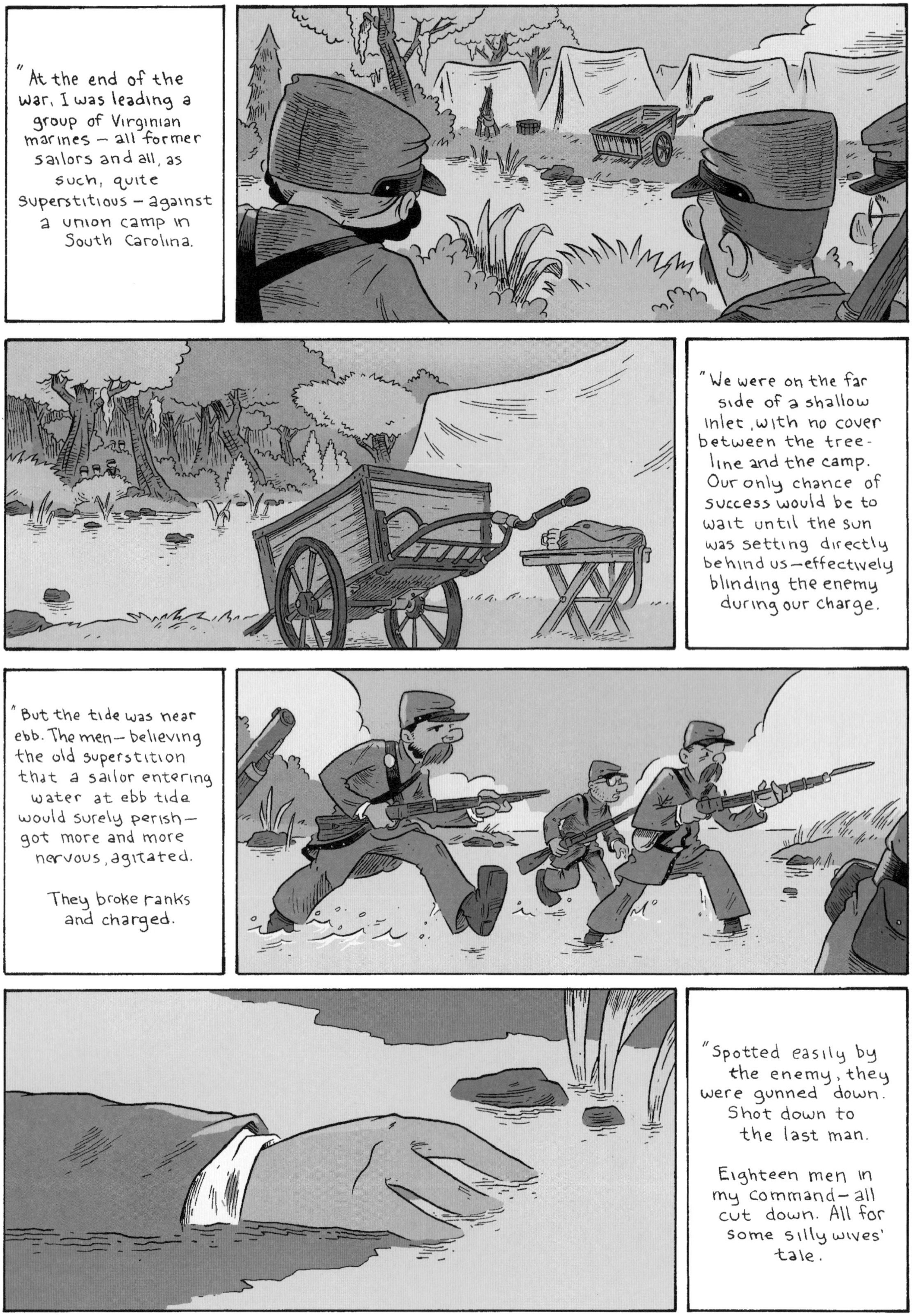
"At the end of the war, I was leading a group of Virginian marines – all former sailors and all, as such, quite superstitious – against a union camp in South Carolina.
"We were on the far side of a shallow inlet, with no cover between the tree-line and the camp. Our only chance of success would be to wait until the sun was setting directly behind us—effectively blinding the enemy during our charge.
"But the tide was near ebb. The men– believing the old superstition that a sailor entering water at ebb tide would surely perish– got more and more nervous, agitated.
They broke ranks and charged.
"Spotted easily by the enemy, they were gunned down. Shot down to the last man.
Eighteen men in my command– all cut down. All for some silly wives' tale.

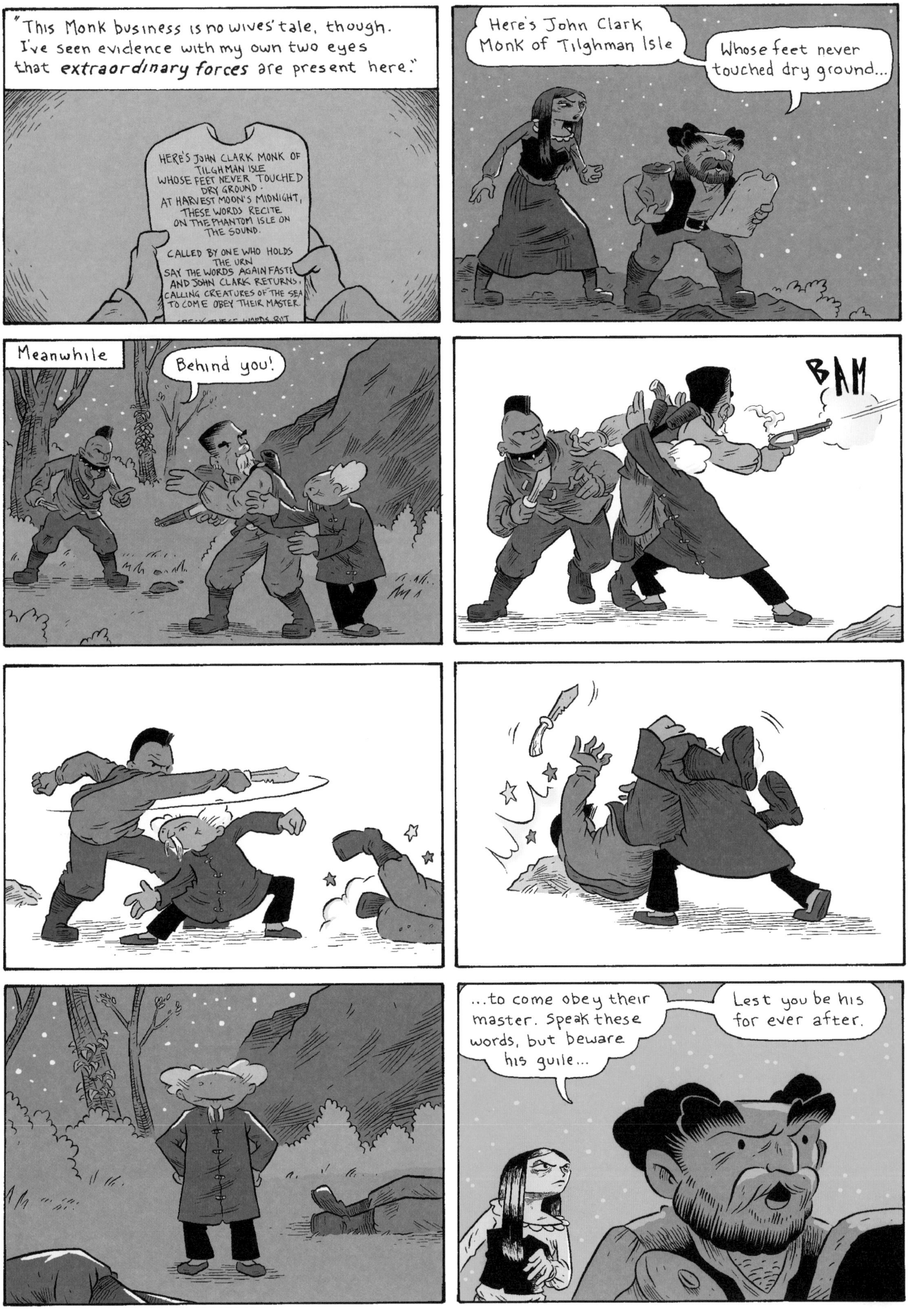
"This Monk business is no wives' tale, though. I've seen evidence with my own two eyes that **extraordinary forces** are present here."
HERE'S JOHN CLARK MONK OF TILGHMAN ISLE
WHOSE FEET NEVER TOUCHED DRY GROUND.
AT HARVEST MOON'S MIDNIGHT, THESE WORDS RECITE ON THE PHANTOM ISLE ON THE SOUND.
CALLED BY ONE WHO HOLDS THE URN
SAY THE WORDS AGAIN FASTE
AND JOHN CLARK RETURNS,
CALLING CREATURES OF THE SEA TO COME OBEY THEIR MASTER.
Here's John Clark Monk of Tilghman Isle
Whose feet never touched dry ground...
Meanwhile
Behind you!
BAM
...to come obey their master. Speak these words, but beware his guile...
Lest you be his for ever after.

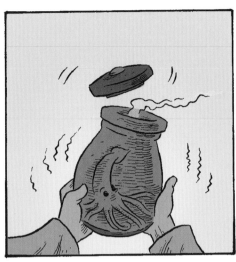

Ju-long, what are *you* doing here?

If you had any sense, you'd be hiding out on the *Layla*.

You just missed running into two of Fink's men in that *very wood*, in fact.

Perhaps you could get us out of these ropes before they return.

Um... Commander...

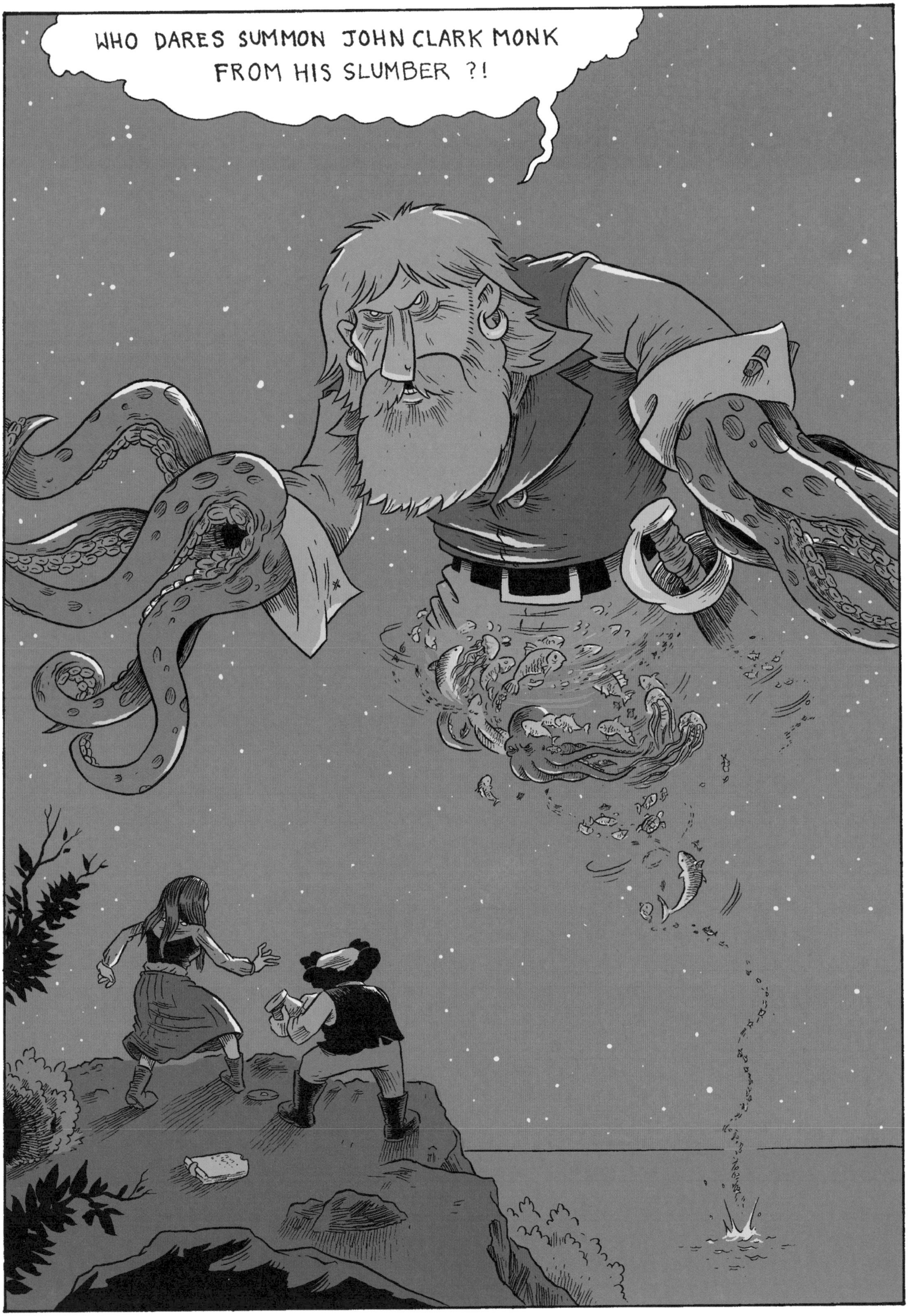
WHO DARES SUMMON JOHN CLARK MONK FROM HIS SLUMBER ?!

CHAPTER TWELVE

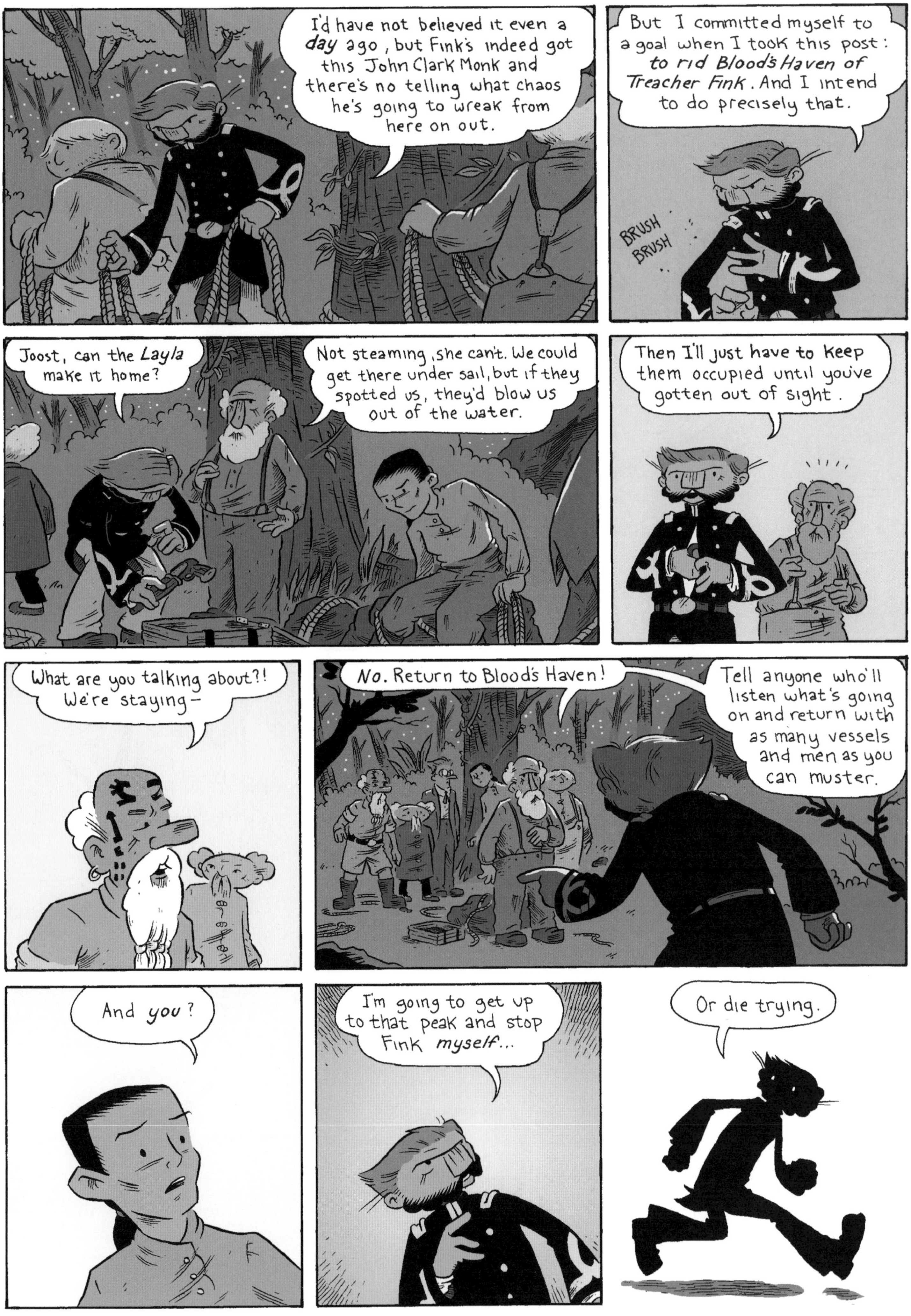
I'd have not believed it even a *day* ago, but Fink's indeed got this John Clark Monk and there's no telling what chaos he's going to wreak from here on out.
But I committed myself to a goal when I took this post: *to rid Blood's Haven of Treacher Fink*. And I intend to do precisely that.
BRUSH BRUSH
Joost, can the *Layla* make it home?
Not steaming, she can't. We could get there under sail, but if they spotted us, they'd blow us out of the water.
Then I'll just have to keep them occupied until you've gotten out of sight.
What are you talking about?! We're staying-
No. Return to Blood's Haven!
Tell anyone who'll listen what's going on and return with as many vessels and men as you can muster.
And *you*?
I'm going to get up to that peak and stop Fink *myself*...
Or die trying.

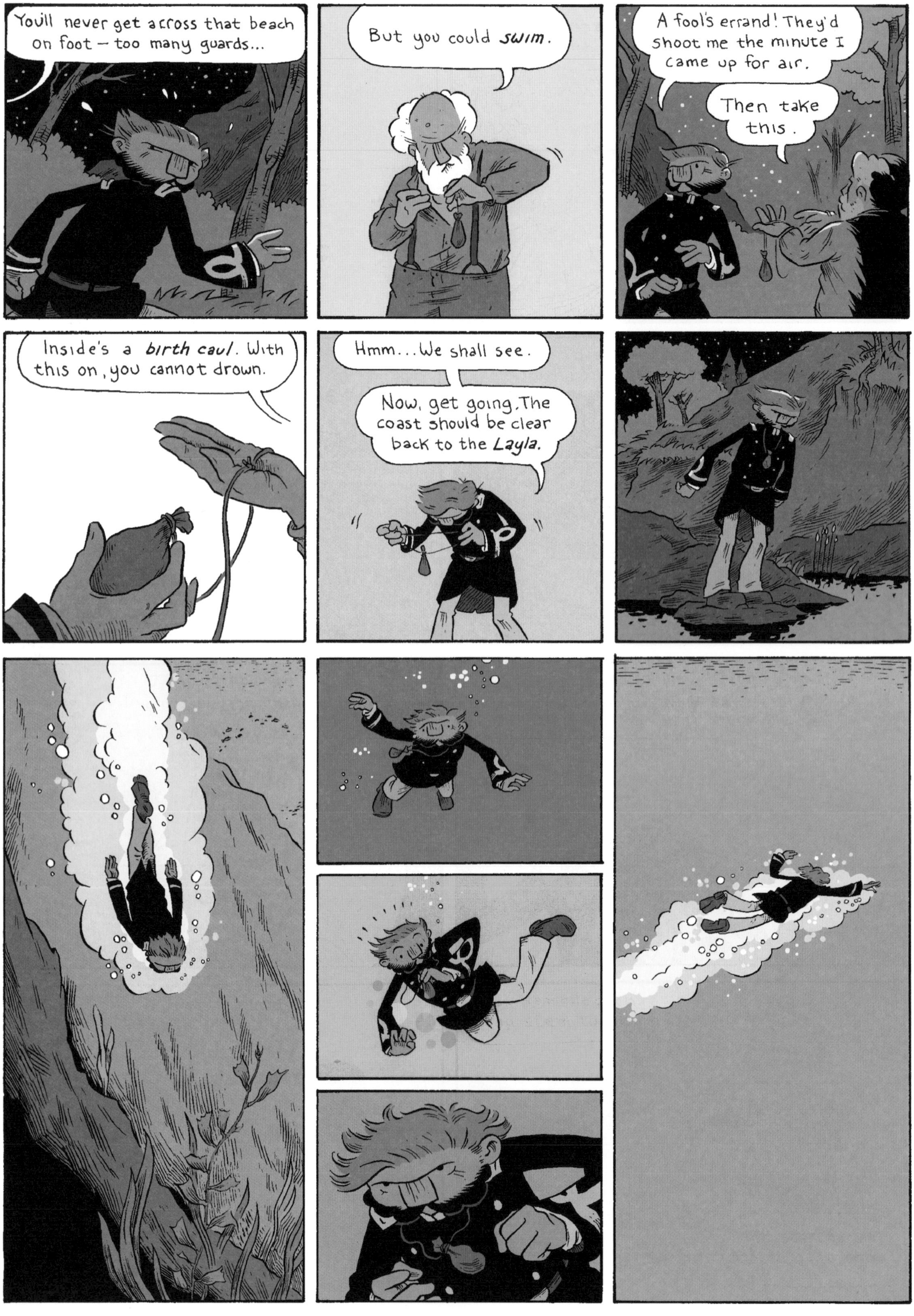
You'll never get across that beach on foot – too many guards...
But you could *swim*.
A fool's errand! They'd shoot me the minute I came up for air.
Then take this.
Inside's a *birth caul*. With this on, you cannot drown.
Hmm... We shall see.
Now, get going. The coast should be clear back to the *Layla*.

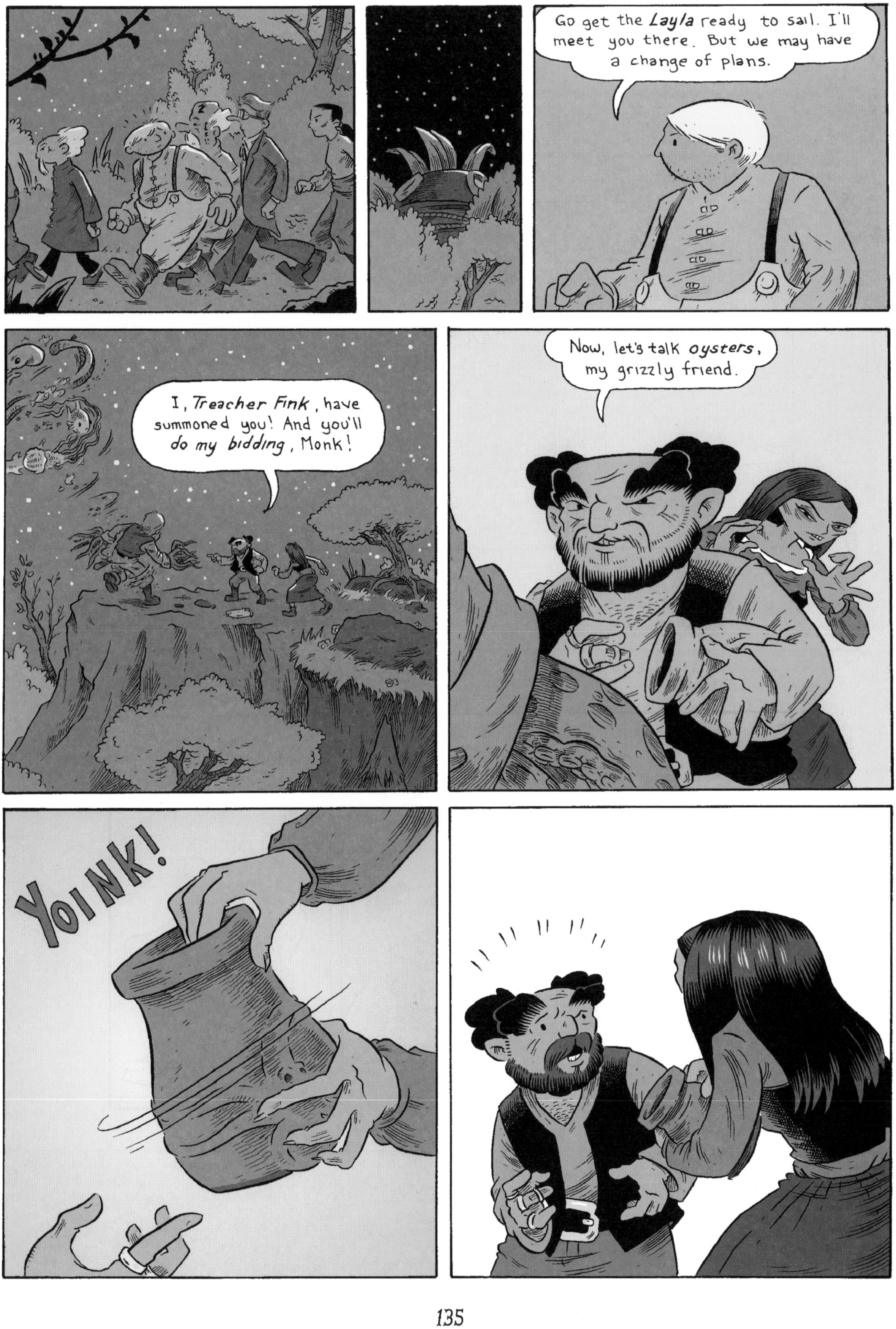

Go get the *Layla* ready to sail. I'll meet you there. But we may have a change of plans.
I, *Treacher Fink*, have summoned you! And you'll *do my bidding*, Monk!
Now, let's talk *oysters*, my grizzly friend.
YOINK!

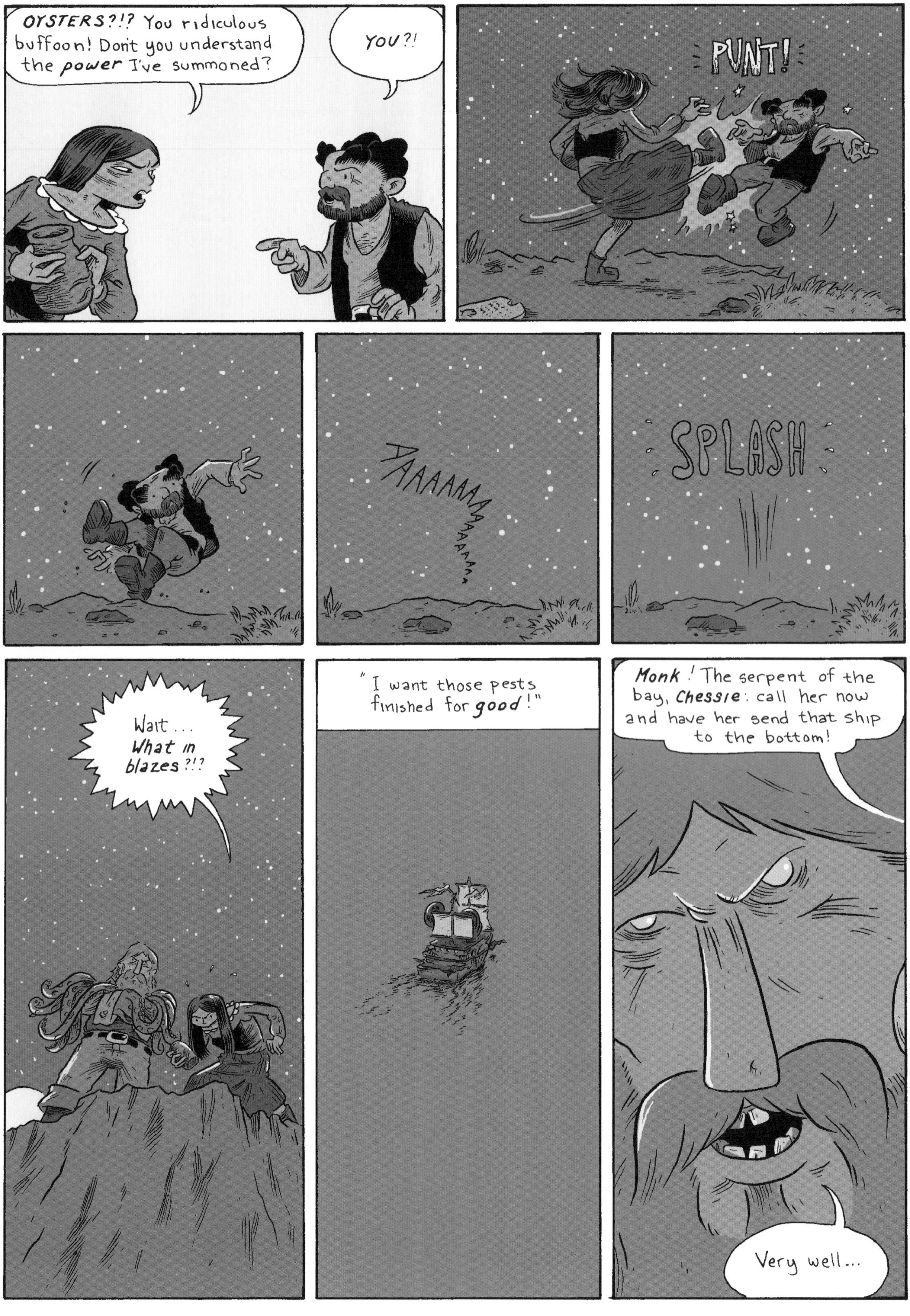
OYSTERS?!? You ridiculous buffoon! Don't you understand the power I've summoned?
YOU?!
PUNT!
AAAAAAAAAAAAAAAAAA
SPLASH
Wait... What in blazes?!?
"I want those pests finished for good!"
Monk! The serpent of the bay, Chessie: call her now and have her send that ship to the bottom!
Very well...

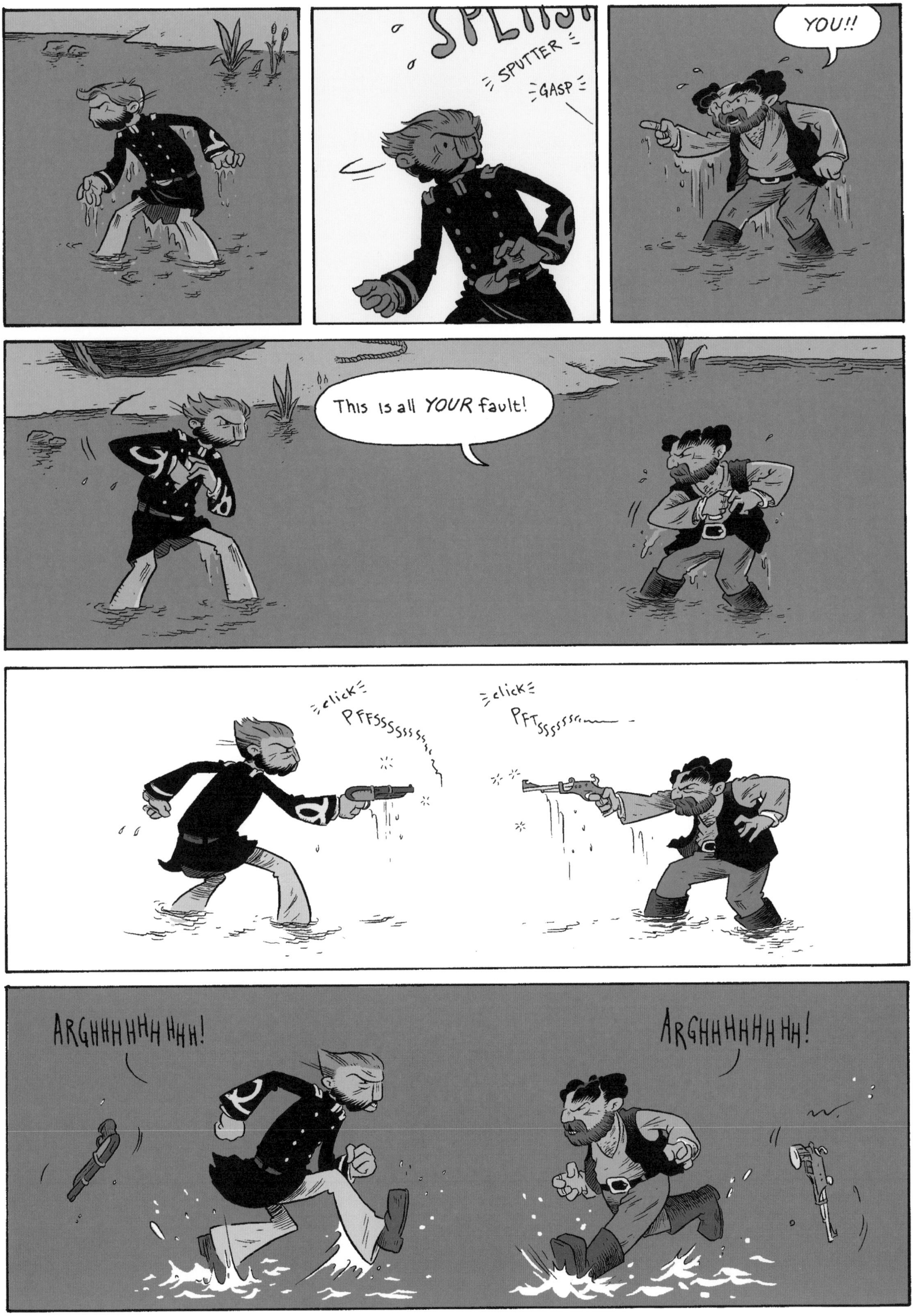
SPLISH
SPUTTER
GASP
YOU!!
This is all YOUR fault!
click
PFFSSSSSSSS
click
PFTSSSSSS
ARGHHHHHHHHH!
ARGHHHHHHHH!

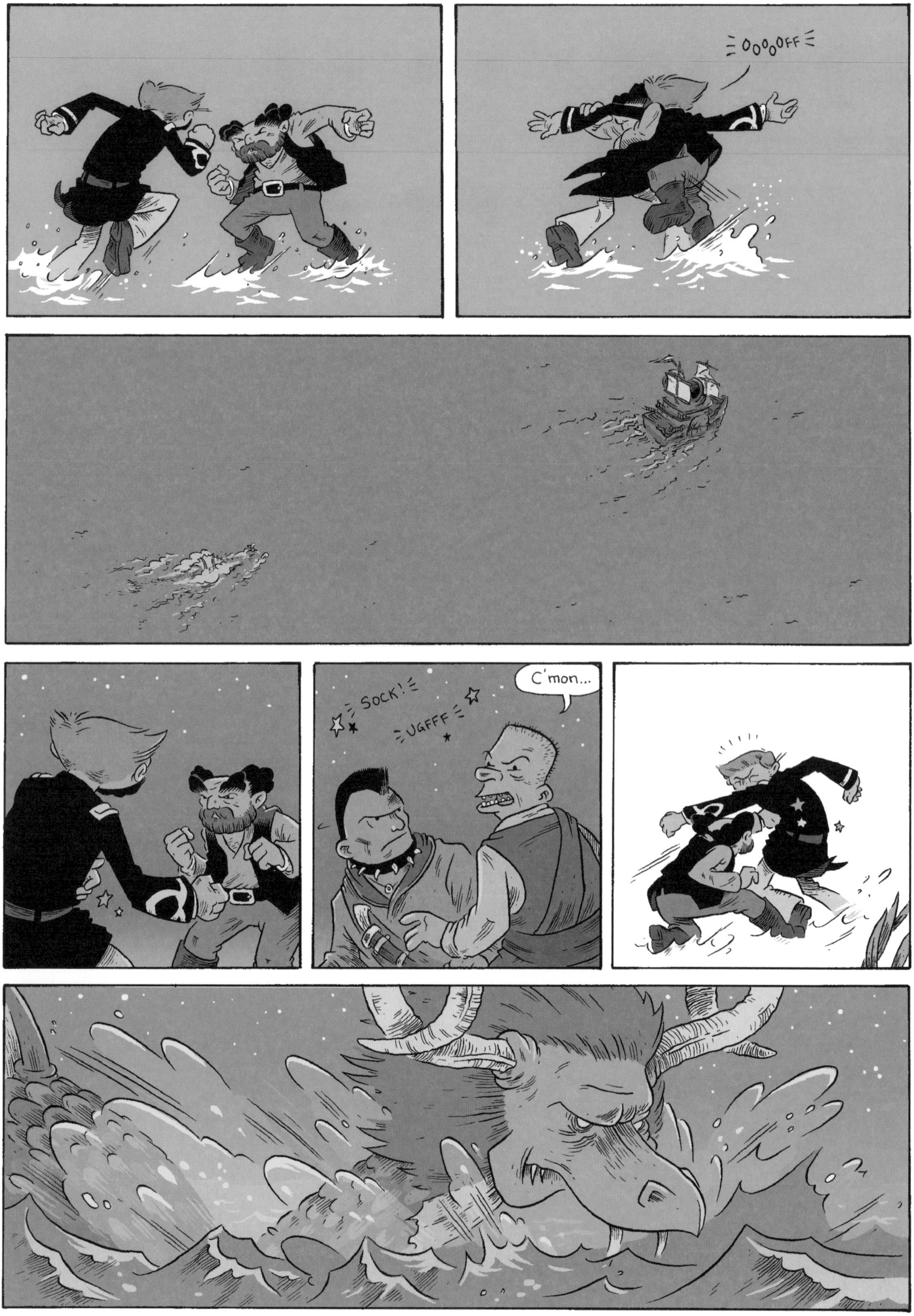
OOOOOFF
SOCK!
UGFFF
C'mon...

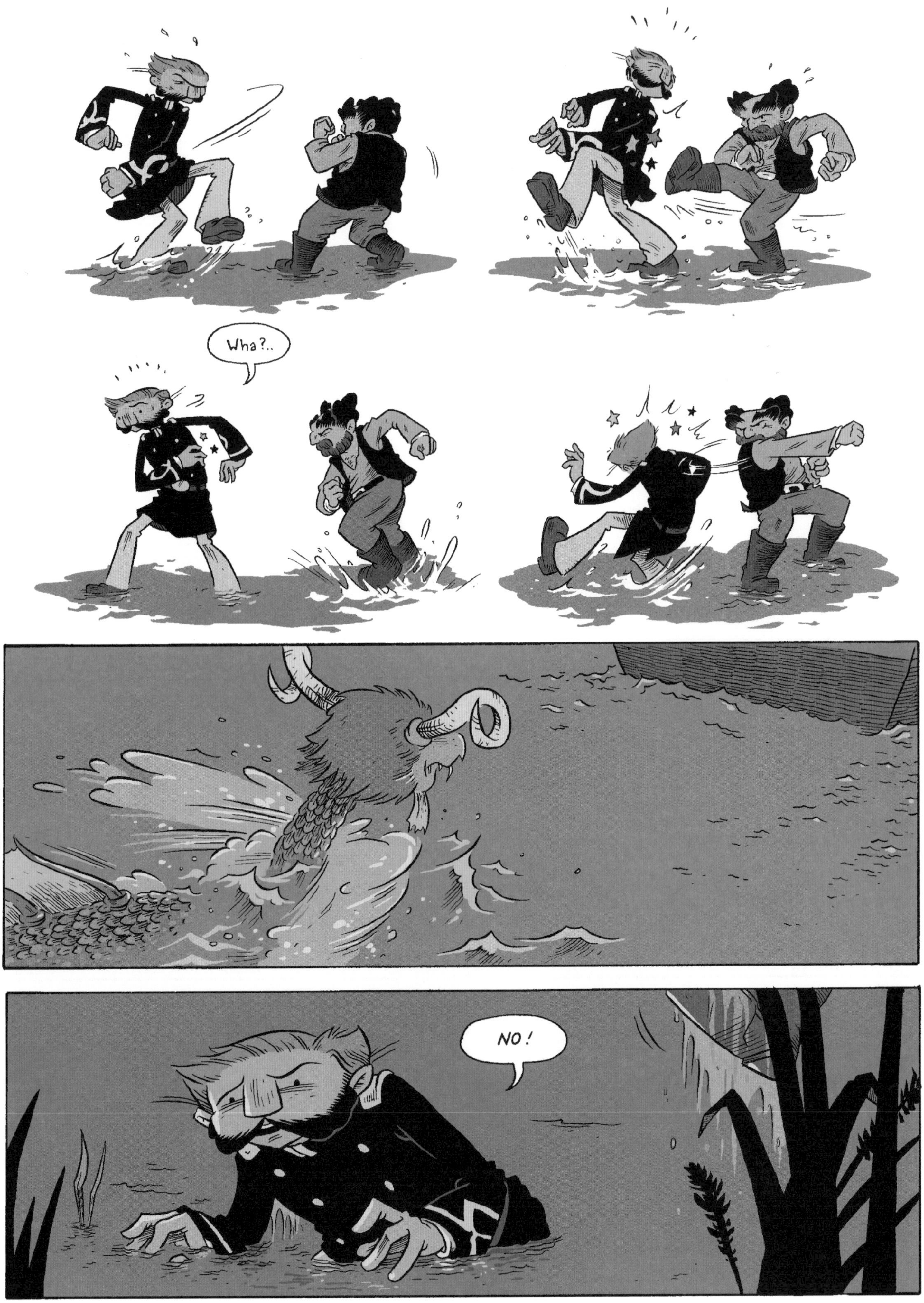
Wha?..
NO!

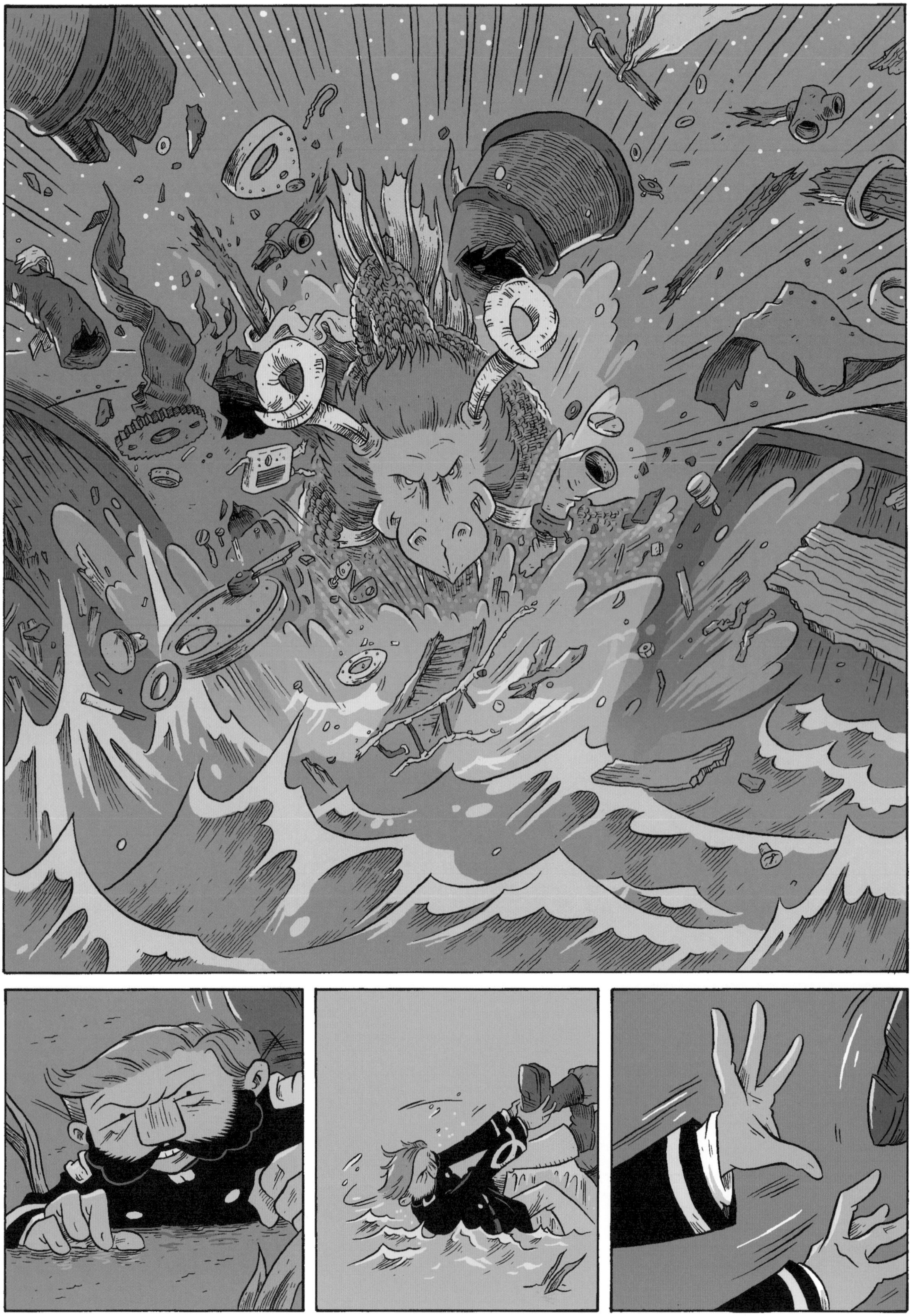

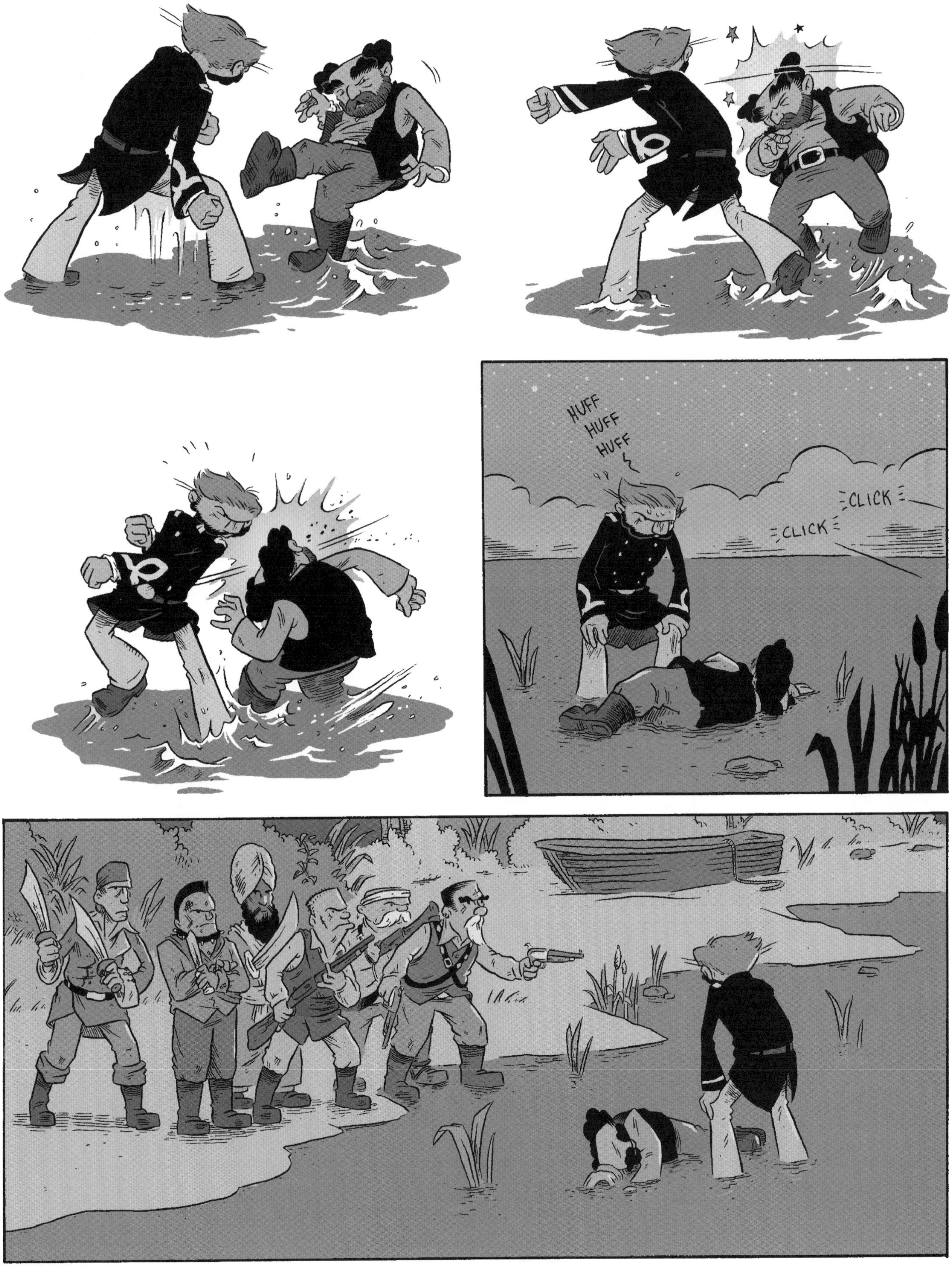
HUFF
HUFF
HUFF
CLICK
CLICK

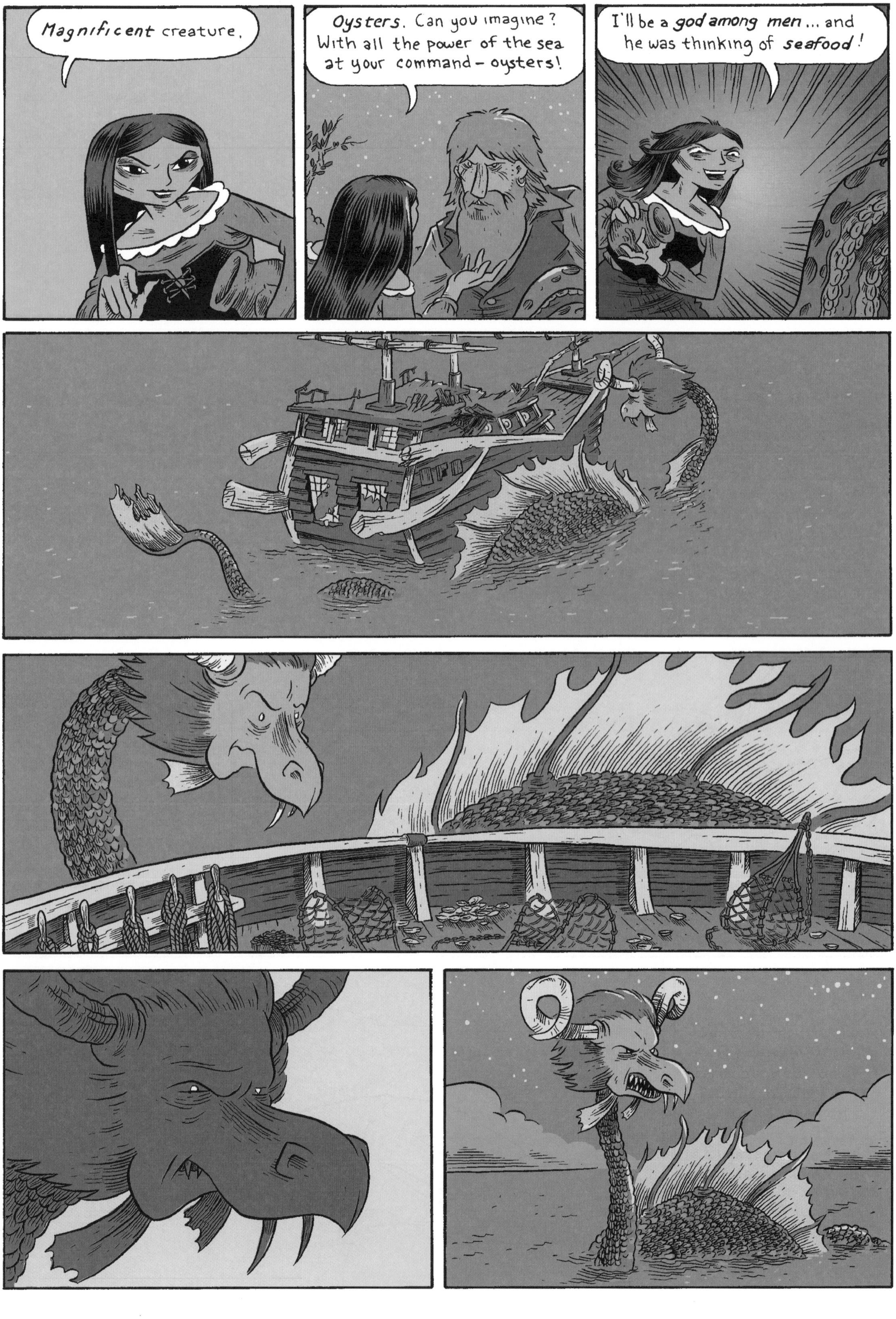
Magnificent creature.
Oysters. Can you imagine? With all the power of the sea at your command – oysters!
I'll be a god among men ... and he was thinking of seafood!

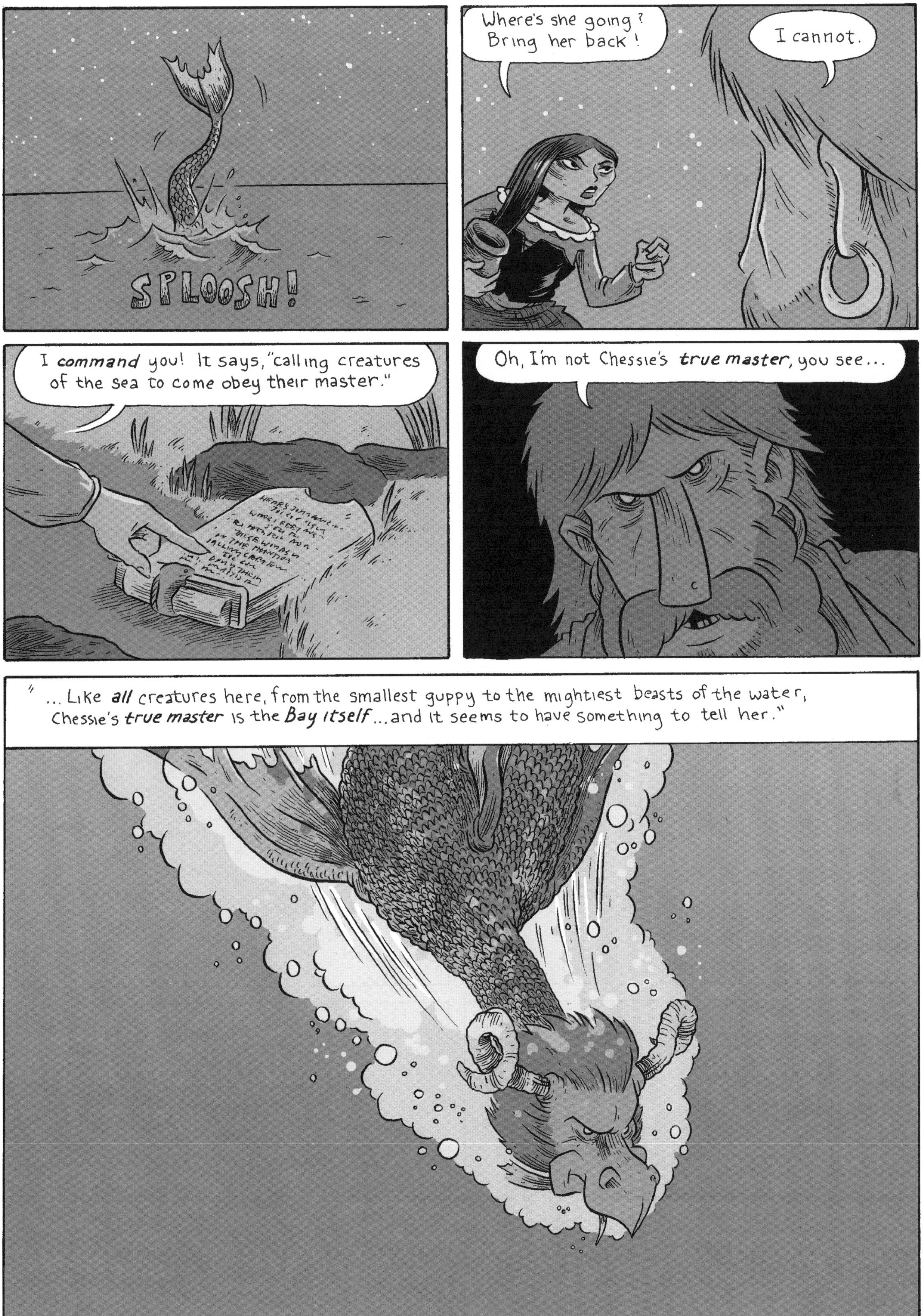
SPLOOSH!
Where's she going? Bring her back!
I cannot.
I command you! It says, "calling creatures of the sea to come obey their master."
Oh, I'm not Chessie's true master, you see...
"...Like all creatures here, from the smallest guppy to the mightiest beasts of the water, Chessie's true master is the Bay itself...and it seems to have something to tell her."

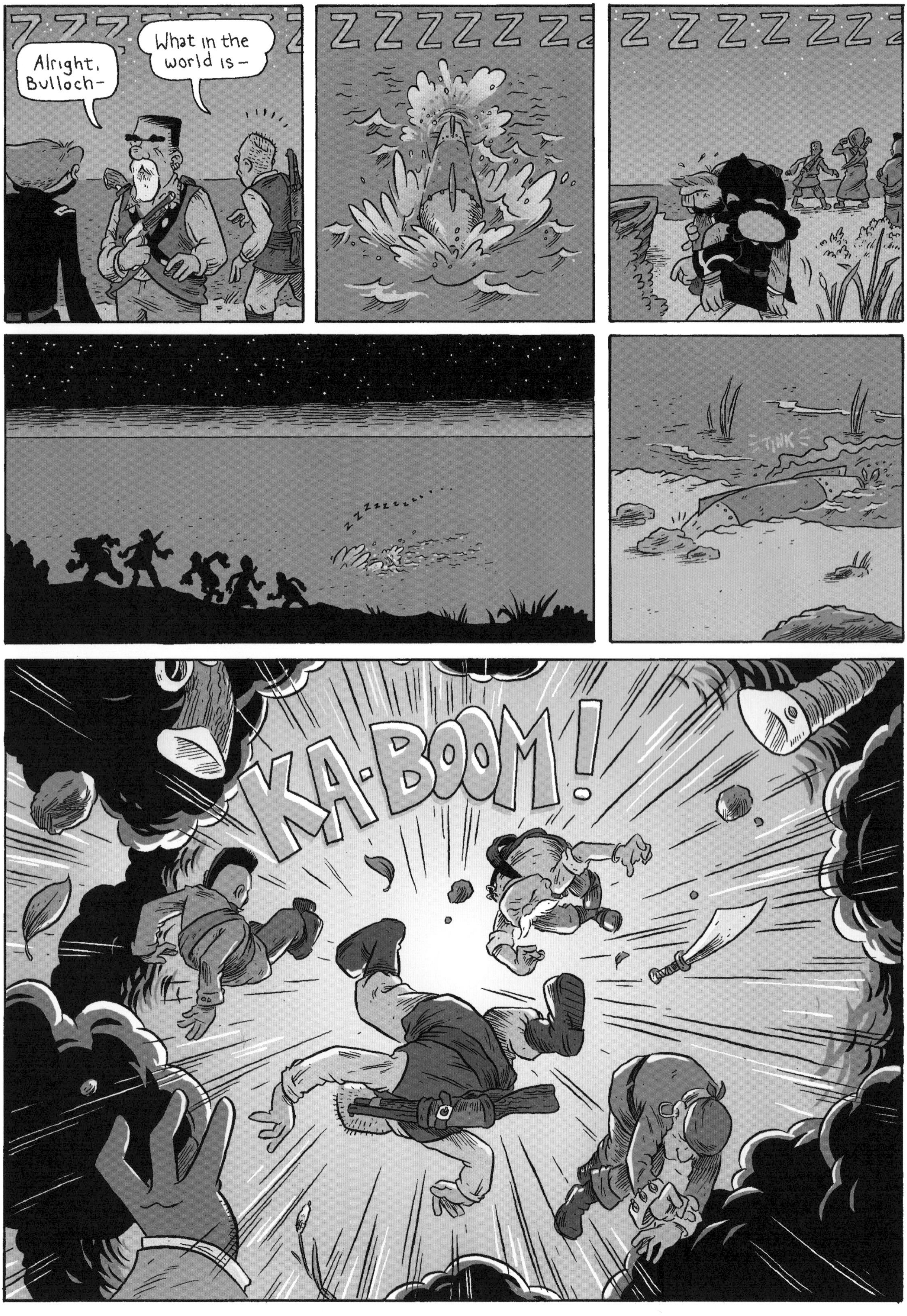
Alright, Bulloch-
What in the world is-
ZZZZZZZZ
ZZZZZZZZ
ZZZZZZZZ
ZZZZZZZ.....
TINK
KA-BOOM!

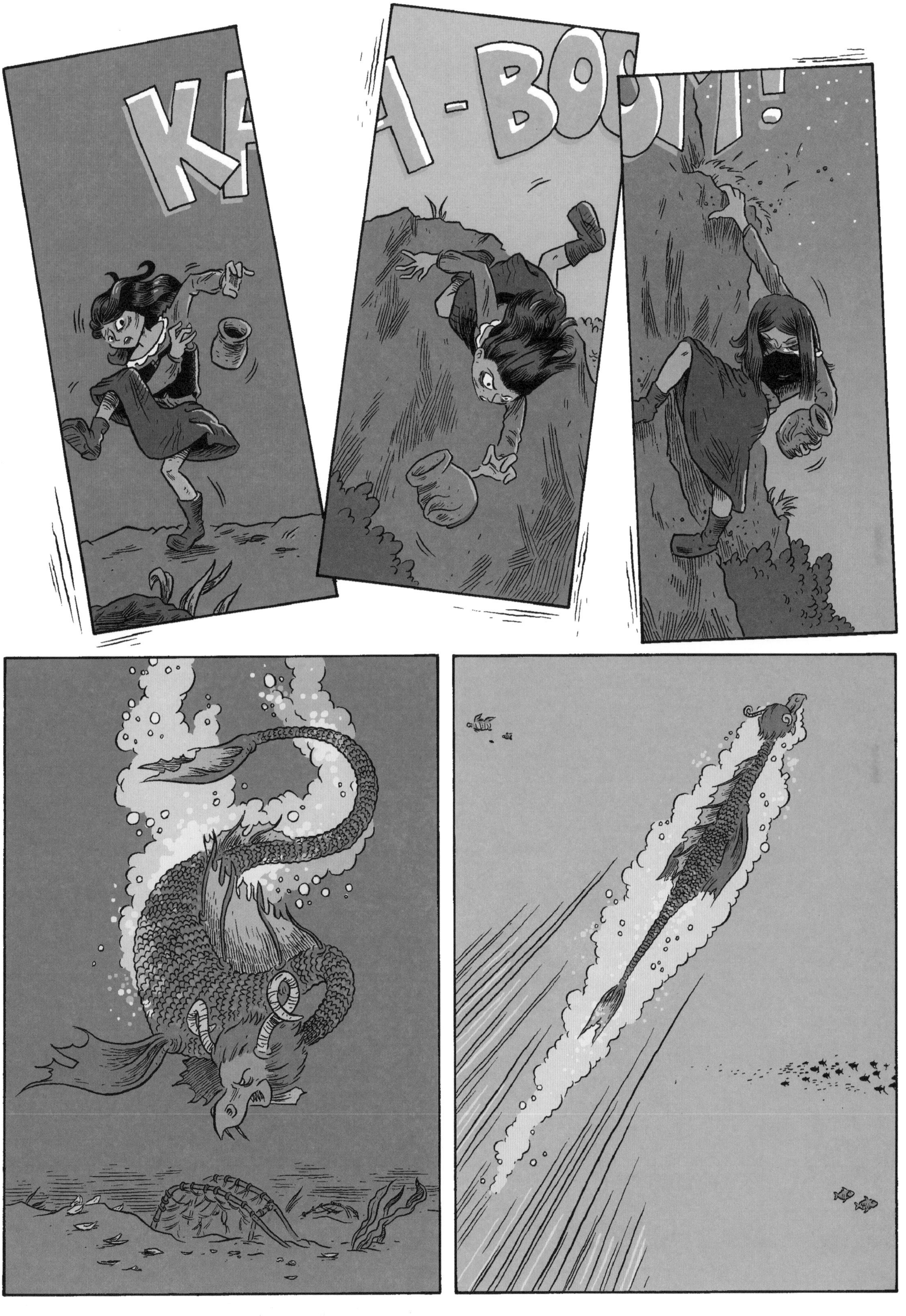
KA-BOOM!

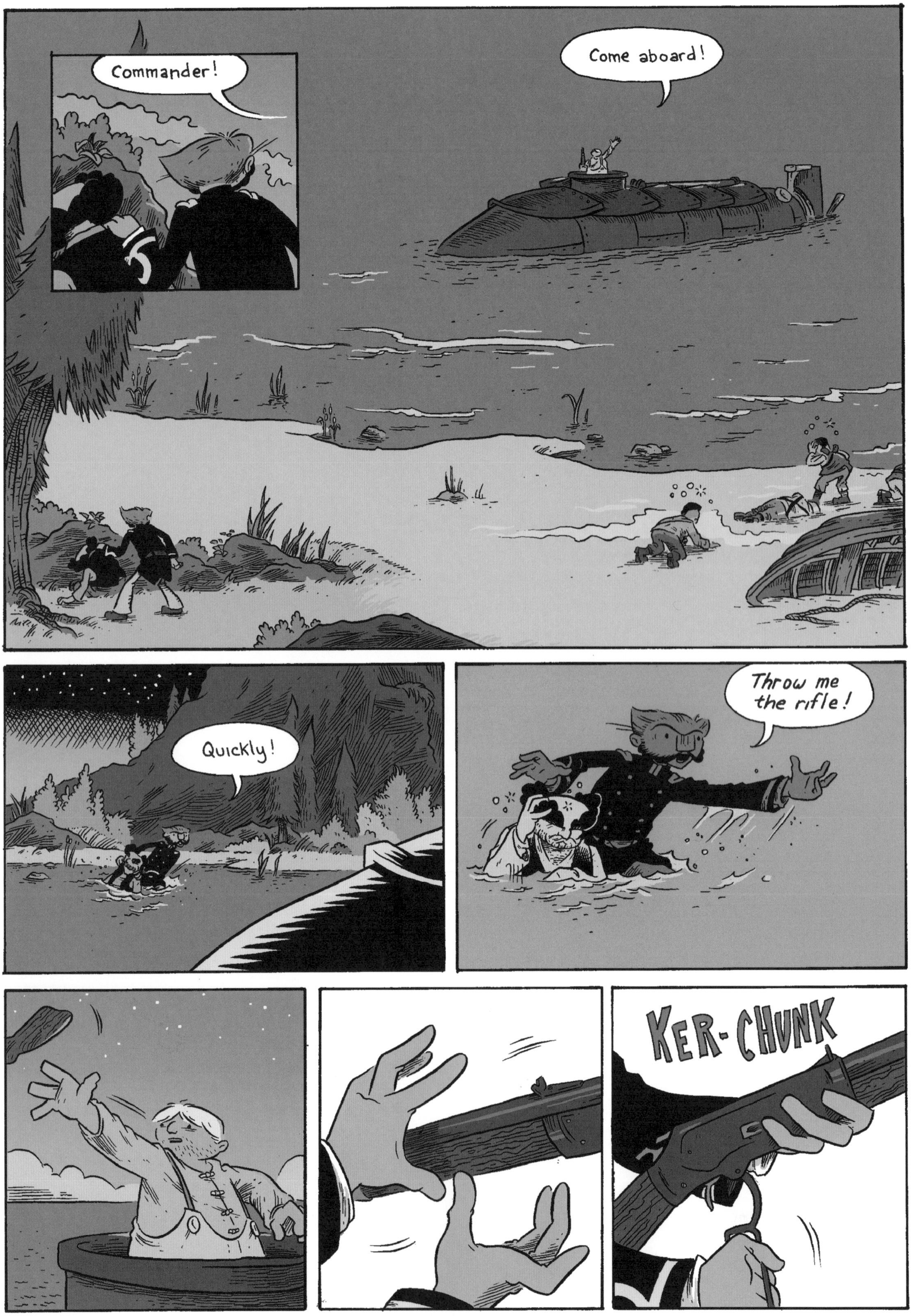
Commander!
Come aboard!
Quickly!
Throw me the rifle!
KER-CHUNK

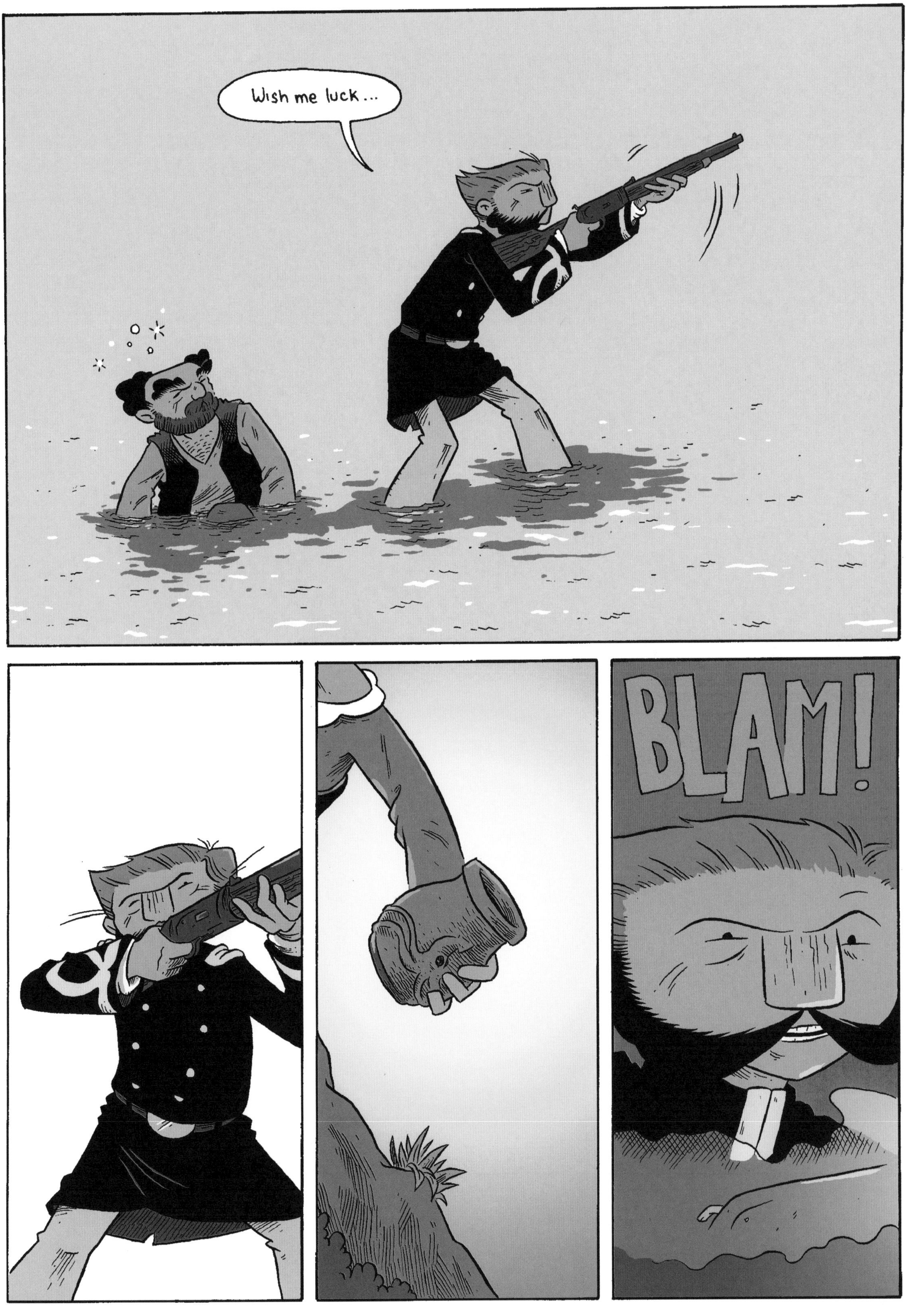
Wish me luck...
BLAM!

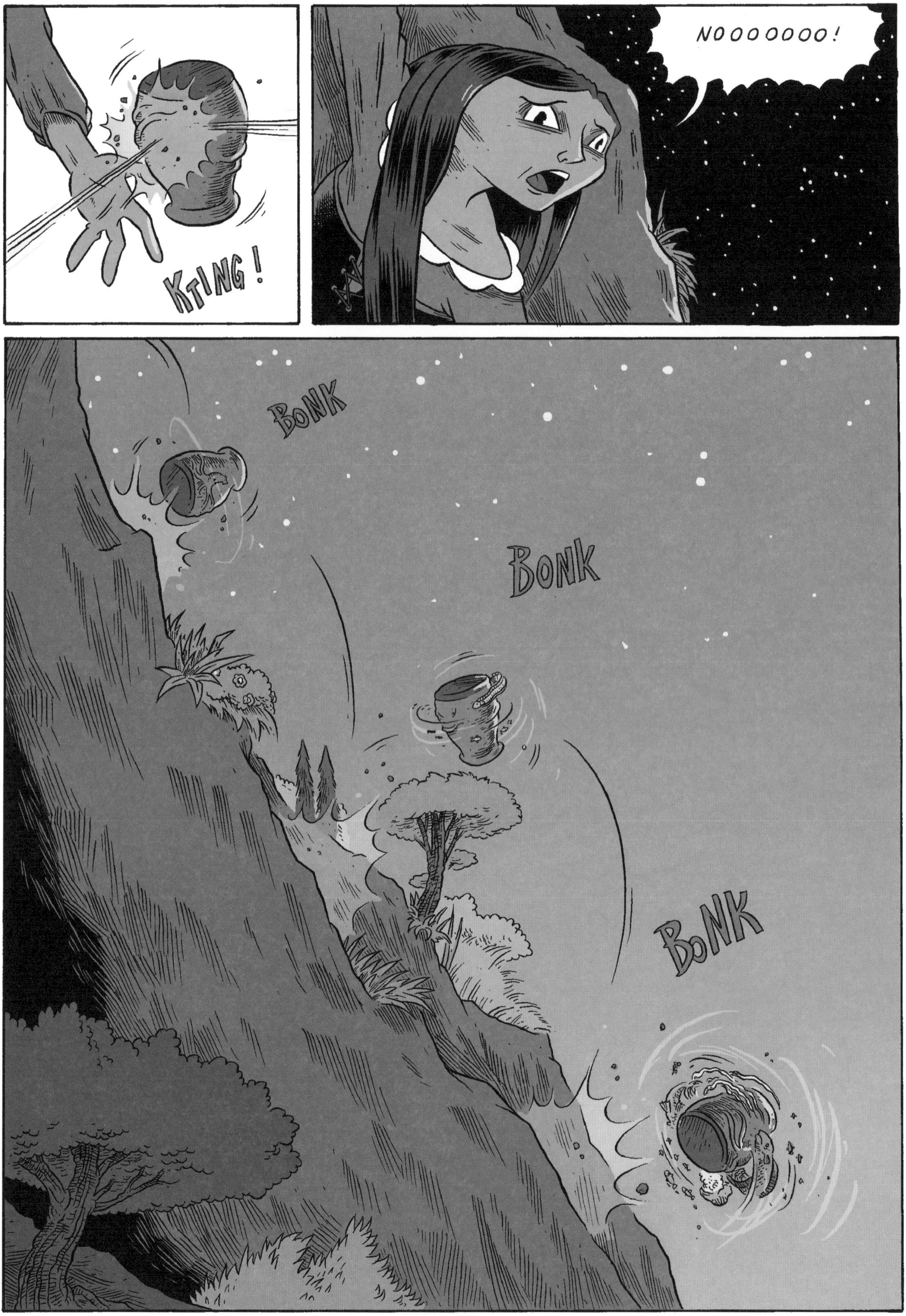
KTING!
NOOOOOOO!
BONK
BONK
BONK

Good day to you, ma'am.

BONK

Sploot!

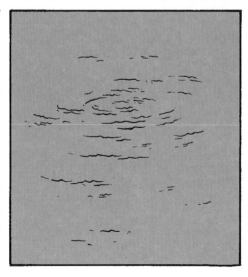

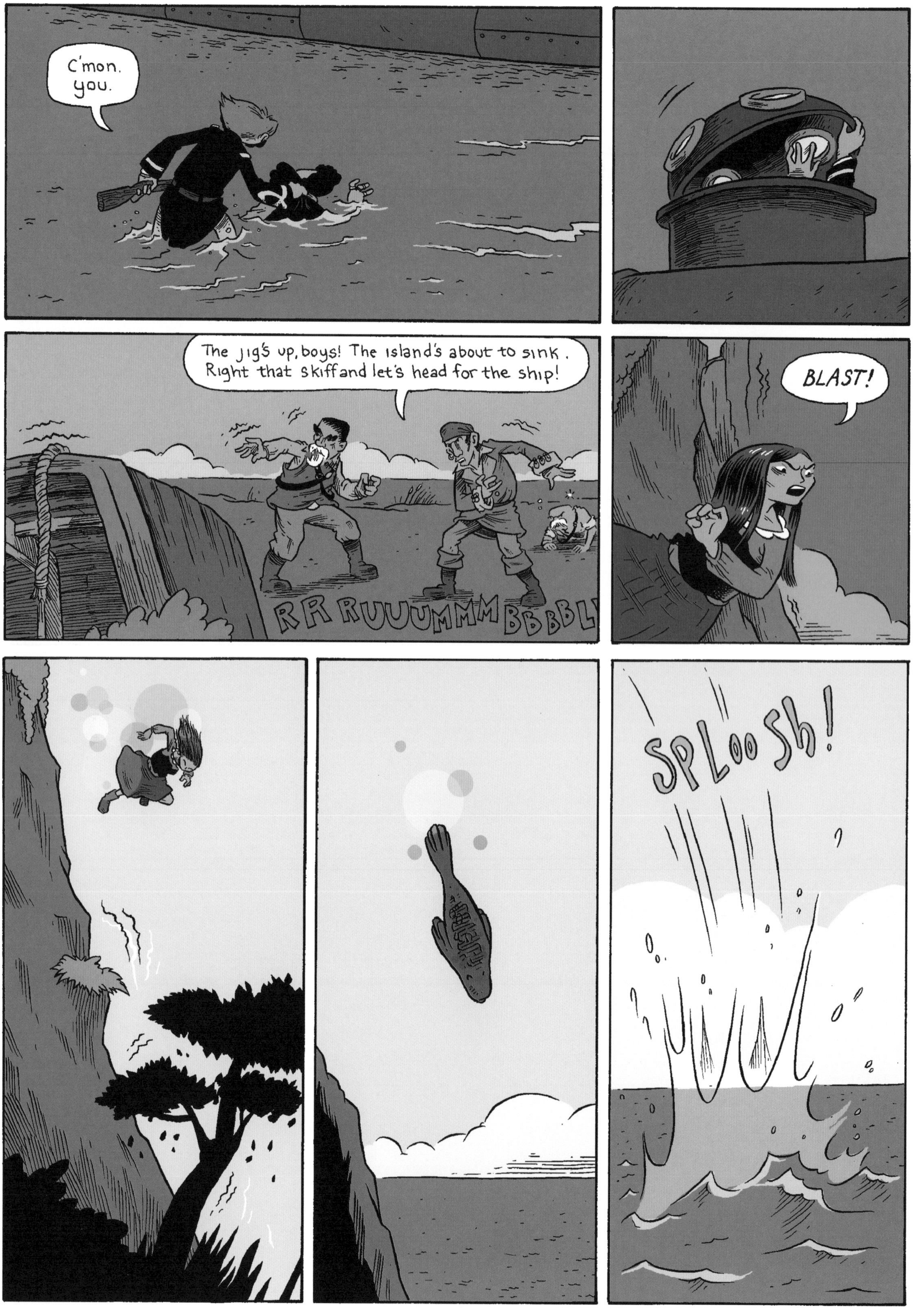
C'mon. you.
The jig's up, boys! The island's about to sink. Right that skiff and let's head for the ship!
RRRUUUMMMBBBBL
BLAST!
SPLooSh!

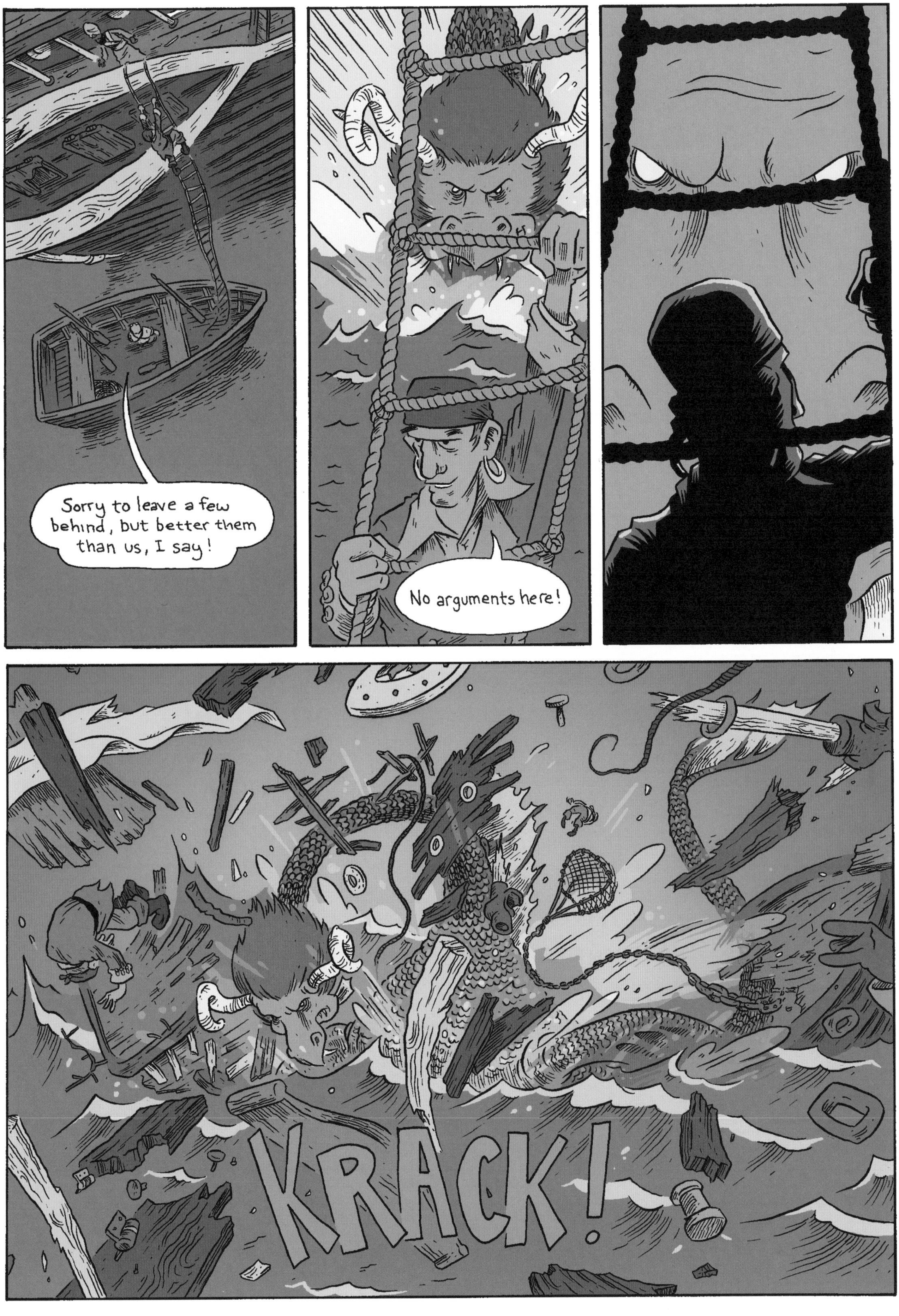
Sorry to leave a few behind, but better them than us, I say!
No arguments here!
KRACK!

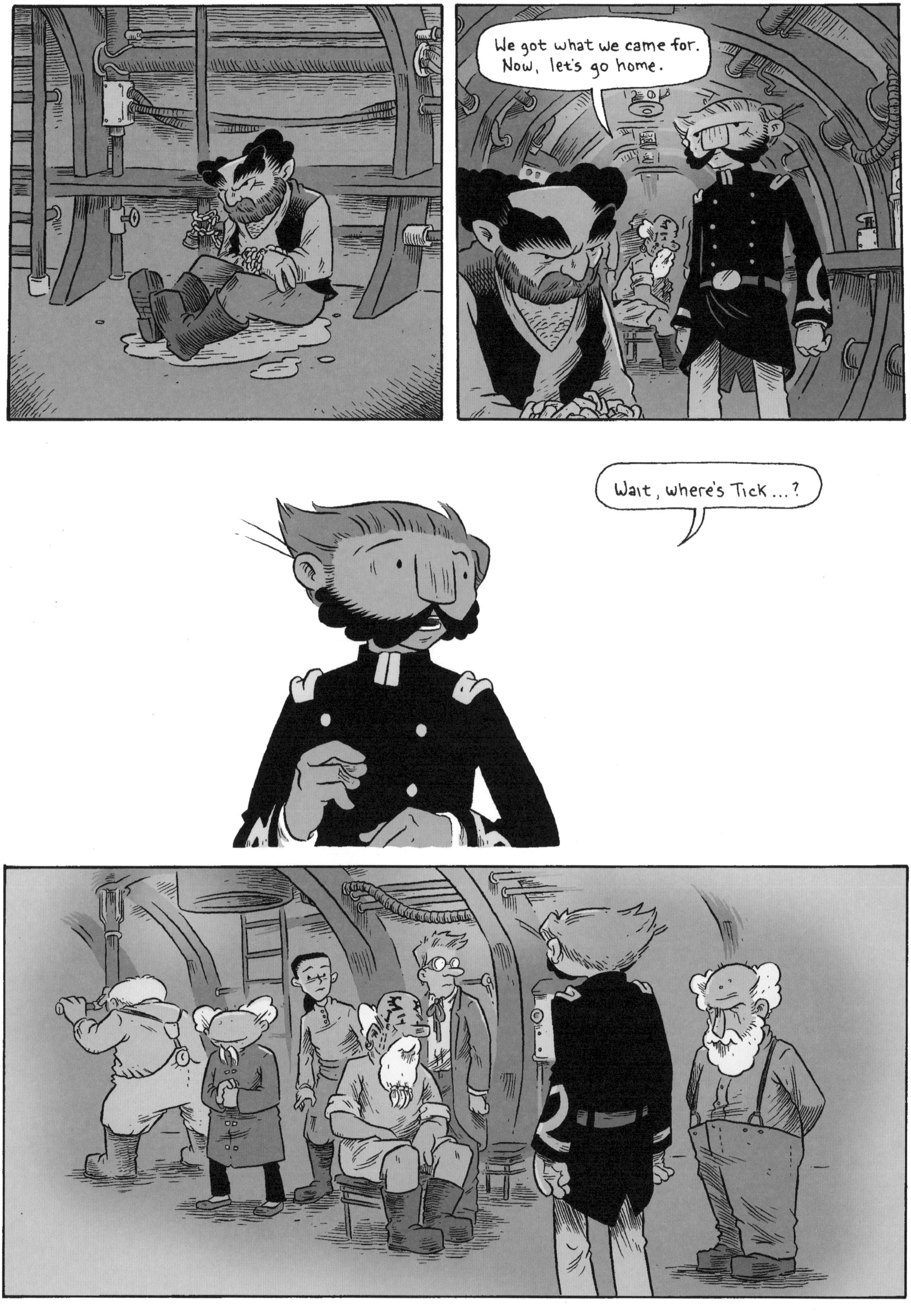
We got what we came for. Now, let's go home.
Wait, where's Tick ...?

EPILOGUE

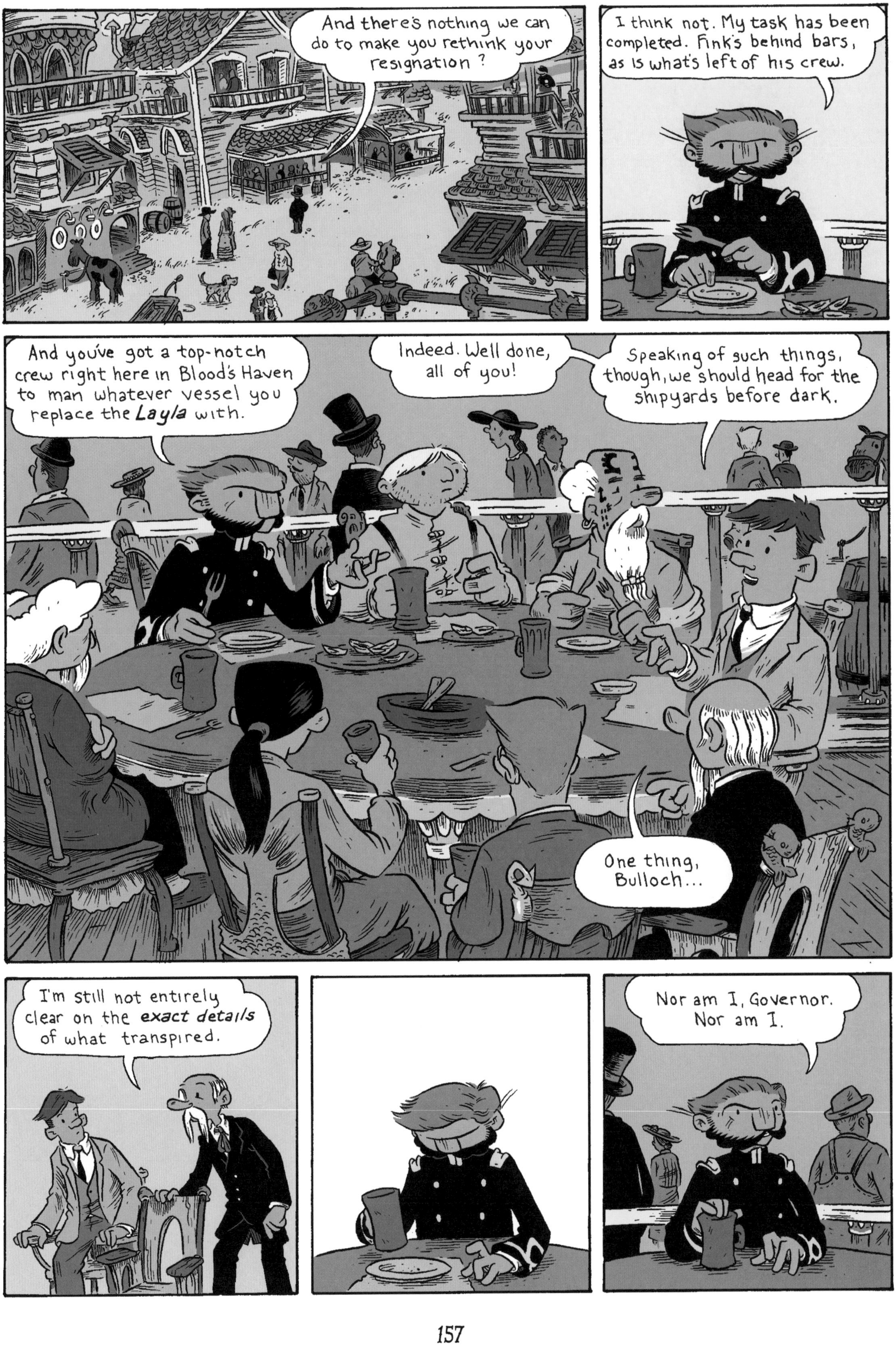
And there's nothing we can do to make you rethink your resignation?
I think not. My task has been completed. Fink's behind bars, as is what's left of his crew.
And you've got a top-notch crew right here in Blood's Haven to man whatever vessel you replace the *Layla* with.
Indeed. Well done, all of you!
Speaking of such things, though, we should head for the shipyards before dark.
One thing, Bulloch...
I'm still not entirely clear on the ***exact details*** of what transpired.
Nor am I, Governor. Nor am I.

So, Commander...

What *are* you going to do now?

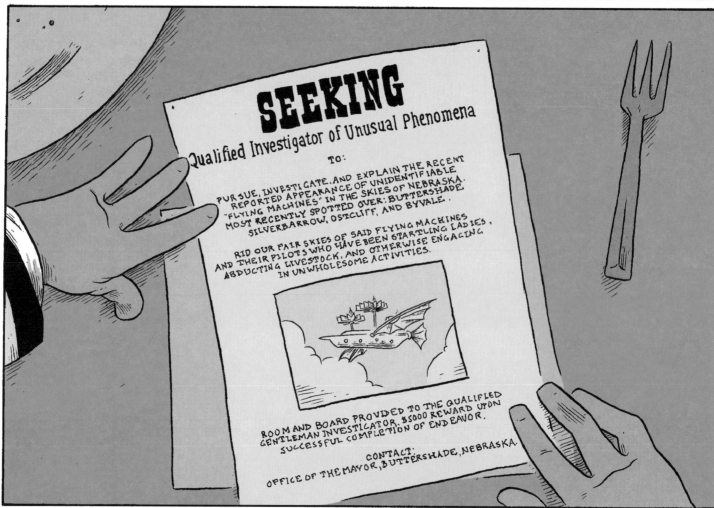

SEEKING
Qualified Investigator of Unusual Phenomena

TO:

PURSUE, INVESTIGATE, AND EXPLAIN THE RECENT REPORTED APPEARANCE OF UNIDENTIFIABLE "FLYING MACHINES" IN THE SKIES OF NEBRASKA. MOST RECENTLY SPOTTED OVER: BUTTERSHADE, SILVERBARROW, OSTCLIFF, AND BYVALE.

RID OUR FAIR SKIES OF SAID FLYING MACHINES AND THEIR PILOTS WHO HAVE BEEN STARTLING LADIES, ABDUCTING LIVESTOCK, AND OTHERWISE ENGAGING IN UNWHOLESOME ACTIVITIES.

ROOM AND BOARD PROVIDED TO THE QUALIFIED GENTLEMAN INVESTIGATOR. $5000 REWARD UPON SUCCESSFUL COMPLETION OF ENDEAVOR.

CONTACT: OFFICE OF THE MAYOR, BUTTERSHADE, NEBRASKA.

As the Greek statesman Demosthenes once said, "Small opportunities are often the banging of great enterprises!"

"The *beginning* of great enterprises."

Indeed!

THE END

Afterword

I hope that *Oyster War* is an example of fiction being stranger than truth. My previous two books, *Amelia Earhart: This Broad Ocean* and *Midnight Sun* (about Earhart's 1929 Atlantic crossing and an airship crash in the arctic in 1928 respectively), were straight historical fiction. By the time I set out to put together *Oyster War*, though, I'd had enough looking up photo reference of period light fixtures and whatnot. I was ready for something more fantastic—something unhinged a bit from the real world. And *Oyster War*—with its ghost captains, magical birth cauls, selkie, and all the rest—is the result. That said, I couldn't resist using some real-life sources as inspiration and story fodder. Here're just a few:

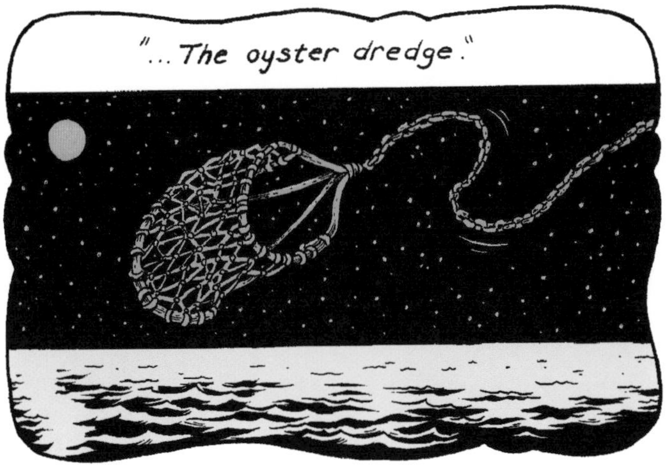
"...The oyster dredge."

Oyster Wars
There was no single oyster war, but rather a series of skirmishes on the Chesapeake Bay over the course of nearly one hundred years (1865-1959) between oyster pirates and authorities from Maryland and Virginia—and occasionally between the two states themselves.

And there's nothing we can do to make you rethink your resignation ?

Blood's Haven

Blood's Haven is entirely fictional. It was partly inspired, though, by Crisfield, Maryland, which was a booming center of seafood commerce in the late 1800s. (Blood's Haven also owes an obvious debt to the village from the 1980 live action film *Popeye*, as well as maybe a bit to Dr. Seuss!)

Chessie

Supposed sea serpent sightings weren't uncommon in the U.S. in the 1800s. The most famous is New England's Gloucester Sea Serpent. The first report of Chessie, the Chesapeake Bay's very own legendary beast, wasn't until the early 1940's, but I'd like to think she'd been in residence for a while.

"...That ship's as empty as last night's jug, or I'm a swag-bellied maid!"

Ju-long

Nearly 70,000 Chinese immigrants arrived in the U.S. in the first decade after the Gold Rush alone, yet Chinese people are strangely absent from most period narratives. America's Westward expansion would not have taken place as it did without them. They're the unsung heroes of the American Frontier. It's not a coincidence that Ju-long is the unsung hero of *Oyster War*.

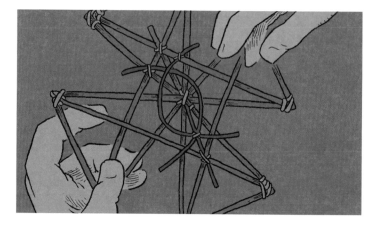

Marshall Islands Stick Charts

Polynesians were master navigators who were able to successfully navigate huge swathes of the Pacific Ocean centuries before the invention of modern navigational aids. One of the means by which they did so was using stick charts to learn the patterns of ocean waves as they reflected off islands and crisscrossed one another. The type of chart Tevia is shown with is a "Mattang," which would actually have only been used for teaching navigation.

Oh, I'm not Chessie's **true master**, you see...

John Clark Monk

Monk (sometimes seen as "Monks") is indeed buried in Maryland. He's come to be known as the "Hanging Sailor of Perryman" because of the unusual circumstances of his burial: he was buried in an underground vault in a metal coffin suspended from chains. Monk was actually a shopkeeper and no one's quite sure how he came to be considered a sailor, nor where all the lore surrounding him originated. Monk's backstory in *Oyster War* is loosely based on an unrelated nautical legend.

Let's Fight!

Ju-long's fighting moves in *Oyster War* are based on taijiquan (or tai chi), a traditional Chinese martial art that I began studying about the time I started brainstorming on this book, and which has become quite important to me since then. Lourdes employs the Portuguese martial art of jogo do pau stick fighting.

KER-CHUNK

Guns

When I originally ran *Oyster War* as a biweekly webcomic, I was surprised by how many comments were about the guns. I'm sad to let folks down, but other than the rifles—which are based on the classic Winchester 1873—all the weaponry in *Oyster War* is pretty much made up.

click
PFFSSSSSSS
click
PFTSSSSSS

The *Alligator*

Both navies in the Civil War were developing submarines, but the Confederates were using them for offensive purposes, whereas the Union was developing them mainly for clearing harbors. The *Alligator* was indeed lost at sea near Cape Hatteras, but has never been found. The real *Alligator* was much smaller than depicted in *Oyster War*, and human-powered, initially by oars and later by a hand-cranked propeller.

-Ben Towle

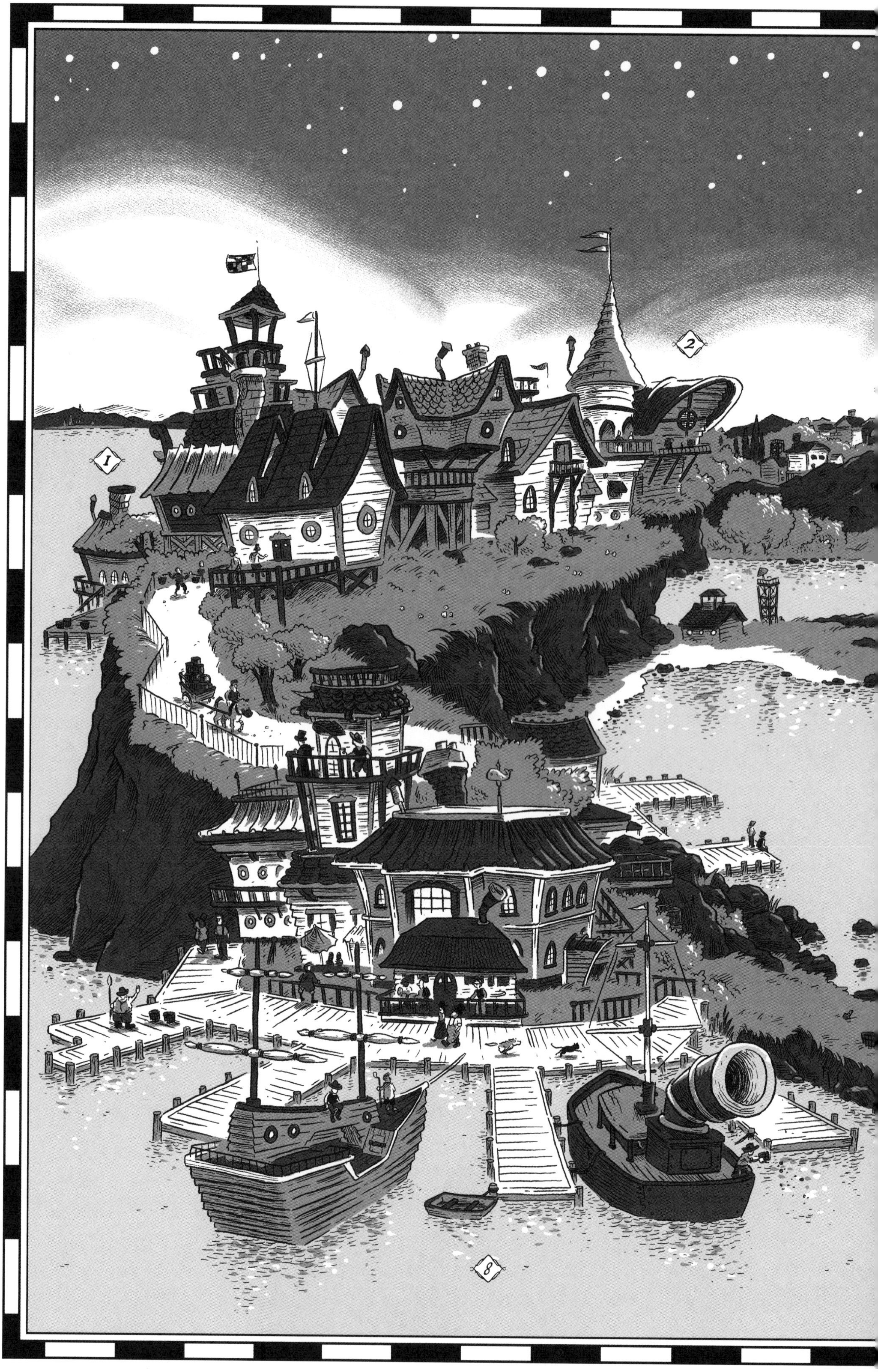
1
2
8

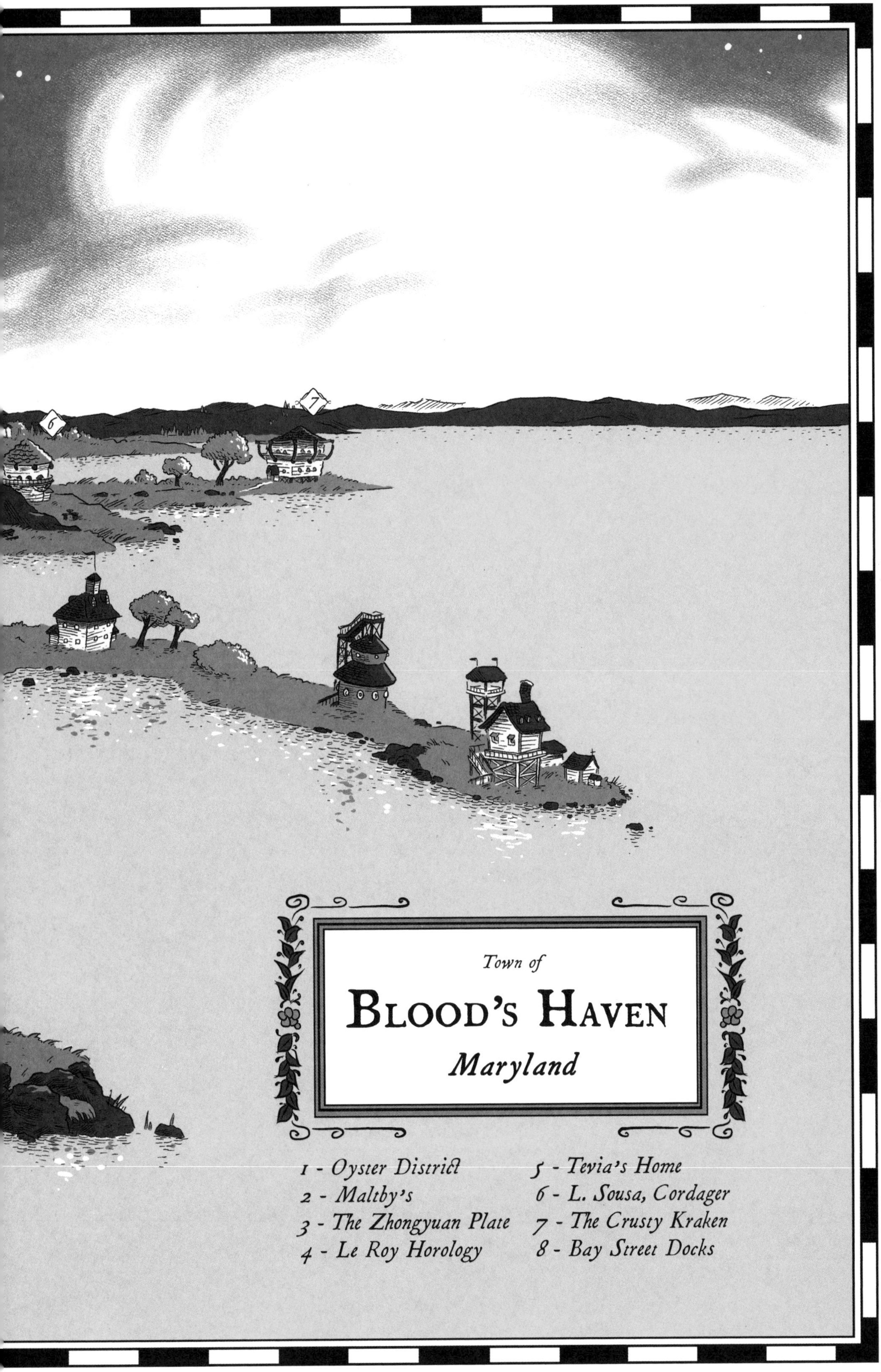
6
7
Town of
BLOOD'S HAVEN
Maryland
1 - Oyster District
2 - Maltby's
3 - The Zhongyuan Plate
4 - Le Roy Horology
5 - Tevia's Home
6 - L. Sousa, Cordager
7 - The Crusty Kraken
8 - Bay Street Docks

Ben Towle is a three-time Eisner-nominated cartoonist whose previous book, *Amelia Earhart: This Broad Ocean* (with Sarah Stewart Taylor), a graphic novel for young adults, was released by Disney/Hyperion Books in 2010. The book has received accolades from such publications as *The New York Times* and *Publishers Weekly* and was a Junior Library Guild selection. His work prior to that includes the historical fiction graphic novel *Midnight Sun* as well as a volume of comics folk tales, *Farewell, Georgia*, both from SLG Publishing. Ben lives with his wife, daughter, dog, and cat in Winston-Salem, North Carolina.

Website: www.benzilla.com

Email: benzilla@benzilla.com

Twitter: @ben_towle

G+: plus.google.com/+BenTowle

I'd like to express my sincerest thanks and gratitude to: the readers and supporters of *Oyster War* in its initial incarnation as a webcomic, everyone who encouraged me and spread the word about *Oyster War* on Twitter and G+, and—most important—my loving wife and daughter, who for some reason put up with my crazy, time-consuming obsession for telling stories with little pictures.

Oyster War is dedicated to the memory of Chris Reilly, 1967-2014, Friend in Comics.

MORE BOOKS FROM ONI PRESS

"CATFOOT'S VENGEANCE IS A MARVELOUS SWASHBUCKLING TALE. CHRIS SCHWEIZER IS AN AMAZINGLY TALENTED CARTOONIST WITH AN EAR FOR DIALOGUE AND AN EYE FOR GREAT STORYTELLING."
-STAN SAKAI, USAGI YOJIMBO
THE WEST INDIES, 1701
THE CROGAN ADVENTURES
CATFOOT'S VENGEANCE
BY CHRIS SCHWEIZER

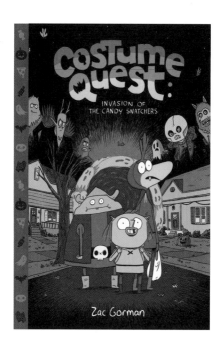

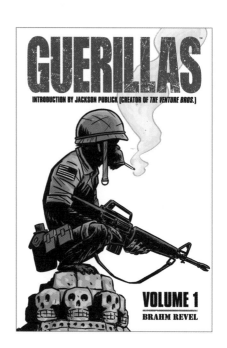

The Crogan Adventures: Catfoot's Vengeance

By Chris Schweizer
200 pages, softcover
ISBN 978-1-62010-203-9

COSTUME QUEST:
INVASION OF THE CANDY SNATCHERS
Zac Gorman

Costume Quest: Invasion of the Candy Snatchers

By Zac Gorman
56 pages, hardcover
ISBN 978-1-62010-190-2

PETROGRAD
PHILIP GELATT • TYLER CROOK

Petrograd

By Philip Gelatt & Tyler Crook
264 pages, hardcover
ISBN 978-1-934964-44-6

Ray Fawkes
ONE SOUL

One Soul

By Ray Fawkes
176 pages, hardcover
ISBN 978-1-934964-66-8

GUERILLAS
INTRODUCTION BY JACKSON PUBLICK (CREATOR OF THE VENTURE BROS.)
VOLUME 1
BRAHM REVEL

Guerillas, Vol. 1

By Brahm Revel
168 pages, softcover
ISBN 978-1-934964-43-9

BAD MACHINERY
THE CASE OF THE TEAM SPIRIT
By John Allison

Bad Machinery, Vol. 1: The Case of the Team Spirit

By John Allison
136 pages, softcover
ISBN 978-1-62010-084-4

ONI PRESS
www.onipress.com

For more information on these and other fine Oni Press comic books and graphic novels, visit our website at www.onipress.com.